Praise for *Bailout Nation*

"The greatest economic calamity in a generation has now swept from Wall Street through Main Street, to Iceland, Europe, and beyond. Barry Ritholtz not only saw the financial tidal wave coming, but tried to warn us before it hit, when few believed anything like it could happen. Now that clean-up is at hand, who better to explain what went wrong? Read this book: when Barry Ritholtz speaks, as the saying goes, attention must be paid."

—Jeff Matthews
Author, *Pilgrimage to Warren Buffett's Omaha*

"This thrilling page-turner is really a doctoral thesis in disguise on the history of financial debacles and the inner workings of the global financial system and modern economics. Barry is truly one of Wall Street's important thinkers and rising stars. Bravo Barry!"

—Jeffrey A. Hirsch
Editor-in-Chief, *Stock Trader's Almanac*

"Barry Ritholtz, long known to readers of *The Big Picture* for telling it like it is, does exactly that in Bailout Nation. With sparkling clarity and his inimitable brashness, Barry names names and tells you where to look for the bodies who are profiting from the unprecedented $8 trillion government bailout."

—Michelle Leder
Author, *Financial Fine Print* and *Footnoted*

"Part history lesson, part social commentary, part in-depth analysis, *Bailout Nation* serves up a riveting indictment of the age of hubris and excess."

—Michael Panzner
Financial Armageddon

"As Wall Street wizards were turning into welfare kings, Barry Ritholtz was there to chronicle every new outrage on his blog, *The Big Picture*. Now he's focused on the really Big Picture—how we got into this mess—with his great new book, *Bailout Nation*."

—Jesse Eisinger
Portfolio

"Barry Ritholtz crystallizes the absurdity of the bailouts and why America's addiction to them is doomed to fail. This should be required reading for every future politician with a conscience."

—Herb Greenberg
former journalist, CNBC, Marketwatch, and now
director of GreebergMeritz Research & Analytics

"Barry Ritholtz is leading the first wave of critical analysts who are trying to make sense of the past year beyond the official explanations. He not only illustrates the conflicts and contradiction in current economic leaders and policies, but suggests some solutions and even opportunities in this sea of global financial misery. I'm already looking forward to volume two."

—Christopher Whalen
Institutional Risk Analytics

"*Bailout Nation* provides a timely review and analysis of the issues and problems that led to and are evidenced in the present financial turmoil. These forensics are much needed today."

—David Kotok
Cumberland Advisors

"Barry Ritholtz has a one-two combination punch of insight and skepticism that leaves financiers, bankers and politicians out cold on the floor. This is pungent and funny required reading about the current crisis."

—Dr. Paul Kedrosky
Infectious Greed
Partner, Ventures West VC

Bailout Nation

Bailout Nation

How Greed and Easy Money Corrupted Wall Street and Shook the World Economy

Barry Ritholtz
with
Aaron Task

John Wiley & Sons, Inc.

Published by John Wiley & Sons, Inc., Hoboken, New Jersey.
Published simultaneously in Canada.

For general information on our other products and services or for technical support, please contact our Customer Care Department within the United States at (800) 762-2974, outside the United States at (317) 572-3993 or fax (317) 572-4002.

Wiley also publishes its books in a variety of electronic formats. Some content that appears in print may not be available in electronic books. For more information about Wiley products, visit our web site at www.wiley.com.

ISBN 978-0-470-52038-3

Printed in the United States of America

10 9 8 7 6 5 4 3 2 1

To Wendy,
who has bailed me out of more than a few jams

Contents

Foreword

Do you find yourself wondering: *How did we get here?*

How did the United States of America get into such a predicament whereby in one year, 2008, the financial system nearly vaporized, the stock market crashed, real estate tanked, and major corporations were being bailed out (or begging to be) on a regular basis. How did our great country, a bastion of capitalism, devolve into a Bailout Nation where the gains were privatized but the losses were socialized?

This terrific book by Barry Ritholtz will explain to you how this sorry state of affairs came to pass. By reading it you will come to understand how we got here, which is a necessary prerequisite for understanding how to navigate the future.

The primary reason that I wrote *Greenspan's Bubbles: The Age of Ignorance at the Federal Reserve* (McGraw-Hill, 2008) was so that when the U.S. credit/housing bubble inevitably burst, people would understand why such enormous financial and economic problems were occurring, seemingly erupting out of nowhere. But they didn't erupt out of nowhere; these problems were created over time by the monetary policies of the Federal Reserve, specifically the targeting of interest rates and the Fed's ongoing refusal to recognize the flaws in this approach.

Although nearly everything that has transpired since my book was published in February 2008 I had expected to occur, I was still shocked by the total collapse of so many major financial firms, such as Bear Stearns, Countrywide Financial, Fannie Mae, and Freddie Mac in such a short amount of time.

But that is what happens to highly leveraged financial entities when significant portions of their underlying assets are found to be essentially worthless. The mind-set of deregulation that was championed by Federal Reserve Chairman Alan Greenspan in the wake of the Long-Term Capital Management (LTCM) bailout in 1998 is partially responsible for the massive overleveraging of nearly the entire financial system in the United States.

That Wall Street bailout (which led to the notion of the "Greenspan put") set the stage for what we are witnessing today in the United States (and in the United Kingdom), with the prudent being forced to bail out the reckless. As Barry notes, "The parallels between what doomed LTCM in 1998 and what forced Wall Street to run to Washington for a handout in 2008 are all there."

The United States has abandoned its capitalist roots, and the country has morphed into a Bailout Nation; now almost any large entity that finds itself in trouble feels the government (taxpayers really) should provide financial support. Similarly, homeowners who overextended themselves also feel that they too should be rescued from their mistakes.

Barry weaves together the problems created by the Federal Reserve's interest rate targeting policies with the determination on the government's part to thwart the "creative destruction" aspect of capitalism. We have now arrived at a juncture where our government seems to embrace free markets only when they deliver the results it wants. If they don't, an attempt is made to alter the outcome, leading to unintended consequences down the road, which often are more severe than the original problem.

Ritholtz also names the villains in this tragedy—the rogues' gallery of politicians and officials who screwed up big time—and demonstrates what they did to make the problem either bigger or worse. He also shows how each bailout throughout modern history has impacted what happens in the future—for example, why Chrysler should have been allowed to fend for itself in 1980, and the impact that has on future bailouts.

This book is the history of how the United States evolved from a rugged, independent nation to a soft Bailout Nation, one in which too few question why we ask the taxpayers "to allow financial firms to self-regulate, but then pony up trillions to bail them out."

However much we dislike the predicament we are in, the only way it can be remedied is if people learn in some detail what has transpired and so, armed with knowledge, demand change. Reading this book will prepare you to be able to do just that.

BILL FLECKENSTEIN
March 2009

Acknowledgments

All books are collaborative efforts, and *Bailout Nation* was more so than most. There were many people whose contributions were crucial to getting this project off the ground, and keeping it going when things started to falter.

Over the course of the past year, I wrote this book while working in an asset management firm, heading a research shop, all the while running a very active blog. This book was possible only thanks to the many helping hands involved.

Much of the book was written in real time, and early versions of parts of this appeared on *The Big Picture* (www.ritholtz.com). I would post ideas a few hundred words at a time, and readers would critique, poke, and prod my thought process along. These brave souls have my everlasting gratitude. Many of the insights, quotes, obscure references, and artworks within the book come courtesy of them.

There were many professional journalists and writers who selflessly shared sources, ideas, and insights with me. In particular, Dan Gross, Jesse Eisinger, Randall Forsyth, and Herb Greenberg all greatly impacted my process. If there are any parallels between my book and Dan's, it's because we batted more than a few ideas off of each other. Special thanks

go to Thomas Donlan of *Barron's*, who took my disjointed ramblings in *A Memo Found in the Street* ("Dear D.C.") and turned them into a concise thing of beauty.

Numerous other authors were helpful with the process of writing a book, as well as influencing my own research and writing. I owe special thanks to Nouriel Roubini, Bill Fleckenstein, and Michael Panzner for advice and comfort. Various fund managers and analysts generously shared their insights, most notably Doug Kass, James Bianco, Scott Frew, Chris Whalen, and David Kotok.

I grew up in a household where stocks and real estate were fodder for dinner-table conversations. My now-retired mother was a successful real estate agent, and used to regale us with dark tales of corruption and criminality in the real estate business (especially about C1 and C2). Her subversive view of the industry she worked in definitely rubbed off on me. (Thanks, Mom!)

The artwork in the book came to me courtesy of a few fantastic artists: John Sherffius of the *Boulder Daily Camera* is the creator of the fabulous jacket illustration to *Bailout Nation*. His political cartoons are also at the beginning of each of the five parts of the book. His dry wit and deft pen strokes communicate more with one picture that I can with thousands of words. J. C. Champredonde is the wicked mind behind the investment banks as casinos illustrations. You will find his work toward the end of the casino capitalism chapter and on the Web at www.stereohell.com. His art perfectly captures the past decade of casino capitalism. Jess Bachman of WallStats.com did amazing work on the Anatomy of a Crisis. R. J. Matson lent us a cartoon—corporate welfare.

Special thanks also go to Bill McBride of Calculated Risk for his informative real estate charts, and to Ron Griess of The Chart Store for the historical market charts.

Few writers particularly enjoy being edited. I was fortunate at TheStreet.com to work with Aaron Task—a rare editor who genuinely makes your work better (as opposed to merely different). When McGraw-Hill first approached me about doing this book (more about them later), I knew without question who I was willing to entrust my words to. Aaron's contributions, organization, and constant urgings forward are the prime reason this book got to the publisher on time in

December 2008. It's been said a book is done when the manuscript is torn from its writer's hands, and Aaron made sure that when that date came, what was being torn was something readable.

Much of this book involves dollar amounts, dates, data, and numbers. Staying on top of that would not have been possible without a crack research team, and I was fortunate to have worked with three of the best: Eugene Ashton-Gonzalez and William J. Miller were terrific, and my research intern, Ariel Katz, deserves special praise for her insights. She graduates from business school in May 2010, and some lucky company should snag her right away. Special thanks also go to Marion Maneker, for his gentle shoves in the right direction and his insights into the world of publishing.

Jeanne Glasser at McGraw-Hill was uniquely patient in dealing with writing a book about live events as they happened. When that publisher took issue with my criticisms of Standard & Poor's (a division of McGraw-Hill), Jeanne fought hard for the book. That the book in your hands ended up at John Wiley & Sons—and Jeanne at FT Press and Wharton School Publishing—tells you something about character. And I would be remiss if I did not add that Lloyd Jassin, my literary agent, went above and beyond the call of duty throughout. As you might imagine, this was not the typical book deal.

Speaking of which: I am thrilled to be published by Wiley. The people there were especially excited about this project. It was a pleasure working with Kevin Commins and Meg Freeborn and the rest of the Wiley crew.

Perhaps this is an acknowledgment first, but I have to give a shout out to Google Docs—the collaborative editing process would have been a bear without it. We had so many different versions of each chapter floating around before we started using it. G-Docs made staying on top of the latest changes and edits a breeze. Chalk one up for cloud computing.

On a personal note, my wife showed infinite patience during this lost year of writing *Bailout Nation*. If it wasn't for her, this book would never have been finished. (*Go for a walk! You're babbling again! Stop procrastinating! And for goodness' sake, will you take a shower already!*)

I must also express my gratitude to my partners at FusionIQ, Kevin Lane and Mike Conte, who gracefully allowed me to take many days off

to finish this beast and to close the door to my office to bang out a few more pages during the workweek.

Many additional authors colored my worldview, and much of what you read is due to the prior work of Roger Lowenstein, Richard Bookstaber, Tom Metz, Paul Desmond, Stephan Mihm, Satyajit Das, Robert J. Shiller, Robert F. Bruner and Sean D. Carr, Reginald Stuart, and Ed Gramlich. Their writings influenced what you now hold in your hands, and if it's any good, it's because I stole only from the very best.

Introduction

Bailout Nation

Owe the bank $100, that's your problem. Owe the bank $100 million, that's the bank's problem.

—J. P. Getty

We like to think of the United States as a rugged country of determined, self-reliant individuals. The iconic image is the American cowboy. You can picture him on a cattle drive, watching warily over his herd. All he needed to get by were his wits, his horse—and his trusty Winchester.

This idealized vision of America is fading fast, rendered moot by present-day cattle rustlers. The new gauchos ride not on the range, but on the financial vistas. Instead of herding cattle, they rope derivatives, wrangle financial instruments, and round up paper wealth. The differences between the modern-day cowboy/bankers

and the ranch hands of the old West are many, not the least of which is monetary—today's banker/rustler makes a whole lot more money than the frontiersmen did in the past.

But there is another crucial difference between the two—the "individualist" part. The newfangled herdsman may look rugged, but he sure as hell ain't independent. The modern cowpoke has become way too reliant on a different sort of cavalry: Uncle Sam—and all the taxpayers that support him.

How did we go from being a nation that revered the idea of the self-reliant broncobuster into something else entirely? What turned us into a nanny state for well-paid bankers?

How did the good ole U.S. of A. turn into a Bailout Nation? That is what this book is about.

It's easy to understand why *bailout* is such a dirty word in the American financial vernacular. There are many reasons, but I want to focus on the three biggest ones.

First, there is something inherently unjust about some people getting a free ride when everyone else has to pay his or her own way. We Americans are always willing to lend a hand to someone down on their luck, but that is not what the current crop of bailouts is about. This is the government financially rescuing people despite—or perhaps because of—their own enormous recklessness and incompetence.

This inequity is especially galling to those of us who work in the financial markets. Wall Street has long been a brutal meritocracy. Success is based on skills and smarts and the relentless ability to identify opportunity while simultaneously managing risk. All of the people I know who work on the Street—whether in stocks, bonds, options, or commodities—have a strong sense of fair play. "Eat what you kill" is the classic Wall Street attitude toward risk and reward, profit and loss.

There are, however, those market players who fail to live or die by their own swords—but then expect to be rescued by others from their own folly. They embody a fair-weather belief in the free market system, somehow thinking it applies only during the good times. This is a high form of moral cowardice, and it is rightly despised by those who play fairly and by the rules.

Since the turn of the twenty-first century, well-connected, moneyed interests have managed to keep all of their profits and bonuses during good times, but have somehow thrown off their risk and the results of their own bad decision making onto the public taxpayers. "Privatized gains and socialized losses" is hardly what capitalism is supposed to be.

Second, the process of how some groups get rescued by the government, while others are left to flounder, is in and of itself suspect. The cliché that "no one should see how laws or sausages get made" is especially true when it comes to bailouts. The political mechanisms—and the dollar amounts involved—are especially egregious. Why? In all modern cases, they are done quickly, on an emergency footing. There is often little or no debate. Transparency has been nonexistent. Many observers not only object philosophically to the concept of bailouts, but are particularly offended by the ham-fisted way they are foisted upon the public. Nearly everything has been done on an ad hoc basis, with little thought and less planning. Who has time for strategy or long-term thinking when we have trillions of dollars to spend?

Third, and finally, there are the costs. If we have learned anything about bailouts over the past hundred years, it is that each rescue attempt is more costly than the one that preceded it. This is usually true in terms of the immediate expenditure, but even more so in terms of the long-term damage done to the financial system. As of February 2009, the costs have raced past $14 trillion. That is an unprecedented sum of money, greater than any other single government expenditure in the nation's history (see Table I.1).

Table I.1 Cheaper to Clean Up After?

Big Budget Expenditure	Cost	Inflation Adjusted Cost
Marshall Plan	$12.7 billion	$115.3 billion
Louisiana Purchase	$15 million	$217 billion
Race to the Moon	$36.4 billion	$237 billion
S&L Crisis	$153 billion	$256 billion
Korean War	$54 billion	$454 billion
The New Deal	$32 billion (est.)	$500 billion (est.)
Gulf War II/Invasion of Iraq	$551 billion	$597 billion
Vietnam War	$111 billion	$698 billion
NASA	$416.7 billion	$851.2 billion
Total		**$3.92 trillion**

Source: Data courtesy of Bianco Research

Beyond the actual out-of-pocket expenses lies the dangerous hazard of corporate bailouts. The government's largesse encourages greater and greater reckless speculation. The ordinary liability and risk that is supposed to go with investing and business ventures seem to have disappeared. A grotesque distortion of normal capitalist incentives is formed. When a sector of the economy expects to be rescued by the government, it loses the healthy fear of financial failure. This leads directly to excessive speculation and reckless behavior—a condition known as moral hazard.

■ ■ ■

Historically, excessive greed, recklessness, and foolish speculation were punished by the market. Speculators lost their capital, their reputation, and their influence. (Back in the day when skyscrapers had windows that opened, some even lost their lives.) Their pools of cash migrated to people who handled risk in a more intelligent fashion. This is—or perhaps was—the great virtue of capitalism: Money finds its way to where it is treated best. Capital gravitates to those who can balance risk and reward, and who can obtain positive investment results, without blowing up. It's no coincidence that the largest venture capital firms, the biggest hedge funds, and the longest-lasting private trusts know how to manage risk. They preserve their capital. They have a healthy respect for losses, and strive to keep them manageable. They do not, as so many have done recently, put all their money on a single number, spin the roulette wheel, and hope for the best.

The present system has lost its auto-correcting mechanism. As economist Allan Meltzer noted, "Capitalism without failure is like religion without sin—it just doesn't work." While the profit motive is alive and well, with rewards potentially in the billions of dollars for some, there is no corresponding and offsetting risk of enormous loss. Any system that allows profits to be kept by a select few but expects the loss to be borne by the public is neither capitalism nor socialism: It is the worst of both worlds.

Government intervention thwarts this migration of capital. Instead of the relentless efficiency of the marketplace—I call it the back of Adam Smith's invisible hand—we have instead politically expedient shortcuts that bypass this process. In the end, this results in a misallocation of capital, and an embracing of risk and short-term motives that leads to utter recklessness. Hence, the mortgage broker who fudges the loan application, the bank that looks the other way to process it, and the fund manager that ultimately buys this crappy paper are all focused not on sustainable, long-term returns, but on the quick buck. As we will see, the implications for the broader economy have been dire.

■ ■ ■

The modern era of finance is now defined by the bailout. *Systemic risk* has become the buzzword du jour. History teaches us that these bouts of intervention to save the system occur far more regularly than an honest definition of that phrase would require. Indeed, systemic risk has become the rallying cry of those who patrol the corridors of Washington, D.C., hats in hand, looking for a handout. As we too often learn after the fact, what is described as systemic risk is more often than not an issue of political connections and politics. Perhaps a more accurate phrase is *economic expediency*.

The past generation has seen increasing dependence on government intervention into the affairs of finance. Industrial companies, banks, markets, and now financial firms have all become less independent and more reliant upon Uncle Sam. This is no longer a question of philosophical purity, but rather a regular occurrence of politically connected corporations—and their well-greased politicians—throwing off the responsibility for their failures onto the public. Any sort of guiding philosophy or ideology regarding free markets, competition, success, and failure seems to have simply faded away as inconvenient. No worries, the taxpayer will cover it.

Some people—most notably current Federal Reserve chairman Ben Bernanke and former chairman Alan Greenspan—seem to feel that it is the responsibility of governmental entities such as the Federal Reserve or Congress to intervene only when the entire system is at risk. The events since August 2007 have made it clear that this is a terribly expensive approach. Perhaps what the government should be doing is acting to prevent systemic risk before it threatens to destabilize the world's economy, rather than merely cleaning up and bailing out afterward. An ounce of regulatory prevention may save trillions in cleanup cures.

The United States finds itself in the midst of an unprecedented cleanup of toxic financial waste. As of this writing, the response to the credit crunch, housing collapse, and recession by various and sundry government agencies had rung up over $14 trillion in taxpayer liabilities, including bailouts for Fannie Mae and Freddie Mac, General Motors and Chrysler (twice, and soon to be three times), American International Group (AIG) (four times), Bank of America (three times), and Citigroup (three times). It has forced capital injections into other major banks, and government-engineered mergers involving once-vaunted firms Bear Stearns, Goldman Sachs, Morgan Stanley, Merrill Lynch, and Washington Mutual (see Table I.1). It has led to the Federal Deposit Insurance Corporation (FDIC) receivership, nationalization and sale of Washington Mutual (now in the hands of JPMorgan Chase), and Wachovia, flipped over the course of a weekend to Wells Fargo.

Yes, that's $14 trillion (plus)—about equal to the gross domestic product (GDP) of the United States in 2007. And as 2008 came to a close, even more industries caught the scent of easy money: Automakers, home builders, insurers, and even state and local governments were clamoring for a piece of the bailout pie.

The implications of this are significant. The current bout of bailouts—the banks and brokers, airlines and automakers, lenders and borrowers in the housing industry—will have significant, long-lasting repercussions.

So far, they have turned the United States into a Bailout Nation.

And that's just the beginning.

Part I

A BRIEF HISTORY OF BAILOUTS

Source: By permission of John Sherffius and Creators Syndicate, Inc.

Chapter 1

A Brief History of Bailouts

"The ultimate result of shielding men from the effects of folly is to fill the world with fools."

—Herbert Spencer, English philosopher

America's relationship with bailouts has been a complex and nuanced affair. It has evolved gradually, morphing through various phases over time. The United States has had several distinct bailout eras, and each has seen an incremental shift in the attitudes toward government rescues. Philosophically, the country has moved from finding the mere idea of a government intervention to any corporation abhorrent, to begrudgingly accepting interventions as a rare but necessary evil. Since the late 1990s, bailouts have been embraced around the world as a near-normal responsibility of government to save the financial markets from themselves. Most recently, a backlash has been building against bailouts as a reward for dumb and irresponsible behavior.

Let us consider an earlier period in U.S. history—the nineteenth century to the pre–Great Depression era. The popular attitude toward

both governments and corporations was very different at that time from today. Government was much smaller, and was not seen as a lender of last resort to either banks or industry. A general suspicion of corporate entities was commonplace among the populace, and there was a near-adversarial relationship between the government and the larger corporate interests.

The federal government's involvement in companies in the nineteenth century was more as an incubator than a rescuer. There wasn't much in the way of venture capital funding then, and a few start-ups sought and received modest amounts of government assistance. Railroad and telegraph firms were given easements and rights of passage, facilitating the government's desire for expansion into the West. Later on, telephone companies also enjoyed government largesse. Eminent domain was used to purchase properties for the benefit of companies as varied as mining, cattle ranches, railroads, and telegraph firms. In each of these early examples, the government's cash outlays were quite modest, and often facilitated a broad public good.

Rather than betting on any single company, the government found it to be in its own interest to jump-start a sector and then allow a brutal Darwinian competition to take place. Ultimately, that left standing only a few survivors as the rest of the industry fell by the wayside. Automobiles, computers, electronics—history is replete with examples of the U.S. government staying out of the way of a competitively developing industry. The government left these companies to follow their own natural life cycle via the mechanics of the free market. In *Pop! Why Bubbles Are Great for the Economy*, Dan Gross details the thousands of railroads, telegraph companies, automakers, and Internet companies that boomed and then eventually went bust.[1] In most industries, this process leaves behind a valuable infrastructure for subsequent companies to build upon. This was Joseph Schumpeter's "creative destruction" at work.

The groundwork for modern bailouts was laid in the early twentieth century, when in 1913, the Federal Reserve System was created. As we will see in a later chapter, this had major implications a century later. As originally envisioned, it was imbued with only modest monetary and fiscal powers. Eventually, these powers were expanded dramatically.

The next phase took place in the 1930s and 1940s, between the Great Depression and World War II. The widespread economic turmoil and political discontent forced the government to engage in a series of economic stimuli designed to generate jobs, income, and economic activity. While some political historians have described this as a bailout, it was not directed toward any specific corporation or economic sector. The public works programs of the Depression era were designed to impact the entire economy, stimulate growth, and reduce the 25 percent unemployment rate.

The latter years of this second era preceded World War II. The U.S. steel industry had previously enjoyed a booming decade in the 1920s, but had collapsed during the economic crisis. The United States, anticipating the possibility of its entry into World War II, recognized the importance of a viable industrial manufacturing sector. Without a healthy steel industry, the country would've been hamstrung in its attempts to build ships, tanks, planes, and other tools of warfare. The munitions industry also received much of Uncle Sam's largesse, as did the metals companies and the rubber industry. Indeed, the ramp-up to World War II saw an enormous amount of government assistance to companies that were war-related.

Were these truly bailouts? It's hard to call any nation's national defense buildup in wartime a true bailout.

After World War II, the United States entered a long period of economic expansion. The building of suburbia, the automobile industry's enormous growth, the expansion of major cities, and the entire postwar baby boom led to salad days for corporate America. There was no further government involvement in corporate America until the rescue of Lockheed Aircraft Corporation in 1971.

What made the Lockheed bailout so pivotal was its status as the first public bailout of a major corporation—and only that corporation. The Lockheed rescue became the blueprint for most future bailouts over the next half century.

The rescue of Lockheed in 1971 ($250 million) led to loan guarantees for Penn Central in 1974 ($676.3 million in loan guarantees), which paved the way for the $1.5 billion rescue of Chrysler in 1980 and then Continental Illinois Bank in 1984 ($1.8 billion loss). This led to the original mother of all government insurance payouts—the savings and loan (S&L) crisis of the early 1990s (total taxpayer cost: $178.56 billion), which led to the stock market rescue of 2000, and so on. Each bailout has

had negative consequences, and the repercussions have often led to the next bailout. Each negative impact seems to have the perverse effect of making future bailouts less surprising and more tolerable—and therefore more likely.

The Federal Reserve's attempted rescue of the credit markets in August 2007 ultimately led to the $29 billion rescue of a single firm—the investment bank Bear Stearns in March 2008. The Fed not only was rescuing Bear Stearns but, indirectly, JPMorgan Chase, the largest derivatives counterparty of Bear Stearns. More important, the Fed was also protecting its original decision to rescue the credit markets. The housing bailout package of July 2008 rationalized the interest rate policies of the early 2000s, and led indirectly to the nationalization of Fannie Mae and Freddie Mac, which not only cost $200 billion, but put more than $5.5 trillion worth of debt back on the books of the U.S. government. Then came the takeover of AIG ($173 billion and counting), the $700 billion Troubled Assets Relief Program (TARP), which featured the forced injection of $250 billion into the nation's largest banks. November 2008 brought another $20 billion capital injection into Citigroup (total $45 billion) and guarantees for $250 billion of its toxic assets. Bank of America also saw its cash injection upped to $45 billion and guarantees of $306 billion on its toxic assets. There was $30 billion for the automakers. 2009 saw a $75 billion rescue for homeowners, and a $770 billion dollar economic stimulus plan.

Perhaps it's best to stop calling these numbers "astronomical." A better term might be "economic numbers"—dollar amounts so vast they dwarf time and space. When you are tossing around those kinds of numbers, what is another $800 billion program for mortgage-backed securities and credit-related assets? And as long as we still have some checks left, we might as well do a government-engineered takeover by JPMorgan Chase of Washington Mutual. The government tried to do the same with Citigroup and Wachovia, but Wells Fargo swooped in with a higher offer, suggesting that even in Bailout Nation, private capital still has its place.

As a nation, we went from never bailing out anyone to somehow finding a seemingly inexhaustible supply of bailout candidates.

I can't wait to see what the hell is gonna happen next month.

Chapter 2

The Creation of the Federal Reserve, and Its Role in Creating Our Bailout Nation

I am a most unhappy man. I have unwittingly ruined my country. A great industrial nation is controlled by its system of credit. Our system of credit is concentrated. The growth of the nation, therefore, and all our activities are in the hands of a few men. We have come to be one of the worst ruled, one of the most completely controlled and dominated Governments in the civilized world.

—President Woodrow Wilson[1]

As much as I tried to steer clear of writing a history of central banking, it was all but impossible. Any examination of bailouts in the United States would be incomplete if the role of the Federal Reserve System were omitted. I will endeavor to keep it brief and relatively painless.

It is crucial to understand the role of the Fed, and how it has radically expanded over time, if you are to have any hope of comprehending the modern era of Bailout Nation. Since March 2008, so many different financial bailouts have been funded directly by the Fed—into investment banks, government-sponsored enterprises (GSEs), brokerage firms, money market funds, even the overall stock market—that we could not discuss bailouts intelligently and avoid mentioning the Fed. It is front and center in this mess.

The role of emergency fixer was not part of the Fed's original mission statement. At the end of the eighteenth century, prior to the creation of a central bank, currencies from as many as 50 nations were circulating in the United States. A single currency, backed by a strong authority, was needed to maintain some semblance of order. For any young and growing country, this was a necessity.

As originally conceived, the central bank had a narrow task. It was brought into existence for eminently reasonable and defensible purposes: to establish financial order, to allow for the creation of needed credit for the country, and to resolve the issue of the fiat currency (money that has value by virtue of the government declaring it has value).

From those relatively modest monetary and fiscal powers, the Federal Reserve has evolved into something that would be unrecognizable to its founders. Under the guise of economic expediency, the Fed has grabbed power, dramatically widening the areas of its responsibility. Since the 1990s, the Federal Reserve System, a private corporation registered in the State of Delaware, has behaved as though it were in charge of anything economic—moderating the swings of the business cycle, maintaining interest rates, supporting the value of depreciating assets, even intervening in the stock market.

During the economic collapse and credit crises, there was a distinct lack of financial leadership in the United States. With President Bush's approval rating at historic lows, the White House showed little inclination to face the storm. As the many crises began heating up in 2007, the leadership vacuum was apparent. It was into this empty space that the Fed inserted itself, seizing more and more authority. It wasn't so much a power grab as a reluctant filling of the void. Steve Matthews, writing for Bloomberg, observed, "What started as a meltdown in the market for subprime mortgages has turned into a worldwide credit and economic crisis. Bernanke, now the Fed chairman, has responded with the most aggressive expansion of the Fed's power in its 95-year history."[2]

Paul Volcker, the well-regarded former Fed Reserve chair, was aghast at how much authority the central bank had claimed as its own. Following the Fed-financed shotgun wedding of Bear Stearns and JPMorgan Chase, he told The Economic Club of New York: "The Federal Reserve has judged it necessary to take actions that extend to the very edge of its lawful and implied powers, transcending in the process certain long-embedded central banking principles and practices."[3]

The Federal Open Market Committee (FOMC), the Federal Reserve's principal tool for implementing monetary policy, has even gone so far as to state that its charge includes preventing "panic" in the markets, a far cry from its official dual mandate of price stability and full employment.

None of these duties were ever part of the Fed's charter.

■ ■ ■

The fourth time's the charm: The institution we know as the United States Federal Reserve is actually the fourth attempt at creating a central banking system in the United States.

To truly appreciate how a limited facilitator of banks evolved into the most powerful central bank in the world, we need to understand a bit of its history. All three previous attempts at creating a central bank in the United States were met with equal measures of concern and controversy. Thomas Jefferson, the principal author of the Declaration of Independence, argued that since the Constitution did not specifically empower Congress to create a central bank, doing so would be unconstitutional. "Banking establishments are more dangerous than standing armies," Jefferson famously declared, and went on to say:

> The central bank is an institution of the most deadly hostility existing against the Principles and form of our Constitution. I am an Enemy to all banks discounting bills or notes for anything but Coin. If the American People allow private banks to control the issuance of their currency, first by inflation and then by deflation, the banks and corporations that will grow up around them will deprive the People of all their Property until their Children will wake up homeless on the continent their Fathers conquered.[4]

The change from the Jeffersonian view toward the Federal Reserve to the modern public's attitude is nothing short of extraordinary.

Like Presidents Jefferson and Wilson, the American people genuinely feared giving this much power to a group of unelected, unaccountable private bankers. The fairly blasé response to the Fed's current expansion of its authority—and trillions in new Fed credit lines—is rather surprising. In light of the antipathy and worry previous central banks had historically evoked, the power grab by the Bernanke Fed and Treasury Secretaries Paulson and Geithner are all the more remarkable. Other than gold bugs and economists from the Austrian school, the public response has been tepid.

■ ■ ■

The first attempt at creating a central bank was made in 1791. The new nation needed a depository for the levies and taxes it collected, and the government required a way to take short-term loans to fill temporary revenue gaps. A simple fiscal institution was created and called the First Bank of the United States. But just to be safe, it had a 20-year charter, which expired in 1811.

Without the existence of a central lending authority, the War of 1812 left the underfinanced nation with a "formidable debt."[5] Private banks issued an ever-increasing amount of notes, leading to a serious bout of monetary inflation. The need for some form of a central bank was readily apparent. Thus, the Second Bank of the United States was chartered in 1816, five years after the demise of the First Bank. It had more funding and therefore greater influence than its predecessor. While both banks were controversial, it was the Second Bank of the United States that was perceived as especially threatening. It became so powerful that "many citizens, politicians, and businessmen came to view it as a threat to themselves and a menace to American democracy."[6]

When the Second Bank's charter lapsed in 1836, there was hardly an appetite for a Third Bank of the United States. But as the young nation grew, its finance and banking system grew haphazardly. Lacking a coordinating central authority, the first hundred years of the country's financial development became a patchwork of private banks, notes, and currencies. Many individual states issued their own legal tender, and private banks had the authority to commission engravers to design banknotes. Insurance companies, railroads, import and export firms, and others all had a similar ability. The anarchy that ensued made the dozens of foreign currencies circulating in the republic's early days look almost organized. In *A Nation of Counterfeiters*, Stephen Mihm writes:

> By the 1850s, with so many entities commissioning banknotes of their own design (and in denominations, sizes, and colors of their own choosing), the money supply became a great confluence of more than 10,000 different kinds of paper that continually changed hands, baffled the uninitiated, and fluctuated in value according to the whims of the market. Thousands of different kinds of gold, silver, and copper coins issued by foreign governments and domestic merchants complicated the mix. Such a multifarious monetary system was not what the framers of the Constitution had intended.[7]

And those were just the legal currencies, notes, and specie. Counterfeiting was fairly commonplace. Estimates were that as much as 10 percent of all currency in circulation was fake.[8]

Beyond forgery, bank runs were common, and bank failures occurred with increasing regularity. It was apparent that the financial system, left to its own devices, could not function properly. It was operating—quite literally—in the Wild West.

The nation's third foray into central banking came about with the National Currency Act (1863), later amended to the National Banking Act (1864 and 1865). This legislation provided for the creation of nationally chartered banks. Requirements included stringent capital minimums, lending limits, and regular bank examinations by the Office of the Comptroller of the Currency. Near-modern banking regulation and supervision thus came into existence.

Although these national banking acts were a significant improvement over the previous regulatory regime, eventually they too proved inadequate. Currency growth was tied to the bond market, not the broader economy. For a rapidly growing young nation, this proved insufficient. An inelastic currency and nonexistent national reserve system led to wild swings in the economy, with oscillating periods of booms and busts. Depressions became a surprisingly common cyclical phenomenon.

These "early experiments in central banking," as the Federal Reserve Bank of Boston called these pre-twentieth-century attempts, were almost quaint in comparison to modern times. The Boston Fed explained:

> As the American economy became larger, more urban, and more complex, the inelastic currency and the immobile reserves contributed to the cyclical pattern of booms and busts. These wide gyrations were becoming more and more intolerable. Financial panics occurred with some frequency, and they often triggered an economic depression. In 1893 a massive depression rocked the American economy as it had never been rocked before. Even though prosperity returned before the end of the decade—and largely for reasons which this nation could not control—the 1893 depression left a legacy of economic uncertainty.[9]

■ ■ ■

How did we end up with such a powerful central bank if the country was originally so opposed to one? After those first three attempts failed, we need to fast-forward to the Panic of 1907. In its aftermath, we find the genesis of the modern Federal Reserve Bank.

As so often happens, a long stretch of cyclical growth led to a boom, bust, panic, and renewal. Rapid industrial growth was the key to the recovery from the depression of 1893. Soon, twentieth-century America was booming. From the mid-1890s to 1906, the nation's annual growth rate was 7.3 percent.[10]

How did the country go from prosperity to panic? It would take a complete book to explain (I recommend Bruner and Carr's *The Panic of 1907*). In brief, the San Francisco earthquake revealed trouble beneath the surface of the nation's finances. The massive scope of the damage impacted financial activity around the world. Relief funds were sent to help resolve nearly $500 million in damages caused by the quake and the ensuing fires. London, Germany, France, New York City, and other financial centers saw significant capital migrate westward.

But it was primarily in London, the capital of the British Empire and the financial center of the world, where the monetary problem gestated. Insurance companies were shipping enormous amounts of gold to San Francisco as policies were paid out. As a result, the money supply in England was becoming inordinately tight. With capital scarce, bankers in the United Kingdom decided to do something about it. Printing presses and helicopters were not a ready solution in 1906; instead, the Bank of England raised rates from 3.5 to 6 percent to attract capital. Soon after, other European banks followed. Money flows to where it's treated best, and after the rate hikes, lots of money found its way back to England.

Consider this modern example of how the more things change, the more they stay the same. In October 2008, after its banking system was devastated by the credit crunch and investment losses, Iceland's central bank hiked its rates to 18 percent for the same reason the Bank of England did a century earlier: to attract capital.

To those who regularly advocate for the dismantling of the Federal Reserve, perhaps the previous tale may prove instructive. Unless all nations agree to do so simultaneously, the dissolving of a central bank amounts to the economic equivalent of unilateral disarmament.

In the United States in 1907, there was no such comparable mechanism to compete with the Bank of England. While the promise of great riches attracts capital during a boom, liquidity flees once the boom turns to bust. The legacy of economic uncertainty tracing back to the 1893 depression, combined with America's acute need to attract capital, set the stage for what came next.

In 1908, Congress was desperately searching for an answer to the ongoing financial crises. Its response was to create the National Monetary Commission, a panel studying potential solutions to the nation's monetary problems. It took five years of political maneuvering, public debate, and legislative proposals to decide whether the United States should have a central bank, and what that bank should look like. It would take yet another book to explain precisely how the Federal Reserve was created in 1913 (and G. Edward Griffin's *The Creature from Jekyll Island*[11] is the Fed hater's standard tome).

For the purpose of understanding how the United States became a Bailout Nation, we need only note that the Federal Reserve System was indeed created, granted extraordinary powers, and set loose upon the world. As we will see, the results of this act will have unforeseen consequences that were not remotely imagined back in 1913.

Chapter 3

Pre-Bailout Nation (1860–1942)

> Capitalism *is not really the best word to describe this arrangement. (The term was coined in the late 19th century as a way to describe the ideological opposite of communism.) Some decades later, people began to use a better term,* "the American system," *in which the government involved itself in the economy primarily to develop what we would now call infrastructure—highways, canals, railroads—but otherwise let economic liberty prevail. I prefer to call this spectacularly successful arrangement* "financial democracy"*—a largely free system in which the U.S. government's role is to help citizens achieve their best potential, using all the economic weapons that our financial arsenal can provide.*
>
> —Robert J. Shiller[1]

The United States as a Bailout Nation is a relatively new phenomenon. In the early and middle parts of our history, the country did not engage in rescue operations of corporations; speculators who got into trouble were on their own.

Government assistance was more likely to be made available during the birth pangs of a new industry—not during a single company's death rattle.

Venture capital firms were nonexistent in the nineteenth century. The early days of the republic did not have the equivalent of a Sand Hill Road. Sometimes Congress was called upon to fund start-ups and new technologies. Classic examples can be found in the expansion of the nation's railroads westward and in the development of the telegraph industry. Both of these industries found a coaxable benefactor in Washington, D.C., and received a helpful push from taxpayer subsidies. Commercialization of the first telegraph line was jump-started by congressional funding; railroads received land grants and other forms of enabling assistance to help them expand westward.

The government's preference was to fund industries that would facilitate the nation's physical expansion, stimulate infrastructure development, and aid economic growth. Once these industrial sectors were up and running, however, they were left to succeed or fail on their own. *How charming! How quaint! What a novel idea!*

Inventors and entrepreneurs were a key part of this process. The telegraph industry began when Samuel F. B. Morse, the inventor of the Morse Code, managed to wrangle $30,000 of taxpayer money out of Congress in 1844. He was credited with establishing the first telegraph line between Washington, D.C., and Baltimore.[2]

So too began the railroad industry. Government grants in 1850 provided lands to Illinois, Mississippi, and Alabama in aid of the Illinois Central Railroad, along with the Mobile and Ohio Railroads. Illinois Central obtained these subsidies through the efforts of a young country lawyer by the name of Abraham Lincoln. The Illinois Central Railroad later repaid the favor by helping Lincoln get elected president in 1860. Perhaps it wasn't such a favor after all; once in office, Lincoln signed land grants to railroads totaling more than 150 million acres of public land. Of the five transcontinental railroads of the day, four of them owed their existence to these enabling subsidies.

The life cycle of all new industries is the same: New technologies experience a period of rapid growth. The opportunities attract competitors. The new industry expands rapidly and soon makes lots of money. This attracts further competition: more companies, people seeking jobs in these growth areas, and even more capital and greater investment. Fresh competition helps the industry develop and mature. Eventually, the boom reaches the point where overinvestment and excess capacity become endemic, leading to brutal price competition and shrinking margins. Strong firms survive while most of the weaker companies fail. Those with poor management, insufficient capital, or inferior technology soon find themselves on the wrong side of Darwin's law. This is a cycle that repeats over and over in the system of free market capitalism.

Beyond the telegraph and railroads, this boom-and-bust cycle has been repeated across all industries. The same pattern has played out in all new technologies: radio, steel, automobiles, television, aviation, electronics, computers, and, more recently, Internet companies. The boom-and-bust cycle in subprime mortgage originators, mortgage brokers, and even real estate agents is no different than prior cycles. And we can expect the same cycle to occur during the next few decades in solar power companies, gene therapy research, electric car manufacturers (again), nanotechnology, stem cell medicine, and all manner of alternative energy production.

Believe it or not, there was a time when this great nation of ours actually believed in allowing consumers in the marketplace to choose the winners and losers of an industry. History has repeatedly shown us that this is a more efficient allocator of capital than representative governments or dictatorial central planners. Alas, it is a lesson easily forgotten.

■ ■ ■

There is a temptation to compare the present-day Bailout Nation—an era of big government bailouts and bigger corporate rescues—to the Great Depression and the New Deal. But there are many obvious differences between the two periods: In the 1930s, the United States was an industrial powerhouse. Steel, manufacturing, railroads, and coal were the dominant industries. Stocks were not that widely owned, so the market crash was initially seen as affecting only the wealthy. The modern era is diametrically different.

There are some similarities between the government's response to the current crisis and Franklin Delano Roosevelt's New Deal, particularly the seemingly endless array of new programs with acronyms like TARP

and TAFFY. But massive government response to a crisis is the effect. What is truly different between the two eras is the cause of the crisis, who got bailed out, and why.

The 1929 stock market crash eventually led to a worldwide depression. It was particularly acute in the United States, where unemployment rose to 25 percent, and nearly one in five homeowners faced foreclosure. Through no fault of their own, the vast majority of Americans were in economic distress. The recipients of government aid had not gotten into these difficult situations by virtue of their own recklessness, speculation, or outright stupidity. Rather, they were the victims of a broad economic collapse, and not its architects. The *Great Gatsby* era certainly had its fair share of excesses; however, the average citizen was not, as Citigroup's Former CEO Chuck Prince once stated, "compelled to dance so long as the music played."

Viewed in this light, it's hard to see the current crop of big corporate bailouts as somehow similar to the government's response to the Great Depression. It is simply not an apt comparison in terms of causes and culpability.

It is true, however, that the 1929 crash and ensuing era led to a vast smorgasbord of government programs. The population demanded action from their government in response to the widespread economic distress. It was intervention into the economy that they wanted; and it was intervention into the economy that they got.

Compare that with the reaction to the bailouts in 2008. It is hard to find many people who supported Secretary of Treasury Henry Paulson's initial plan to spend $750 billion buying troubled assets from banks and brokers. As originally conceived, the Troubled Asset Relief Program (TARP) was intensely disliked by the country (and people didn't exactly embrace it as it evolved). Calls to members of Congress ran 10 to 1 against the enormous spending package. Perhaps that is why it was voted down on the first attempt in the House of Representatives. The citizenry opposed the idea of casino capitalism, a system where privatized profits stayed in the hands of fair-weather capitalists, but all the risks were borne by the public. There was minor outrage over bailing out the very firms that had caused such widespread economic distress.

In the 1930s, there was very little in the way of objections from the public. In fact, the biggest applause line in FDR's 1933 inaugural address was not "We have nothing to fear but fear itself" but his repeated calls for action: "This nation asks for action, and action now."[3]

Here is a neat reversal of roles: Business leaders in the 1930s strongly objected to the government oversight and regulation that came with taxpayer largesse. In the modern era, it is the taxpayers who are objecting, while business leaders take private jets to Congress to go on bended knee and request bailout bucks.

Consider the steel industry, long a symbol of American might, as an example of economic distress that led to a major government intervention. From its precrash peak in 1929, the steel industry had fallen into utter disarray just three years later. Production had all but collapsed, cascading from more than 63 million net tons of ingot iron produced in 1929 to barely 15 million tons produced in 1932. This more than 75 percent drop in manufacturing output took production to the lowest levels since 1901, more than a third of a century earlier. Bethlehem Steel, which had been running at 90 percent of capacity before the crash, was operating at 13 percent of capacity by 1932.

Steel was emblematic of the rest of the U.S. economy: It had ground to a virtual standstill after the crash. The extreme economic conditions led to extreme responses. The government's focus was not on rescuing a single company or industry, but rather on resuscitating a once-great economy. As such, it's hard to think of these actions as bailouts—at least in the same way we view modern-day corporate bailouts. A look at the details reveals why.

From its 1929 peak to the ultimate low in 1932, the Dow Jones Industrial Average fell some 89 percent. The 1929 market crash was far broader than the technology crash in 2000. The broad indexes in 1929 lost more than three-quarters of their value. Most of the losses in the 2000–2002 crash were concentrated in technology and telecommunications and the new dot-com stocks. The benchmark Standard & Poor's 500 index lost only 50 percent, while the Dow Industrials fell a mere 38 percent.

The current downturn is one for the record books, at least in terms of speed: From their October 2007 all-time highs, the Dow and the S&P 500 were cut in half barely a year later. This was one of the steepest falls and fastest drops in market history. This downturn has seen major wealth destruction—but the effects in the overall economy have yet to

reach the same damage as in the Great Depression. Perhaps it is the safety nets that are in place; maybe the 1970s prepped us for this downturn. It may simply be that we have yet to plumb the full depths of this downturn.

Regardless, the impact of the 1929 market crash was far worse than anything we've seen since. The ensuing economic contraction was a uniquely devastating event in modern history. During the Great Depression, the U.S. economy simply collapsed into shambles. Lenders faced heavy investment losses, communities were unable to collect property taxes, the construction industry was all but frozen. Unemployment rates ran over 25 percent. Industrial capacity plummeted. Municipalities were badly in need of funds. The automobile industry ground to a full halt. During the worst of the Depression, one in five homes was in danger of foreclosure.

Even the worst of the complex difficulties of the 2008–2009 credit crunch and housing recession were mere sun showers compared to the financial hurricane of the Depression era: Banks have failed, but the FDIC's guarantees have prevented widespread panic. Unemployment has risen, but far below the worst levels of the 1930s. And the two million or so foreclosures over recent years are far less, on a percentage basis, than the nearly 20 percent foreclosure rate in the 1930s. In short, while the broad economy circa early 2009 is ugly, it remains far healthier than during the Great Depression.

President Roosevelt's response to the economic crisis has become known as the New Deal. It involved spending programs, aid to industry, new job creation, public works programs, and lending assistance to homeowners. Significant new legislation attempted to restore faith in the American banking system and credit markets, in the equity markets, and in the U.S. economy. It was the single most comprehensive and far-reaching set of legislative programs in American history.

The housing sector was a key part of the economy devastated by the Depression. It may be instructive to examine how homeowners benefited from intelligent government-sponsored lending.

When considering whether this was a bailout, one needs to consider the context of this massive intervention. The market for financing homes was quite different in the 1920s and 1930s than it is today. There were no such things as 30-year, fixed-rate mortgages. Instead, the typical mortgage was an interest-only loan for a period ranging from three to five years. These nonamortizing mortgages called for a balloon payment upon maturity. Most were renewed without much fuss—assuming the borrowers had maintained their jobs and payment histories.

As the 1930s economy went from bad to worse, this cozy home financing arrangement ran into trouble. Home prices entered into a steep decline. A cash-strapped populace, suffering from massive job losses, was frequently unable to meet its mortgage payments. In *History and Policies of the Home Owner's Loan Corporation,* C. L. Harriss writes, "What had generally been regarded as a reasonably sound arrangement by all parties concerned proved to be very weak when a set of interrelated forces combined to bring on a severe depression after 1929 and to disrupt seriously the structure of home-ownership finance."[4]

At its worst, mortgages were being foreclosed at the rate of 1,000 per day.[5] Moreover, as demands for cash increased from depositors, many lending institutions were faced with the issue of their own insolvency. Some lacked the capital to roll over mortgages. Others saw their credit lines disappear. Real estate assets were sold off of their books as many banks went bankrupt and had their assets seized by creditors.

All in all, the housing finance system was breaking down.

The Home Owners' Loan Act of 1933 (HOLA) was President Roosevelt's response to the wave of foreclosures. It directed the Federal Home Loan Bank Board to create the Home Owners' Loan Corporation (HOLC) with $200 million in Treasury funds, and authorized the HOLC to issue not more than $2 billion in bonds for the purchase of mortgage bonds. Ultimately, this amount was more than doubled to $4.75 billion. Loans were limited to distressed homeowners of units of one- to four-family residences. Homes valued at less than $20,000 were eligible, so long as the mortgage was recorded prior to HOLA (June 13, 1933).

By just about any conceivable measure, the Home Owners' Loan Corporation was a wild success. When the HOLC was liquidated on March 31, 1951, it did so at a slight profit, returning to the Treasury an accrued surplus of $14 million.[6] The rest of its performance was just as impressive:

- From June 1933 to June 1935, the HOLC received 1,886,491 applications for $6.2 billion of home mortgage refinancing, an average of $3,272 per application.[7]

- Seventy-five percent of loans were for less than $4,000, and amounted to about 69 percent of the HOLC appraised value of the property.[8]
- The HOLC made more than one million loans, lending more than $3.5 billion and refinancing 20 percent of the mortgaged homes in the country.
- At one point in time, one in five mortgages in the United States was owned by the HOLC.
- The total lending amounted to 5 percent of GDP.[9]

As part of the effort to revive the economy as a whole, the HOLC rescued the American housing sector. And it did so with little cost to the taxpayer. It is hard to think of this program as a true bailout, especially in comparison to modern bailouts. Homeowners who ran into trouble did so through no fault of their own. They hadn't purchased homes they could not afford. Home buyers of the day did not dabble with exotic mortgages, but instead used conservative financing to make their purchases. They did not engage in flipping, spec building, or other forms of speculation. There were no liar loans back then. The homeowners of the 1930s who were rescued by the HOLC did not contribute in any appreciable way to the economic mess of the time. Because of these many factors, the term *bailout* is not the correct title for this act; *rescue* is the more appropriate term.

The specifics of the HOLC were the secret to its success. HOLC loans were for as much as 80 percent of the appraised property value, but no greater than $14,000 under any circumstances. The HOLC exchanged Treasury bonds (4 percent interest rate) for mortgages. The Treasuries were triple tax free (exempt from local, state, and federal income taxes). The homeowner was charged a 5 percent interest rate over a 15-year loan term. At the time, prevailing rates were above 6 percent, so the HOLC terms were a substantial discount from what might otherwise be available. In some cases mortgages were interest only for the first three years, followed by the 15-year amortization period.

> It was the mortgage issuers who absorbed the loss between the value of the refinancing and their interest in the distressed loans. This was a preferable outcome to the certain loss a foreclosure was sure to cause in the very difficult real estate and credit markets of the time. The guaranteed HOLC bonds, and their tax-free status, encouraged the acceptance of HOLC bonds by mortgage issuers. Banks in receivership also were able to exchange mortgage holdings for HOLC bonds.
>
> But the HOLC was not a giveaway program. The program took over more than 200,000 houses by foreclosure.[10] In some states the HOLC foreclosure rate was quite significant. In New York and Massachusetts, over 40 percent of the government loans made were foreclosed.

■ ■ ■

In 1932, President Herbert Hoover called for the creation of the Reconstruction Finance Corporation (RFC) in a State of the Union address. In its first year, the RFC primarily made loans to banks and financial institutions. Later, its role was dramatically expanded to include loans to railroads, agriculture, and the steel industry. The RFC was initially created with $500 million of capital from the Treasury (the RFC was eventually authorized to borrow $1.5 billion more). During its years of existence, the RFC borrowed $51.3 billion from the Treasury and $3.1 billion from the public.[11]

Under Roosevelt, the government's response was greatly expanded. The New Deal was a bevy of legislation and government funding, including the National Industrial Recovery Act (NIRA), the Home Owners' Loan Act of 1933 (HOLA), and the Defense Plant Corporation (DPC). (See Table 3.1.) The NIRA "provided a legal framework under which both government and business acted together to raise prices without fear of anti-trust punishment."[12]

The creation of the FDIC in 1933 and the expansion of FDIC insurance in 2008 served similar purposes. Then, as now, the financial system was prone to panics and bank runs. By establishing deposit insurance for

Table 3.1 New Deal Programs

Act or Program	Acronym	Year Enacted	Significance
Agricultural Adjustment Act	AAA	1933	Protected farmers from price drops by providing crop subsidies to reduce production; provided educational programs to teach methods of preventing soil erosion.
Civil Works Administration	CWA	1933	Provided public works jobs at $15 per week to four million workers in 1934.
Civilian Conservation Corps	CCC	1933	Sent 250,000 young men to work camps to perform reforestation and conservation tasks. Removed surplus of workers from cities, provided healthy conditions for boys, and provided money for families.
Federal Emergency Relief Act	FERA	1933	Distributed millions of dollars of direct aid to unemployed workers.
Glass-Steagall Act/ Federal Deposit Insurance Corporation	FDIC	1933	Created federally insured bank deposits ($2,500 per investor at first) to prevent bank failures.
National Industrial Recovery Act	NIRA	1933	Created the National Recovery Administration (NRA) to enforce codes of fair competition and minimum wages, and to permit collective bargaining of workers.
National Youth Administration	NYA	1935	Provided part-time employment to more than two million college and high school students.
Public Works Administration	PWA	1933	Received $3.3 billion appropriation from Congress for public works projects.
Rural Electrification Administration	REA	1935	Encouraged farmers to join cooperatives to bring electricity to farms. Despite its efforts, by 1940 only 40 percent of American farms were electrified.

Table 3.1 (*Continued*)

Act or Program	Acronym	Year Enacted	Significance
Securities Exchange Act/Securities and Exchange Commission	SEC	1934	Regulated the stock market and restricted margin buying.
Social Security Act		1935	Response to critics (Dr. Francis Townsend and Huey Long); it provided pensions, unemployment insurance, and aid to blind, deaf, disabled, and dependent children.
Tennessee Valley Authority	TVA	1933	Federal government built series of dams to prevent flooding and sell electricity. First public competition with private power industries.
Wagner Act/National Labor Relations Board	NLRB	1935	Allowed workers to join unions and outlawed union-busting tactics by management.
Works Progress Administration	WPA	1935	Employed 8.5 million workers in construction and other jobs, and, importantly, provided work in arts, theater, and literary projects.

SOURCE: Greg D. Feldmeth, www.polytechnic.org/faculty/UShistory

all banking deposits, the government sought to alleviate the fear of loss that potential bank failures were causing. Panics were all too frequently developing. Bank runs became self-fulfilling prophecies, ultimately leading to institutions failing. Many of the banks held railroad bonds, and as the railroads succumbed to the economic contraction, the banks suffered also.

Unlike the current crisis, the Great Depression was not primarily located in any one sector; it was endemic to every corner of the economy. The government tried to reinvigorate the broader economy and to recapitalize the financial sector. It provided funding and a mechanism to allow homeowners who could afford to rework their mortgages to do so. The focus of the many government programs was to

shore up the financial institutions. Once that was accomplished through government guarantees—insurance for deposits, credit availability for banks—only then did the population start developing faith in these institutions.

Yet, there are a few parallels between today and the 1930s. Rampant speculation among Wall Street players set up the initial market crash in both eras. In both cases, the primary vehicle for leverage was unregulated credit or derivatives. Leverage added fuel on the way up, and it caught fire on the way down. Once all this liquidity began to dry up, the leverage led to a myriad of interconnected problems throughout the economy. Growth rapidly contracted. The initial government reaction was tepid, with key players mostly in denial about the extent of the economic damage. As the damage became increasingly difficult to ignore, the governmental response became broader, with major corporate bankruptcies spurring action. Then came a presidential election and new administration promising significant change.

One of the government's early responses to the crisis of the 1930s was to provide loans for railroads. The goal was to maintain the value of their bonds and therefore indirectly strengthen the banks' balance sheets. In the current era, loans to banks and brokerage firms—initially to keep them liquid, but ultimately to keep them solvent—has been one of the early Federal Reserve responses.

Here's a fun trick: Take any Depression-era railroad lending legislation, and place it into a document. Now do a "find & replace," substituting the words "home mortgages" for "railroad bonds." You very nearly end up with what became known as the Emergency Economic Stabilization Act, also known as the Troubled Assets Relief Program (TARP) passed on an emergency basis on October 3, 2008.

Current Fed chairman Ben Bernanke is a renowned student of the Great Depression, so perhaps similarities in the legislation are a bit of an homage. But Bernanke may have missed the biggest lessons of when and why massive government intervention is warranted—or at least may have turned them on their head, as we'll see in ensuing chapters.

Chapter 4

Industrial-Era Bailouts (1971–1995)

When things are going well, the companies stress the idea of free enterprise, with no need for government regulation. But when things aren't going well, they suddenly become a close partner with the government and want it to bail them out. All they have to do is threaten to collapse and the government pours in more money.

—A. Ernest Fitzgerald, civilian cost analyst and Management Systems Deputy to the Air Force Assistant Secretary for Financial Management

The previous era of government interventions focused broadly on emergency economic and prewar relief: Housing, jobs, finance, industrial production, and wartime preparation all received enormous aid.

The era that followed took a new and different path: bailouts of individual companies. This represented an enormous break from past philosophies, government activities, and use of taxpayer proceeds.

■ ■ ■

The year 1971 was a sea change in the history of American bailouts. That was the year when, for the very first time, the United States bailed out an industrial firm whose own financial mismanagement had driven it to the brink of extinction. The company was Lockheed Aircraft Corporation, and the bailout was in the form of loan guarantees worth $250 million.

Prior to the Lockheed rescue, the United States had never acted *in loco parentis* for any single firm. Previous rescue operations were intended to help the nation work through difficult times. During the Great Depression, one in four workers was unemployed, and the nation's economy was contracting 15 percent per year. The fear of further economic damage and civil unrest essentially forced the government's hand. During the period prior to U.S. entry into World War II, the government gave aid to steel, munitions, and rubber companies. As much as any governmental interventions, before or since, it is difficult to call these actions bailouts—they were acts of national self-preservation aimed at entire wartime industries, not individual private enterprises.

Lockheed was an unprecedented and, to many people, alarming new development. Never before had the government effected a rescue operation of a single company.

The firm had been having financial troubles for several years, posting losses in 1969 ($19.5 million) and 1970 ($86.3 million). Management had repeatedly made significant miscalculations on major projects: The company had won a $1.9 billion defense contract for the C-5A military transport plane in 1965, underbidding Boeing by $300 million.[1] Lockheed's optimistic projections led to enormous cost overruns. Separately, the firm's attempt at building passenger aircraft—the L-1011 TriStar—was also problematic. On top of these, Lockheed also had cost overruns on three other large military projects.

All in all, the firm was in dire financial straits due to its own actions and mismanagement.[2]

Despite its bumbling missteps, Lockheed hadn't become the nation's largest defense contractor because its management was foolish. They may have been marginally competent when it came to managing large military projects, but their true genius lay in the procurement process. By 1971, they had learned to quite skillfully navigate the vast bureaucracy of the U.S. military. And since the majority of Lockheed's revenues were already coming from the taxpayers, it did not require a big stretch to identify the federal government as the most likely potential rescuer of the company's precarious financial condition.

Facing continual cost overruns with four major U.S. military projects, as well as delays in the development of the TriStar, Lockheed saw no alternative. The firm formally petitioned the government for assistance on March 2, 1970, via a letter from Chairman Daniel Haughton to Deputy Defense Secretary David Packard. The company asked for a whopping $600 million in government assistance. That would be the 2007 equivalent of $3.2 billion.

The emergency loan package for Lockheed Aircraft was highly contested in Congress. The term *corporate welfare* was coined by Wisconsin Senator William Proxmire (D) to describe the proposed bailout. The House just barely voted in favor of the Emergency Loan Guarantee Act of 1971, 192 to 189. The bill almost didn't make it through the Senate; Vice President Spiro Agnew cast the deciding vote, winning passage 49 to 48.

SOURCE: © 2008, R. J. Matson, *St. Louis Post Dispatch*, politicalcartoons.com. Reprinted by permission.

Something else happened in 1971 that many believe was a critical catalyst to the United States becoming Bailout Nation: Richard Nixon took America off the gold standard.

As World War II came to its bloody conclusion, the Bretton Woods agreement had established the dollar as the world's reserve currency and set a fixed rate for the dollar's value versus an ounce of gold (3.5 ounces per $1,000). On August 15, 1971, just a few weeks after Congress approved the Lockheed bailout, Nixon broke that dollar-gold relationship.

It's difficult to show any direct causation from Nixon's act to the massive bailouts of modern times. But what is uncontested is that the U.S. federal debt and money supply exploded in the years subsequent to 1971, while the dollar steadily declined in value:

- In 1971 the total U.S. federal debt stood at $436 billion. Today, that number exceeds $10 trillion.
- From about $800 billion in 1971, the total broad-based money supply (M3) increased to a staggering $10.2 trillion at the end of Alan Greenspan's tenure as Federal Reserve chairman in 2006.
- After the first quarter of 2006, the Fed stopped reporting M3 money supply, a story for another book entirely.[3]

As long as foreigners were willing to buy U.S. Treasury securities, it became easier as the years went by for politicians and policymakers to approve bailouts that were largely financed by debt. Nearly 40 years later, Americans have become shockingly comfortable with Congress raising the U.S. debt ceiling in order to pay for various and sundry expenditures, including by $1.5 trillion in the summer of 2008 alone for the Housing Bill and Paulson's TARP plan.

The dollar was literally losing its value, but that was almost an afterthought.

> It took a while for politicians and policymakers to grasp the significance of just how much you can buy on credit when corporate welfare was in its infancy in 1971. But Lockheed was the proverbial Pandora's box that unleashed a generation of evils on American capitalism.

Even as they tackled Lockheed's rescue, members of Congress were already contemplating an even bigger bailout: Penn Central Railroad. Faced with mounting losses and unable (or unwilling) to pay its creditors, Penn Central declared bankruptcy in 1970. "In his petition to the court, Chairman Paul Gorman said that the line was 'virtually without cash, unable to meet its debts, [and] has no means of borrowing.' "[4]

At the time, Penn Central was the nation's largest railroad, and the Nixon administration proposed allowing the Defense Department to underwrite $200 million in loans to the struggling firm. But Congress balked. "The potential for political mischief really scared people," one observer told *Time* magazine in a statement that sounded serious at the time but now seems quaint. *Time* reported:

> In an effort to revive the failing intercity passenger rail service, Congress enacted the Rail Passenger Service Act (RPSA) in 1971. The RPSA authorized the creation of the National Railroad Passenger Corporation, a federally funded corporation better known as Amtrak [*and what a winner that turned out to be*].
>
> When it became apparent that it was not possible to reorganize a viable rail system solely through the Bankruptcy Case, Congress, drawing upon its bankruptcy power and the eminent domain authority available to it under the Commerce Clause, enacted the Regional Rail Reorganization Act of 1973 (the Rail Act) to ensure the existence of a viable rail system in the Northeast.[5]

In the end, Congress provided $125 million in loan guarantees to Penn Central's creditors and spent $7 billion in direct federal operating subsidies for Conrail, which Congress created in 1976 from the carcass of Penn Central and five other struggling East Coast rail lines.

If Lockheed was the government's first sip of bailout elixir, Penn Central was a big gulp that opened the floodgates for the bailout binge that was about to come.

In 1971, corporate welfare was just a baby. By 1980, it was a baby no more.

■ ■ ■

There is a strong case that such help rewards failure and penalizes success, puts a dull edge on competition, is unfair to an ailing company's competitors and their shareholders, and inexorably leads the Government deeper into private business. Why should a huge company be bailed out, say critics, while thousands of smaller firms suffer bankruptcy every year? Where should the Government draw the line? GM Chairman Thomas A. Murphy has attacked federal help for Chrysler as "a basic challenge to the philosophy of America."

—*Time*, 1979[6]

Throughout the 1970s, American automakers were being challenged as never before. The luxo-barges they were building had become stale and tired looking; they did not lend themselves easily to higher fuel efficiency changes or attractive redesigns. Creating a manufacturing system that produced mechanically reliable vehicles seemed to be beyond their ken. The companies themselves had become bloated bureaucracies with far too many layers of management to be able make significant changes.

Besides, change was not their forte.

Then came the oil embargo of 1973. Skyrocketing energy inflation was the new reality. As gasoline prices soared, the devastation was most acutely felt in Detroit, where America's biggest and least fuel-efficient cars and trucks were manufactured.

In the 1950s, *Barron's* described the Detroit automakers as the big two and a half—with Chrysler Corporation, the perennial sales laggard, as the half. When the embargo hit, Chrysler suffered the most of the Big Three.

By the mid-1970s, the company was hemorrhaging cash. Chrysler lost $52 million in 1974, and a record $259.5 million in 1975. As smaller, less expensive and more fuel-efficient cars from Japan and Europe gained increasing market share in 1970s, Chrysler found itself in an ever-deepening hole. It looked like it might have to declare bankruptcy.

But the United States is a big country, filled with big-assed people who love their big, comfy cars. As soon as the energy crisis ended, it was back to business as usual. The return of Motor City muscle made 1976 a hugely profitable year: The company's net income was $422.6 million.

Make small, efficient vehicles? The idea was laughable. The oil embargo was looked at as an aberration, and once prices had stabilized, it was back to manufacturing big iron. Despite the drop in fuel prices, though, Honda and Toyota continued to make steady gains in market share that decade—and beyond.

Although Chrysler had renegotiated terms with its top lenders, this merely bought the automaker a few years, allowing it to survive from one crisis to the next. The year 1977 was profitable, but less so: Net income was $163.2 million. Chrysler's models were getting long in the tooth, and retooling factories was an expensive process. By late 1978, the company was again running in the red, losing $204.6 million, as the fall of the Shah of Iran and a new oil embargo sent fuel prices to record high levels. By 1979, Chrysler was looking at its first billion-dollar annual loss.

As the decade came to a close, it was apparent to management that they were running out of money and would be unable to resolve their financial situation on their own.

Management decided it was time to visit Uncle Sam.

The Chrysler bailout was everything Lockheed—its predecessor in the bailout time line by nine years—was, and more. It was bigger and more expensive. Lockheed had loan guarantees worth $250 million; Chrysler's were for six times that amount. The rationale for the rescue of Lockheed, the country's biggest defense firm, was national defense. With Chrysler, it was the U.S. economy, and saving 200,000 jobs.

But the big difference between the two was that the Chrysler rescue package was much more complex. The terms of the Chrysler loan guarantees required an additional $2 billion in commitments or concessions from "its own owners, stockholders, administrators, employees, dealers, suppliers, foreign and domestic financial institutions, and by State and local governments."[7]

The Chrysler bailout of 1980 was not quite a prepackaged bankruptcy reorganization. It left the company with the same management team, the same union contracts, the same pension obligations, and the same health care coverage; all the bailout did was buy the company a few more years. Indeed, the prebailout industry looked almost identical to the postbailout industry. None of the Detroit automakers, Chrysler included, received any long-term benefits from the bailout.

What Congress did was postpone the inevitable.

■ ■ ■

In the television series *Star Trek*, Captain Kirk is accidentally transported to another starship *Enterprise* in an alternative universe ("Mirror Mirror"). Kirk quickly figures he is in a changed parallel universe, as the entire social fabric is radically different. Not only that, but his science officer, Mr. Spock, wears a beard. What was the cause of these changes? It turned out that because of a single change in the earlier history of that universe, everything else was radically different.

If only we had access to the universe with the bearded Spock.

This is the investigative challenge of any philosophical inquiry into bailouts—there is no control group. We don't get to examine the counterfactual outcomes had the government not intervened into the private markets. Hence, we have only the net result of taxpayer largesse as our frame of reference in the real world. We can, however, imagine the possible what-might-have-beens had a few votes been changed.

Without seeing the alternative, it is easy for Chrysler's congressional supporters to point to this as a successful bailout: After all, the government-guaranteed loans were repaid, employees' jobs were saved, and eventually Chrysler itself was purchased by Mercedes-Benz. The German company even managed to find a greater fool, Cerberus, to take the Detroit dog off its hands.

But was Chrysler really a successful bailout after all? Judged on the shortest-term basis of mere survival, we can begrudgingly say yes. Lacking access to our alternative universe—one where bailouts were voted down in Congress, and companies such as Lockheed and Chrysler had to fend for themselves in the private sector—we can only imagine how things might have turned out.

Let's use the Chrysler bailout as a hypothetical model of what might have happened in the event the government did not succumb to political pressure to bail out Chrysler.

We do not know precisely what that world would have looked like if Chrysler were forced to fend for itself in the marketplace, like all other competitive companies in the United States. But we can easily imagine it. Chrysler executives said had they not received government assistance, they would have had to file not Chapter 11 reorganization, but Chapter 7 bankruptcy.

Let's consider this alternative universe—where Spock wears a beard, and where Chrysler was allowed to suffer its own timely demise. A Chrysler in bankruptcy may very likely have caused several distinct business shifts, with far-reaching repercussions for the American automobile industry and the broader economy at large.

■ ■ ■

The sight of Chrysler in flames may very well have sent paroxysms of fear into the senior management of General Motors and Ford. All three companies had been engaged in long, slow declines, but the baby boomer generation's growth and consumption habits had masked the decline somewhat. Sure, the Big Three were selling more and more vehicles each year, but they were losing market share; their slice of the expanding pie was shrinking.

It is easy to see why. Their cars were no longer attractive, and the vehicles' reputation for mechanical reliability had deservedly slid in the face of superior German and Japanese machinery. Gas mileage was consistently mediocre. Rather than working to engineer improved mileage, corporate management chose to wage a political fight against Corporate Average Fuel Economy (CAFE) standards instead. It is one of many post-Chrysler actions that in hindsight have proven to be disastrous.

Had senior management been forced to confront one of the Big Three actually going under, it would have served as a wake-up call to the (all too many layers of) management of the remaining two companies.

What happened instead was a failure of imagination at Ford and GM. Instead of causing introspection and contemplation, there was snickering and gloating. Neither company recognized that they were both suffering

from the same disease that afflicted Chrysler—costly union contracts, expensive pension funding obligations, and ruinous future health care costs. The perennial third-place Chrysler was simply weaker, and so it showed the effects of its poor capital structure sooner than the other two.

A Chrysler bankruptcy could have been the impetus for major changes in Dearborn and Detroit. Instead, both firms generated more of the same ungainly, oversized, ugly cars. Quality wouldn't dramatically improve for two decades, and the cars lagged in mechanical reliability for years. Fuel efficiency also lagged, especially against Japanese vehicles.

Chrysler survived, but a slow necrosis gradually handed over the dominance of the U.S. automobile market to the Japanese, Koreans, and Germans. For the first time ever in May 2008, the majority of automobiles sold in the United States were not made by U.S. companies. In 1980, the U.S. manufacturers' market share had been 75 percent.

If that's your idea of a successful bailout, I'd hate to see what your idea of a losing one is like.

■ ■ ■

Had Chrysler gone belly-up, the loss of 123,000 jobs at Chrysler would've scared that the bejesus out of the United Auto Workers (UAW). The union had grown powerful and influential over time, and had developed a ruinous us-versus-them mentality with the management of the Big Three. A massive loss of jobs would have served notice that the current state of business was simply unsustainable and could not continue without major repercussions in the future.

One can imagine that in the face of such tragic economic destruction, the UAW might have begun negotiations with a completely different set of objectives. The UAW's senior management should have been tossed out, and a new operating arrangement negotiated.

Indeed, one can even imagine a more enlightened set of union representatives who would have been willing to horse-trade much more than they did, giving up pension and health care benefits, in exchange for a significant stake in the companies their union members worked for. Perhaps a more "Silicon Valley stock option" approach might have been the way to go. Employees could give up some health care benefits and pension guarantees, and receive in exchange equity in the form of stock options. I would imagine that this ownership arrangement would have worked miracles on worker productivity, too.

This would have left the remaining Big Two in a much healthier financial condition going forward.

The bailout sure didn't do the auto workers' union any long-term favors. The UAW's membership peaked in 1979, with some 1.5 million members. Twenty-seven years later, UAW membership had fallen by two-thirds to 538,448 (2006). And year-over-year totals are still falling by significant amounts. In the last full year of data we have (2006–2007) the union lost another 73,538—a 14 percent annual membership decrease. Membership is now below half a million, and rapidly heading toward 400,000.

Perhaps that's not such a coincidence, given what we know about the other implications of this bailout.

■ ■ ■

In the event of a Chapter 7 bankruptcy, we don't know that Chrysler would have disappeared from the face of the Earth. Unlike us mortals, large corporate entities, with valuable physical assets and intellectual property, stand a very real chance of some form of reincarnation. Chrysler owns valuable manufacturing facilities, trademarks, patents, and designs, along with three-quarters of a century of manufacturing know-how. At pennies on the dollar, these assets would have been attractive to a third-party purchaser.

Had Chrysler been allowed to slip the surly bonds of Earth in 1980, it's not too difficult to imagine a vulture investor obtaining all of the aforementioned assets, and putting them to good use. Maybe it would have been a group of wealthy auto enthusiasts, or perhaps the budding Korean manufacturers. Whoever it might be, just picture the newly refurbished Chrysler Corporation recapitalized, minus the onerous labor contracts, pension obligations, and health care overhead. Its new owner would have been free to pursue new manufacturing methods, new automobile designs, even new markets—with all the advantages Chrysler itself had, but without the defunct company's baggage.

A postbankruptcy Chrysler would have been leaner, meaner, and more cost-efficient, and maybe even a more fuel-efficient machine than

the rest of Detroit. Surely it could have been willing to take chances on some new designs that would break free of the stodgy old boring boxes put out by Detroit in the 1970s and 1980s.

Not only would Chrysler have been much more competitive in the U.S. and world markets, its mere existence would have forced GM and Ford to streamline their own processes and improve their vehicles in terms of attractiveness, mechanical reliability, and fuel efficiency.

■ ■ ■

It is quite reasonable to conclude that the bailout of Chrysler in 1980 prevented significant market forces from doing their best to reboot the entire U.S. auto sector.

The short-term gains of the bailout to save some jobs in the auto industry ended up costing a million more jobs over the ensuing decades.

Avoiding some immediate pain now seems to invariably lead to much greater pain down the road. This is a pattern we see repeated over and over again.

INTERMEZZO

A Pattern Emerges

As we progressed deeper into the history of bailouts, comparing them to the present, it became increasingly obvious that just about all American bailouts follow a consistent blueprint. This consistency was remarkable from event to event, regardless of the underlying corporate sector, the amount of money involved, or even the decade in which the bailout took place.

What does the prototypical bailout look like? Something like this:

Ten-Step Bailout Pattern

1. **Risk event:** Typically of the company's own making, it might be something as general as leverage or as specific as collateralized mortgage-backed securities. Regardless of the particular causes or complexities of these risk events, rest assured that a very significant amount of money is at risk. It is not only the company, but a series of related investments that are also endangered. This means monied parties—usually well connected on Wall Street and in Washington, D.C.—have a vested interest in not allowing the natural course of events to occur.
2. **Preawareness:** At first, the risk event is known to only a small coterie of experts such as junior researchers who are easily dismissed, and academics, easily derided as nonpractitioner theorists. The early observers during the precrisis write papers, attend conferences, and discuss industry specifics. More recently, they swapped e-mails and linked to blog posts.

Despite the warnings, the industry itself continues with business as usual. Cries of "Chicken Little" and "Cassandra" greet the early warnings.

3. **First reactions:** Key employees and industry insiders know something is amiss. But they continue to put on a happy public persona. Those pointing to the warning signs are denigrated with increasingly hostile rhetoric as the entrenched interests hope to scare or shame them into silence.
4. **Bigger reactions:** The risk event continues to grow in magnitude. It slowly leaks to the press—industry-specific journals at first, then general-interest media. By that point, it is very slowly beginning to seep into the public's consciousness. This is a process that typically occurs over months and indeed years.

   By the time the public has a widespread awareness of the issue, the problem has grown into something understood as significant, but not yet dangerous.
5. **"Interested party" agitation:** A group of self-interested parties have taken notice of the situation. Corporate management starts to become increasingly concerned—mostly with their own self-preservation, but with health of the corporate entity as well. There may be a subset of fund managers who perceive the situation as either threat or opportunity, and they seek to protect their assets from damage—or profit from some entities' demise.

   Eventually, the regulatory agencies become aware that something is awry, and at that point, it's a given that the politicians will soon figure out that something big is brewing.
6. **Official concern:** By now, some elements of the risk event have impacted the company's stock price. It is widely perceived as a temporary circumstance—and an opportunity to "buy while the shares are on sale."

   Shortly thereafter, the stock price declines even further. Short sellers may be castigated for their nasty rumormongering, and perhaps management blames Wall Street for being too focused on the short-term profits. Regardless, we receive assurances that this is a temporary setback, and the company's fundamentals are solid.

   Large institutional interests typically have billions of dollars that are put at greater possible loss due to the risk event. Whether they are hedge funds or mutual funds, investment banks or pension funds, the financial sector especially has the ear of the Federal Reserve and the U.S. Treasury secretary. When markets go through their regular cyclical downturns, public officials become increasingly pliable.

Ironically, it is often those who have built their names and reputations on free-market bona fides who plead and scream for intervention. *Creative destruction* is a brilliant concept to discuss in grad school, but with real money on the line, it becomes readily dismissed as an abstract academic concept.

7. **Broader worry, deepening panic:** The public's prior hazy understanding is coming into sharper focus: Some company or industry is less than healthy.

   We now enter the acceleration phase.

   There are more stock price declines, as it becomes apparent this is a very significant issue. As it progresses, the forecast of repercussions expands from worrisome to dire. By now, the mainstream media are covering the issue much more closely. The public is increasingly concerned.

   Those with the most money at stake have become downright frightened. Some have bought the stock or sector the whole way down. Others have been frozen, unable to move, watching the car wreck in slow motion while capital got destroyed. Various options are explored. Alternative plans are discussed. Insiders slowly come to realize that none of these plans can happen fast enough or generate enough capital to resolve the issue.

   The risk event is rapidly approaching the point of no return.

8. **Major intervention/bailout:** The political class eventually finds itself unable to resist temptation, and answers the call of some constituency or political campaign donor. We begin to hear phrases like "systemic risk" or "economic catastrophe." There is a tremendous incentive to overly dramatize the risk event, so as to improve the likelihood of some form of legislation passing.

   Invariably, some well-meaning politician, columnist, or other observer will warn about the negative consequences that will accompany this intervention. The phrase "moral hazard" will be bandied about. Most often, these arguments are summarily dismissed.

Sometimes events move so quickly there's no time for a full and open debate, leaving that discussion to the historians.

Finally, the bailout plan comes together. It is quickly signed by the president and is perceived as the lesser of two evils, a better alternative than letting Joseph Schumpeter's creative destruction have its way with the subject of our concern.

9. **Rationalizations and apologies:** In a manner bereft of contrition, officials explain why this was absolutely necessary. They warn of the horrors that would have befallen us all if the bailout hadn't been enacted in haste. Congressional hearings are held, often with the same executives who lobbied for the bailout testifying before the very same members of Congress who approved the package.

   The executives use phrases like "100-year flood" and "act of God," and say they "feel terrible for the employees who dedicated their lives to the firm and now have seen their life savings and pensions wiped out by this perfect storm of unforeseeable events."

   The members of Congress say: "My constituents are outraged!" "How could you let this happen on your watch?" "Why were the warning signs ignored?" "You made *how* much money last year?" "Thanks for the campaign donations."

10. **Expected results and unintended consequences:** The bailout is put into effect sooner rather than later. It usually has some degree of curative properties, as large piles of money often do. We learn of errors and problems fairly quickly, but usually some measure of victory is declared. Minor abuses come to light—a little fraud here, some oversight snafu there. These are par for the course, and mostly ignored.

    Without fail, the unintended consequences of the bailout begin working their way through the system. The repercussions are felt years and even decades later.

▪ ▪ ▪

We have seen this exact pattern with the various industrial bailouts of the 1970s and 1980s, the savings and loan (S&L) crisis of the early 1990s, and the Long Term Capital Management (LTCM) crisis of 1998. More recently, the tech wreck of 2000–2003, the credit crisis, the derivatives disaster, and the housing collapse all went through similar phases.

Each of these events followed the usual progression. Indeed, all of the current bailouts are repercussions—the step 10—of previous bailouts.

And we have yet to learn the unintended consequences of the credit crunch bailout, the housing rescue plan, the American International Group (AIG), Citigroup (C), Bank of America (BAC) rescues, the General Motors (GM) loans, or the Fannie and Freddie conservatorship. We seemed to be rushing headlong through steps 1 through 9; step 10 is off in the future.

But rest assured, we will discover, as we always do, some terrible repercussions down the road. They will be substantive and substantial—and very, very expensive.

Part II

THE MODERN ERA OF BAILOUTS

Source: By permission of John Sherffius and Creators Syndicate, Inc.

Chapter 5

Stock Market Bailouts (1987–1995)

The essential Greenspan legacy . . . is the idea that the Fed will allow nothing to go really wrong.

—James Grant, publisher of *Grant's Interest Rate Observer*[1]

So far, we have looked at various interventions—in the economy (1930s); in individual companies (Lockheed, Chrysler); and in entire sectors (banking). The next step on our path to becoming a Bailout Nation was when we went beyond any given company or sector bailout. We moved into uncharted territory when the U.S. Federal Reserve began intervening in the *entire stock market.*

Of course, the Federal Reserve has indirectly impacted all markets by performing its ordinary duties: maintaining price stability and maximizing employment. The Fed engages in a variety of targeted actions, such as changing interest rates, adding or subtracting liquidity, buying and selling Treasuries. These all have an impact on the markets, for better or worse. But that impact is incidental to the operations of the Fed's normal central banking activities. The results are a by-product, not the goal of the central bankers.

Where investors—and taxpayers—should become concerned is when the Fed goes far beyond ordinary central banking operations and seeks to maintain or support asset prices. This is a slippery slope, and, as we shall see, it leads to consequences that have been utterly disastrous.

How the Federal Reserve morphed from a lender of last resort to a guarantor of asset prices is a long and tortured tale. We will skip most of the boring history, and instead focus on the era dating from the 1987 crash forward. Traditionally, the Fed's mandate has been to "foster progress toward price stability" and to "promote sustained real output growth." For our purposes, let's call these fighting inflation and smoothing out the excesses of the business cycle.

Change came to the Fed in the form of a new Federal Open Market Committee (FOMC) chairman. Alan Greenspan took the reins in 1987, and he radically broke away from his predecessors' philosophies. Under the new chairman, FOMC policy incrementally moved toward supporting asset prices. As so often happens with these things, it began with a major disruption. In Greenspan's case, it was the 1987 market crash.

Initially, 1987 was a good year for the markets. By August, the S&P 500 had gained about 40 percent year-to-date. September was a bit rocky, sliding 10 percent from the highs—but that was to be expected. Nothing goes up in a straight line forever, right?

But then came October. Things took a turn for the worse, as the Dow Jones Industrial Average slid 3.8 percent on Wednesday, October 14. On Friday, October 16, the blue chips lost another 4.6 percent. The crash occurred on Black Monday (October 19)—when the Dow plummeted a harrowing 22.6 percent.

We can spend many hours going over all of the conditions precedent to the crash, but that is another book entirely (the interested should read *Black Monday*, by Tim Metz). While there is still academic debate over the causes of the crash, for our purposes, let's note as sufficient causal elements the combination of portfolio insurance—a derivatives product that utterly failed to work as advertised (*let's hear it for innovation!*)—a creaky New York Stock Exchange (NYSE) infrastructure, and Treasury Secretary Baker's remarks over the weekend implying we were no longer supporting the dollar.

The actual crash is a fascinating part of stock market history. Those of you who wish to become serious students of the market must familiarize yourself with what occurred. Panics may vary from generation to generation, but we learn that human nature is immutable.

It is not the crash itself, however, but rather the actions of various parts of the government that are of particular interest to us.

The response from the Federal Reserve was swift. Before the market's opening on Tuesday, October 20, the Fed issued the following statement: "The Federal Reserve System, consistent with its responsibilities as the nation's central bank, affirmed today its readiness to serve as a source of liquidity to support the financial and economic system."

Note that the address is to the system, threatened by the large movement downward of *asset prices*. The central bank then added substantially to reserves through open market operations. Over the next two weeks, the federal funds rate fell to 6.5 percent from 7.5 percent just prior to the crash.

But the Fed's pledge was not sufficient to halt the sell-off. According to Tim Metz, author of *Black Monday* (Beard Books, 2003), there was a slight problem prior to the opening of the markets the next day: Most of the NYSE floor specialists were technically insolvent. Not only had they absorbed enormous losses during the crash, but the various bank lines of credit they used each day had disappeared. It looked like the crash was going to continue Tuesday, with the Dow off 6 percent in the morning. It wasn't until New York Federal Reserve President Gerry Corrigan jawboned banks into restoring credit lines—and somehow turned off futures information between New York and Chicago—that the mother of all Turnaround Tuesdays took place.

It is a classic example of the authority of the Fed being used to avoid what looked like a full-blown liquidity crisis.

". . . the Fed's responsibilities to serve as lender of last resort was intended to reverse the *crisis psychology* and to guarantee the safety and soundness of the banking system" was how Robert T. Parry, president of the Federal Reserve Bank of San Francisco, described the Fed's actions at a University of California at Davis conference 10 years later.[2] He affirmed what the Fed saw as its proper role.

Now, it's at precisely this point in our narrative that we must stop for a moment to point out something you may not have taken the trouble to

consider before. Exactly why did the Fed become in charge of psychology? The central bank was originally established to bring financial order to the early Wild West days of banking. Somehow, resolving fiat currency issues and supervising credit morphed into a far more subjective role. Michael Panzner, author of the prescient doomsday tome *Financial Armageddon* (Kaplan Business, 2007), calls it "mission creep."

We know what happened next: Over the ensuing years, the role of the Fed crept significantly, from that of inflation fighter to market therapist, and ultimately to the guarantor of asset prices.

After the 1987 crash, Wall Streeters were relieved. Instead, they should have been concerned. They had unknowingly made a deal with the devil, one that would prove quite costly down the road. The supposedly unique Federal Reserve intervention after the 1987 crash was hardly a one-off—it became the Fed's modus operandi which continues to this day.

■ ■ ■

The 1987 crash laid bare many of the structural flaws of the market. During trading of the highest-ever volume on Black Monday, the market's internal plumbing had failed. Orders were not executed for hours, quotes did not update, and specialists were overwhelmed at their posts. At brokerage firms, phones rang and rang unanswered.

The mechanical functioning of the NYSE was not the result of any intelligent design. The conventions for executing equity orders had evolved on an ad hoc basis. It took the stresses of the crash to reveal the market's warts.

The President's Working Group on Financial Markets

In 1988, President Ronald Reagan issued Executive Order 12631 establishing the President's Working Group (PWG) on Financial Markets. The goal of the PWG was to "enhance the integrity, efficiency, orderliness, and competitiveness of our Nation's financial markets while maintaining investor confidence." (Once again with the *psychology*.)

Twenty years later, it remains a secretive organization, one whose formalized meetings keep no minutes and whose functions are poorly understood. There is surprisingly little academic publishing on this body. Due to its secretive nature, the PWG's workings are often described in market folklore as "*they*," as in "*They* won't let the market drop, *they* were in buying today."

It wasn't until 1997 that the PWG received the name by which they are best know today: the Plunge Protection Team (PPT). That was the headline of a Sunday *Washington Post* article by staff writer Brett D. Fromson.[3]

For our purposes, the PPT is an irrelevant footnote.

Why? First off, it is hard to imagine a secret cabal manipulating markets, deploying billions or even trillions in capital, with a nary a shred of evidence ever surfacing. The Bush White House couldn't illegally fire nine U.S. attorneys without the political motivation being discovered and a major investigation launched.[4] Could the markets be supported via massive trading, and no one anywhere would ever see proof and come forward? It's hard to imagine that big a secret being kept for so long.

Second, and more important, the PPT, well, they really suck at their jobs. If the conspiracy theorists are correct and this group is supposed to prevent market meltdowns, they are not exactly hitting the cover off the ball. The late George Carlin had a routine on American Indians' military organizational structure. They weren't bad fighters, he said, just because they started out defending Massachusetts and ended up in Santa Monica.

And so it is with the PPT. How is *their* fighting prowess? Well, consider that starting in 2000, the NASDAQ fell from over 5,100 to about 1,100—a plunge of nearly 80 percent in about two and a half years. And in 2008, the PPT performed even more miserably. Bloomberg reported that as of November 19, 2008, markets were suffering from "the worst annual decline in the Standard & Poor's 500 index since 1931."[5] The carnage "dragged down

(*continued*)

(*continued*)

every industry in the benchmark gauge and 96 percent of its stocks. Four hundred eighty-two companies slipped as the 500-stock index slumped 46 percent, poised for its biggest yearly retreat in eight decades." And after the major indexes ended 2008 down more than 40 percent for the year, the first 10 weeks of 2009 saw the markets fall another 22 percent.

Worst annual decline in eight decades? Down another 22 percent in two months? Geez, how incompetent must a secret market-manipulating organization be before someone gets fired?

■ ■ ■

History teaches us that the development of Bailout Nation, Wall Street edition, was not done in secret meetings. Rather, it occurred in the very public functions of the Federal Reserve, and the subsequent results of its policy actions.

The Greenspan Fed created an endemic culture of excessive risk taking. The U.S. central bank created moral hazard not by targeting inflation or the business cycle, but instead by focusing on asset prices. From the squishy focus on psychology, it was merely a short hop to asset prices. After all, when prices go down, it negatively impacts sentiment, right? This was the Fed's fatal flaw under Greenspan's leadership. As we shall see, once those in the capital markets realized that the Fed stood ready to protect the downside via monetary reflation, all bets were on higher prices.

It's worth recalling that the 1987 crash came mere months into Greenspan's tenure. The rookie Fed chairman earned high praise for his handling of the situation. There were reports of a mysterious trader entering the S&P futures pits in Chicago to make a large buy order, which helped finally stem the decline; whether that person was an agent of the federal government or just part of Wall Street mythology remains a mystery. But the truth is enough people believed Greenspan's Fed would approve such an intervention that it helped restore confidence in the markets.

Indeed, one can make a case that Greenspan learned early on that the solution to every problem was to throw money at it—*liquidity* in the parlance of central bankers—even though doing so ultimately leads to bigger problems down the road.

The 1987 crash was unusual, in that it was a market-based—as opposed to an economic—event. After a 40 percent rise in the first eight months of the year, prices had simply gotten way too far ahead of themselves.

The 1990–1991 recession was a more typical economic event.[6] A variety of macroeconomic factors contributed to the slowdown: The S&L crisis, a real estate slump, the first Gulf War, and a spike in energy prices had all taken their toll. Chairman Greenspan found himself hobbled by a near open revolt of FOMC governors. The Fed "curtailed the authority of its chairman, Alan Greenspan, to reduce rates on his own" in between meetings.[7]

It seems that Greenspan couldn't help himself: He cut rates half a point just days prior to the February FOMC meeting, despite signs of an economic recovery in the making. This upset the FOMC Board of Governors a great deal.

Why would a Fed chair risk the ire and support of his board—and only a few days before the next FOMC meeting? Perhaps a chart of the equity markets might provide some insight (see Figure 5.1).

Note: The small circles are quarter-point rate cuts; the large circle is a half-point cut. The last cut in 1990 and the first two in 1991 were intermeeting. There would be seven more quarter-point cuts in 1991, and a half-point "Christmas present cut" in late December 1991. By the end of 1992, Fed rates would be as low as 3 percent—and would stay that low until February 1994.

One cannot help but notice how unusual this action was: a half-point cut, made by a Fed chair acting alone, mere days before the next FOMC meeting and with the Dow already in rally mode. While one can never know exactly what another person is thinking, Greenspan's actions certainly have the appearance of attempting to spur the equity markets.

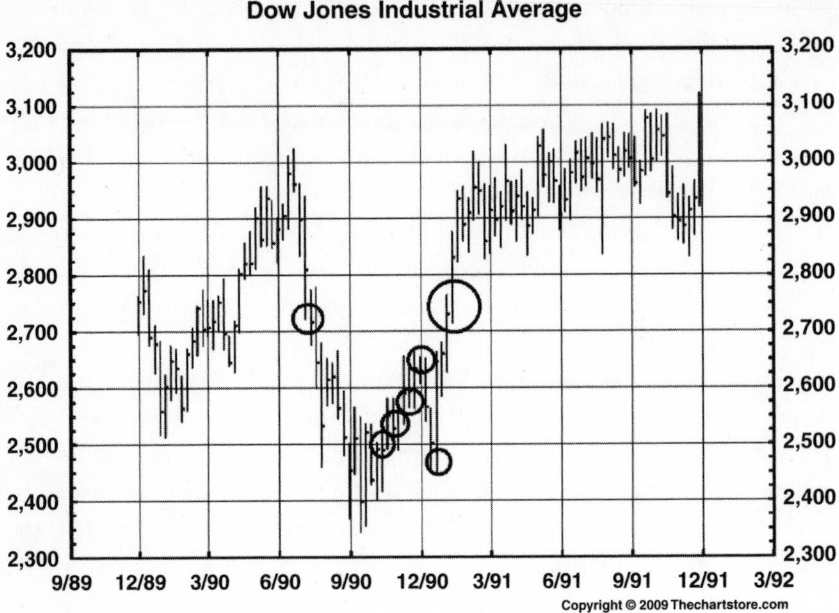

Figure 5.1 Dow Jones Industrial Average, 1990–1991

By itself, this action can be in part rationalized by other factors—the economic slowdown, the high price of oil, perhaps even the presidential election the following year. However, placing this into the context of Greenspan's tenure as Fed chairman, one gets a very different impression. This was standard operating procedure for Greenspan throughout his Fed career. Targeting asset prices is seen consistently throughout the 1990s. Even his nickname, "the Maestro," came about due to the way he skillfully "conducted" the markets.

The Fed's power to change interest rates as a way to promote and protect asset prices is the key to understanding the Greenspan era. Indeed, it is the crucial economic element that was the precursor to the late 2000 bailouts. Rather than seeing markets as a sign of the economy's health, the Fed chair tended to see asset prices as an end unto themselves. What this led to was the treatment of symptoms, rather than underlying causes. The markets' health, rather than the economy's, seemed to be what was of paramount importance.

Nobel laureate Paul Krugman, writing presciently in *U.S. News & World Report* in April 1991,[8] noted the sticky issues that the Fed would be facing in the near future:

> Even if the U.S. economy begins to recover soon, the current recession will leave a lasting legacy in economic policy making. The downturn has undermined public confidence in the Federal Reserve Board because the Fed missed the slump's early warning signs. *A weaker Fed will now find it harder to resist political pressures to keep interest rates low and growth high.* (emphasis added)

Krugman was way ahead of the curve: The public faith in the Fed didn't falter until after the market crash was well under way (2000–2002). And Greenspan's reputation didn't really unravel until the credit crisis and housing collapse were in full bloom (circa 2006–2007). By 2008, the man formerly known as the Maestro saw his reputation in tatters.

But the key to our tale was the low interest rates. Whether it was a result of political pressure or by his own hand, the story of the Federal Reserve under Greenspan is a tale of acquiescence to those pressures. By February 1994, it had been five years since the Fed had last tightened rates.[9] It was a preview of what would occur a decade later—only the rates would be taken even lower, and the economic damage would be immeasurably greater.

The tail was just starting to wag the dog.

■ ■ ■

Over the next few years, numerous events would test the bull market that began in 1982. After the recession of 1990–1991, the next major wobble would be the bankruptcy of Orange County, California, late in 1994. That story is yet another book—try *Big Bets Gone Bad* by Philippe Jorion (Academic Press, 1995)—but for our purposes, we need only note that it caught the Fed's attention.

Two weeks later Mexico devalued the peso.

Markets shook off the bad news. The Dow ended the year under 4,000, but began rising shortly after the calendar flipped. By the middle of 1995, the blue chips were well over 4,500—more than a 13 percent gain in half a year. But concerns about Mexico's stability and its currency

issues began to catch up with the indexes. Markets began to stall in midsummer (see Figure 5.2).

On July 6, 1995, Federal Reserve Chairman Alan Greenspan reversed the string of seven rate increases of the prior 12 months and cut the federal funds rate 25 basis points. The Fed would follow with another 25 basis point rate cut in December and yet another in January of the following year.

The Fed justified the July and December rate cuts as done to "decrease slightly the degree of pressure on bank reserve positions." The January 31, 1996, rate cut was put forth because "moderating economic expansion in recent months has reduced potential inflationary pressures going forward. With price and cost trends already subdued, a slight easing of monetary policy is consistent with contained inflation and sustainable growth."

Wall Streeters saw it as Alan Greenspan helping them out.

And it was just the beginning.

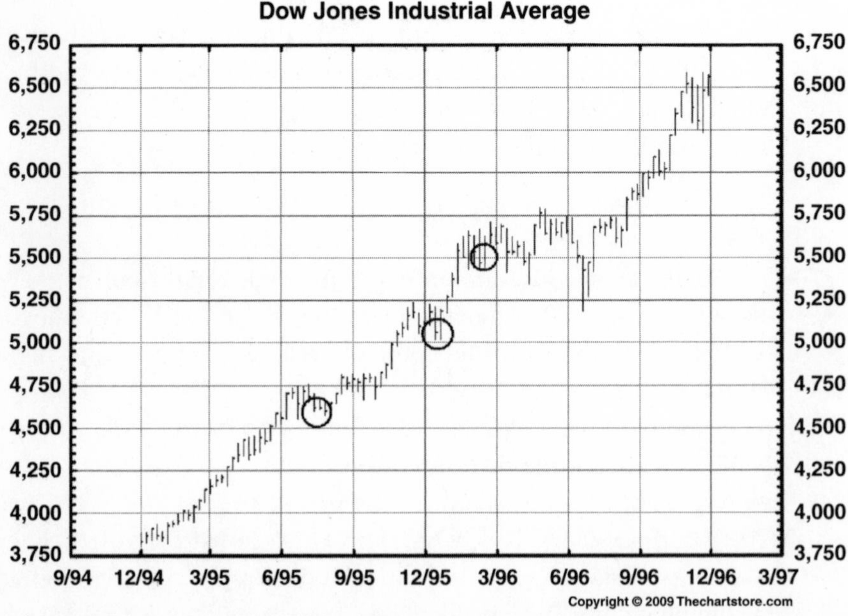

Figure 5.2 Dow Jones Industrial Average, 1994–1995

Chapter 6

The Irrational Exuberance Era (1996–1999)

[The Fed chairman's job is] to take away the punch bowl just as the party gets going.

—William McChesney Martin Jr.

All in all, 1995 had been a damned good year for the markets. The broad indexes gained over 34 percent, more than triple the average annual return. It was the first 30+ percent gain for the S&P 500 in 20 years. The last rally as strong was in 1975 (31.1 percent), following the disastrous recession bear market of 1974 (-29.6 percent).

The 1990s sure weren't the 1970s. This was the early days of a huge tech boom: Semiconductors, software, PCs, the Internet, mobile communications, data storage, and related technologies were all in the early "hockey stick" phase of their growth. When Netscape floated its initial public offering (IPO) in August 1995, it exploded, gaining nearly 500 percent during the first day's trading. Even bigger IPO opening days would soon follow.

The gains were all the more remarkable considering how 1994 had ended: bankruptcy for the nation's wealthiest county (Orange County, California) and a rapidly developing Mexican peso crisis. But the economy was expanding *and* the Federal Reserve was cutting rates—all was right in the world of stocks and finance.

The year 1996 was nearly as good, tacking 20.3 percent on top of the prior year's gains. In less than two years, the Dow had soared from 3,800 to over 6,600. The market was hot that year—and getting hotter.

■ ■ ■

It was in this environment that Alan Greenspan first floated the phrase "irrational exuberance." In a December 1996 speech, Greenspan raised the exuberance issue—and then nearly as quickly dismissed it.

> But how do we know when irrational exuberance has unduly escalated asset values, which then become subject to unexpected and prolonged contractions as they have in Japan over the past decade? And how do we factor that assessment into monetary policy? We as central bankers need not be concerned if a collapsing financial asset bubble does not threaten to impair the real economy, its production, jobs, and price stability.[1]

That speech became infamous for introducing the "irrational exuberance" phrase to the financial lexicon. To the Bailout Nation, there were even more profound reasons the speech was notable. In it we find the basis of not one, but two major Greenspan policies—both of which would emerge to significantly impact markets in the future. They were not recognized as such at the time, but with the benefit of hindsight—and an ensuing decade of Greenspan's Federal Open Market Committee (FOMC) policy—they are readily apparent to us today.

The first policy shift was Greenspan's focus on asset prices. This wasn't a subtle or abstract implication; Greenspan explicitly stated as much in the same speech:

> Indeed, the sharp stock market break of 1987 had few negative consequences for the economy. But we should not underestimate or become complacent about the complexity of the interactions of asset markets and the economy. Thus, evaluating shifts in balance sheets generally, and in asset prices particularly, must be an integral part of the development of monetary policy.[2]

The Fed's previous rate cuts had only *implied* a concern over asset prices; now, the chief explicitly affirmed the fact. The Fed was not concerned just about inflation and employment; asset prices were an "integral part" of its calculus, too.

This was revolutionary. Fed chiefs didn't usually care so much about stock prices; they were more concerned with the bond market. After all, it was the fixed-income traders—known as bond ghouls for their morbid affection for bad economic news—who set interest rates. Worries about deficits, inflation, and trade balances all found a receptive audience among the bond traders.

Once Wall Street figured out Greenspan was concerned about equity prices, it wasn't too long before it learned how to play the Fed like the devil's fiddle. When rate cuts did not materialize, the Street would have itself a hissy fit. It is always ill advised to anthropomorphize markets, but observing the market kick and scream when cuts weren't forthcoming was akin to watching a two-year-old throw a tantrum.[3] It may be illegal to manipulate markets, but no trader will ever get thrown in jail for manipulating Alan Greenspan.

The other policy shift hinted at in the "irrational exuberance" speech was the concept of cleaning up after, rather than preventing, asset bubbles and their aftermath. That was precisely what Greenspan implied when he made the incredible statement that "central bankers need not be concerned" about a bubble collapse, so long as it doesn't leak into the real economy.

Years later Greenspan said: "It is far from obvious that bubbles, even if identified early, can be preempted at lower cost than a substantial economic contraction and possible financial destabilization—the very outcomes we would be seeking to avoid."[4]

This is, as any student of market history will tell you, an utterly absurd statement. As we have seen time and again, manias and panics invariably spill over into the real economy. The speech suggests that Greenspan learned precisely the wrong lesson from the 1987 crash. Market bubbles always destroy capital, ruin speculators, and cause all manner of heartache. From the Dutch tulip craze in 1636–1637 and the South Sea bubble in 1720 to the Nifty Fifty stocks in the 1960s, the dot-com bubble in 2000, the housing and credit boom and bust in the 2000s, and the credit and derivatives debacle in 2008, the final results of all investment crazes are lost treasure, blood, and tears.

What the astute student learns from the history of speculative frenzies is that the 1987 crash was a unique aberration, an unusual outcome relative to past collapses. The combination of a hot equity market and the new innovation called portfolio insurance combined with the messy New York Stock Exchange (NYSE) plumbing to create an unusually short-lived, market-driven event in an otherwise robust economy.

The 1987 crash seemed to be the only crash that was (sorry to use a dirty word) "contained."

Greenspan completely missed this point. The 1987 crash was the rare exception, not the rule. That the chairman of the Federal Reserve failed to recognize this is nothing short of astonishing. Prior to 1987, numerous books had detailed the phenomenon of manias, and the economic fallout that occurs upon their collapse.[5] Greenspan was evolving a belief system unsupported by facts or history—and not for the last time, either. That a false premise became the cornerstone of his monetary philosophy goes a long way in explaining what happened next.

But we do not need to theorize to test Chairman Greenspan's hypothesis. We have explicit proof of the falsity of the thesis: The costs of the 2008–2009 credit bubble and collapse have been astronomical. As of December 2008, the United States has rung up over $14 trillion in bailout-related expenses—and counting.

Thus, we have the rarest of dichotomies: a Fed chair who appears to be concerned with falling asset prices—cutting interest rates in response to minor market stumbles—and yet who is at the same time a central banker who claims to be comfortable with collapsing bubbles.

These two views are inherently at odds with each other. The only way to reconcile the conflict is to recognize the latter statement as sheer nonsense. It is a dangerous, shameless, foolish rationalization—one that allowed the Fed to look the other way as markets began overheating in the late 1990s.

As we will soon see, each of these changes in emphasis and policy will have dramatic repercussions in the years to come. Not the least of these are in the asset prices themselves: as of March 2009, the S&P 500 was back at levels below where it was when Greenspan gave his 1996 "irrational exuberance" speech. If you bought the broad index the day after the speech, some 13 years later you would have nothing to show for it. What a long, strange trip that's been.

■ ■ ■

The end of the 1990s would see the philosophies of the Maestro, as he was known before his impact on markets was more widely understood, in full throat. The Fed chief would be repeatedly tested—by a currency crisis, a major hedge fund collapse, and a technology bubble. He rose to every challenge essentially the same way: increased liquidity and lower rates. Each time, the market would cheer, rallying to new heights.

Ultimately, this would become known as the Greenspan put.

The Greenspan Put

A put is an option contract that gives its owner the right to sell a stock at a specific dollar amount (the strike price). The put holder has total downside protection, regardless of how far a stock or index might fall; in this event, the put holder has the right to sell it at the much higher strike price.

As you might imagine, a put gives any speculator a tremendous degree of comfort. It allows speculators to engage the markets with a high degree of self-confidence. They know they are protected from market turmoil. But there is a dark side to this.

Consider, for example, automotive innovations such as antilock braking systems (ABSs) and supplemental restraint systems. Despite the new technological safety features, automobile fatality rates have hardly improved. It turns out owners of cars with more safety features end up traveling faster and taking more chances than they might in lesser-equipped vehicles. Hence, the gains of ABSs and airbags are offset by overconfidence. Perversely, these safety features can make for less safe drivers.

So, too, it is with financial markets. The moral hazard of the Greenspan put was that it encouraged greater speculation, more aggressive trading, and more use of margin. Once traders figured out Greenspan had their backs, they lost much of their restraint.

(*continued*)

(continued)

The net result was a market with a strong upward bias, and a five-year run of double-digit returns.

S&P 500	**Returns**
2002	−23.37
2001	−13.04
2000	−10.14
1999	19.51
1998	26.67
1997	31.02
1996	20.27
1995	34.11
1994	−1.47

In 1997, the Asian contagion struck. The Thai government cut the peg of its currency, the baht, from the U.S. dollar. The decision to let the baht float was disastrous. The currency collapsed, and caused a chain reaction throughout Asia. From Thailand, the so-called Asian flu raced through Indonesia, South Korea, Hong Kong, Malaysia, Laos, and the Philippines. China, India, Taiwan, Singapore, Brunei, and Vietnam were also affected.

The United States was mostly insulated from the Asian problems, but for a one-day wobble in the markets: On October 27, 1997, the Dow Jones Industrial Average fell 554 points, then its biggest-ever one-day point drop, and the New York Stock Exchange briefly suspended trading. But bulls perceived the 7.2 percent sell-off as a buying opportunity. The markets snapped back the very next day. Markets had begun 1997 around 6,400 on the Dow, and finished the year just under 8,000.

The year 1998 saw the last opportunity to avoid moral hazard on a grand scale. A huge opportunity was lost, and the genesis of our current crisis was born.

The missed opportunity in question involved Long-Term Capital Management (LTCM), a hedge fund that specialized in fixed-income arbitrage. Using enormous amounts of leverage—about $100 billion in borrowed money—the fund bought thinly traded assets that were difficult to value. (*Gee, why does that sound so familiar?*)

Long-Term Capital Management's investing philosophy and prowess were based on the idea of mean reversion. When spreads—the difference in prices between two bonds—on emerging market debt widened in reaction to the Asian contagion, the hedge fund bet heavily that those instruments would return to normal levels. Because of its early success and the pedigrees of its principals—including former Salomon Brothers bond chief John Meriwether and Nobel Prize-winning economists Myron Scholes and Robert Merton—LTCM was able to use leverage to amplify its bets many times.

Thanks to leverage, LTCM's exposure was greater than $100 billion. Furthermore, the fund was able to negotiate cut-rate prices for financing from many Wall Street firms, who were enamored of and infatuated by the fund's mysterious nature. So great was the allure of LTCM that many of its financiers mimicked the fund's trades (see Figure 6.1).

Thus, many big Wall Street firms were exposed to similar risk throughout 1998. When Russia defaulted on its debt in August of that year, spreads on emerging market bonds not only didn't revert to normal levels, but continued to widen. The widening credit spreads were taking an unhealthy bite out of LTCM's portfolio. In less than four months, the fund lost nearly $5 billion.

As LTCM's losses began to accumulate, the fund had no choice but to liquidate whatever it could to stay afloat. Markets had been digesting its gains since April, but speculation about LTCM's troubles was starting to make the rounds. As rumors of the fund's losses spread, the Dow fell from its high near 8,700 in mid-August 1998 to as low as 7,400 in early September—a rapid-fire 15 percent decline.

The Asian flu took place halfway across the world, and required little in the way of a Fed response. LTCM, by contrast, was in Greenwich, Connecticut—much closer to home. Most of the 19 primary dealers—banks and brokerages that directly trade government securities with the Federal Reserve—were involved. They all had lent LTCM much of its leverage, and stood to lose $100 billion if the firm collapsed.

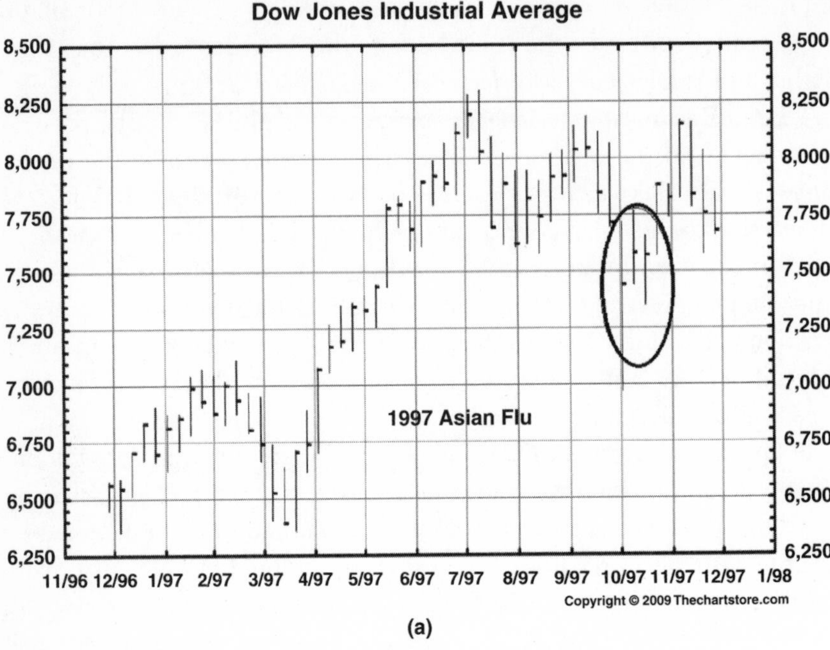

(a)

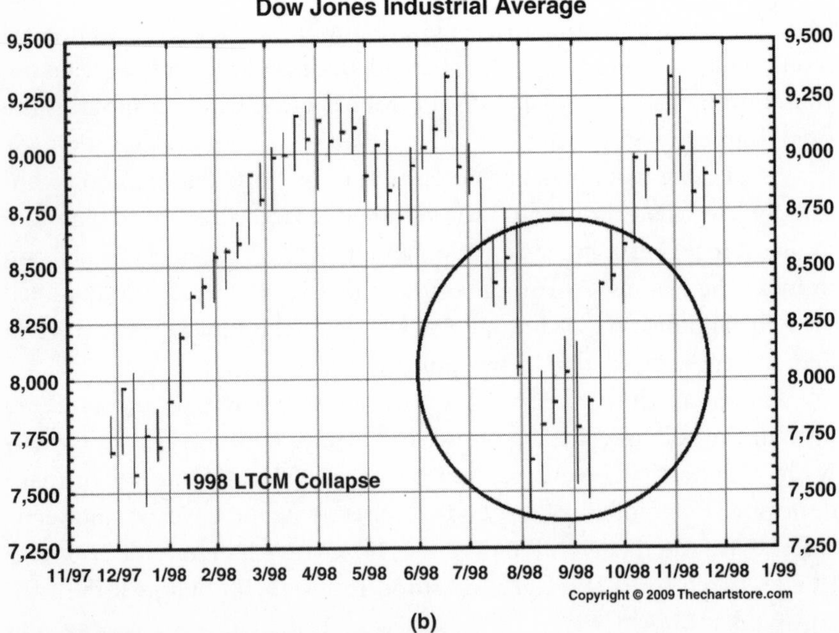

(b)

Figure 6.1 1997 Asian Flu, 1998 LTCM

Too Smart for Their Own Good

Long-Term Capital Management (LTCM) used sophisticated trading techniques, but its business model was fairly simple. Using proprietary software, the traders identified price spreads that were wrong according to the quants' models. However, these price discrepancies were very small on a percentage basis. In order to make money doing this, they had to use leverage to make the price differentials add up to anything significant. This meant LTCM borrowed lots and lots of money against their investors' cash, and then put that to work following the computer's algorithms.

Since the bond market is so deeply traded—millions of traders trade trillions of dollars' worth every day—even with the leverage, their choices were limited. So they took the road less traveled, or in LTCM's case, the bond less traded. Ordinary Treasuries could not satisfy their itch; instead, their proprietary models found ever rarer and more exotic fixed-income instruments. These were not well followed or understood, nor were they deeply traded. The quants at LTCM thought this gave them an advantage, as they understood these instruments better than many, indeed most. Off they went in search of lesser-known markets. Leaving the main river, they soon found themselves in unknown eddies, trading exotic fixed-income markets—like those soon-to-be defaulting Russian bonds.

This worked well, so long as prices were behaving as the models forecast. Wide spreads were supposed to tighten, and rising prices were supposed to keep rising. Once prices stopped behaving as the models forecast, however, trouble soon followed.

The leverage that so enhanced returns on the way up began to slaughter capital on the way down. For those trading their capital without leverage, a 10 percent loss is a relatively minor inconvenience. If you are leveraged 10 to 1, however, a 10 percent loss wipes you out totally.

And if you're leveraged 100 to 1 like LTCM was, well, then you're just begging for trouble.

To someone whose only tool is a hammer, pretty soon everything begins to look like a nail. Greenspan cut rates 25 basis points on September 29, 1998. Two weeks later on October 15—between meetings!—he cut another 25. A scheduled Fed meeting on November 17 brought yet another quarter-point cut. In seven weeks, "Easy Al" lopped off 75 basis points from the federal funds rate.

The statement after the November cut was unusually telling: "Although conditions in financial markets have settled down materially since mid-October, unusual strains remain."[6]

Thus, the Greenspan put was born.

About the same time Easy Al was cutting rates that September, William J. McDonough, the president of the New York Federal Reserve Bank, was having a little get-together one Tuesday evening at the Fed's fortresslike building on Maiden Lane. He called for a meeting of the *patresfamilias*—the heads of the 16 largest banks, along with the New York Stock Exchange chairman. The discussion was over what to do about the imminent collapse of Long-Term Capital Management.

Roger Lowenstein's narrative, *When Genius Failed* (Random House, 2000), is a fascinating read for anyone interested in the grisly details of LTCM. For our purposes, we need only note two facts:

1. The Fed was cutting rates.
2. The Fed was using its authority and prestige to help work out the demise of what was a private partnership.

The central bankers jawboned the 14 largest banks—with the notable exception of future bailoutee Bear Stearns—into kicking in $3.65 billion to buy out the assets of LTCM. These included leveraged assets of over $100 billion and derivatives with a notional value of over $1 trillion.

The belief that LTCM had to be bailed out was widely held. It was 1987 redux, and the media accolades poured in. In the aftermath of the LTCM rescue, *Time* put Alan Greenspan, Robert Rubin, and Larry Summers on the cover as "The committee to save the world."[7]

The chaos surrounding a liquidation of LTCM would cause the markets, in Chairman Greenspan's words, to "seize up."

But this raises uncomfortable regulatory questions. If this huge leveraged fund presented such systemic risk, then why weren't there regulations limiting the size and the leverage that hedge funds could use?

Note the ideological quandary this created for the chairman who believed markets could "self-regulate." Either these funds are too dangerous to be allowed to exist without strict oversight and controls, or this was not a case of systemic risk. There can be no middle ground; he had to either change the rules or change his belief system.

Of course, that's not how Greenspan saw it. The failure of LTCM would have had a very negative impact on psychology. Woe to the Fed chair who allows traders to become morose! That was how Mr. *Atlas Shrugged* rationalized the intervention. (Thank goodness Ayn Rand was already dead.)

Whether that would have turned out to be true is a matter of much dispute. The evidence leads me to surmise that not only would LTCM's demise *not* have caused the system to collapse, it would have done a world of good. Indeed, the best possible outcome would have been for LTCM to go belly-up and take a big bite out of the investment banks dumb enough to lend all that money to LTCM.

Consider what was at stake: First, LTCM's portfolio had $100 billion in leveraged paper. But it was the leverage, not the paper, that was the issue. Everything LTCM owned wasn't Russian debt heading to zero; some of it had real value. The problem wasn't the quality of the assets; it was using $1 to buy $100 worth of paper. It doesn't take much spread widening to lose a substantial amount of capital when you are running that much leverage. As we will see in Part IV, that would have been a ripping good lesson for the investment banks to have learned.

What the banks actually learned was that the Fed (and by extension, Uncle Sam) would be there to back them up when they ran into trouble. This is precisely what moral hazard argues against: Encouraging risk-taking to become separated from its consequences.

The other issue was the trillion dollars in derivatives. How did an unregulated, three-year-old, heavily leveraged partnership manage to have so much in "insurance" entrusted to it by counterparties? The only answer I can deduce is that the number of idiots on the planet is greater by several orders of magnitude than previously believed. If you have been paying any attention, that many of them work in finance should come as no surprise.

This was yet another lesson sorely not learned.

What would have happened had this notional amount of derivative paper become worthless? Short answer: not a whole lot.

The loss would have been the premiums paid to LTCM, not the trillion-dollar notional value. If your car insurance company disappeared tomorrow, you wouldn't lose the value of your vehicle—only the premium payments you made. This is why it's advisable to do business with firms such as the Government Employees Insurance Company (GEICO) or Allstate, and not Billy Bob's Bait Shop & Auto Insurance Co.

The penalty for getting into bed with a counterparty that was young, untested, highly leveraged, and reckless should have been expensive. Instead, it was a minor inconvenience. It was yet another lesson not learned from LTCM, and contributed mightily to moral hazard. Future repercussions would be severe.

Had LTCM been allowed to fail naturally, perhaps a lesson might have been learned: Risk and reward are sides of the same coin. Alas, it was a missed opportunity for the traders and risk managers at major banks and brokers to learn this simple truism. The parallels between what doomed LTCM in 1998 and forced Wall Street to run to Washington for a handout in 2008 are all there, and the significance of these missed opportunities is now readily apparent.

In sum, Long-Term Capital Management was the dress rehearsal for the great credit crisis of 2008—and a missed opportunity to prevent the ongoing tragedy.

Chapter 7

The Tech Wreck (2000–2003)

I would not only reappoint Mr. Greenspan—if Mr. Greenspan should happen to die, God forbid . . . I'd prop him up and put a pair of dark glasses on him and keep him as long as we could.

—John McCain, GOP debate, 2000

Up until now, Alan Greenspan had merely been dabbling. Yes, his frequent interventions in markets were worrisome, unprecedented by historical Federal Reserve standards. But as we shall see, they were merely a warm-up for what was to yet come.

In July 1998, the NASDAQ Composite had just cleared the 2,000 mark for the first time. At the time, the tech-heavy index was dominated by active traders, ranging from big momentum funds to small day traders. The prior few years had been good to those NASDAQ traders, with strong gains in 1995 (39.9 percent), 1996 (22.7 percent), and 1997 (21.6 percent). And 1998 was looking like a good year also, until the unpleasantness with Long-Term Capital Management began. At the

first inkling of trouble, the so-called momo traders dumped their shares. As the depth of the LTCM hedge fund's problems became clear, the NASDAQ got pounded. From its July peak of 2,000, the NASDAQ lost nearly one-third of its value, trading down to near 1,350 in less than three months.

To a Fed chair obsessed with asset prices, this was of grave concern.

Hence, the LTCM bailout. If Greenspan hoped the rescue plan would act as a salve to traders, he sure got his wish. Confidence levels recovered just as quickly as they had faltered. Once the threat from Long-Term Capital Management was past, the bull market reasserted itself. The S&P 500 and the Dow Jones Industrial Average each had respectable years in 1998 and 1999. But it was the NASDAQ—heavily weighted with the hot technology, telecom, and Internet IPOs—that exploded. Despite that 30 percent midyear haircut, the NASDAQ cleared its old highs, and by December 31 it was near 2,200—up 39.6 percent for the year. Even more remarkably, from those October lows, the tech index gained 63 percent in less than three months. It was in every way an astonishing performance.

And why not? Traders knew the Fed chief had their back. The Greenspan put was fully operational, interest rates were low, and technology was booming.

It was the new era of *rational* exuberance.

NASDAQ Returns

12/31/95	39.92%
12/31/96	22.71
12/31/97	21.64
12/31/98	39.63
12/31/99	85.59
12/31/00	–39.29
12/31/01	–21.05
12/31/02	–31.53

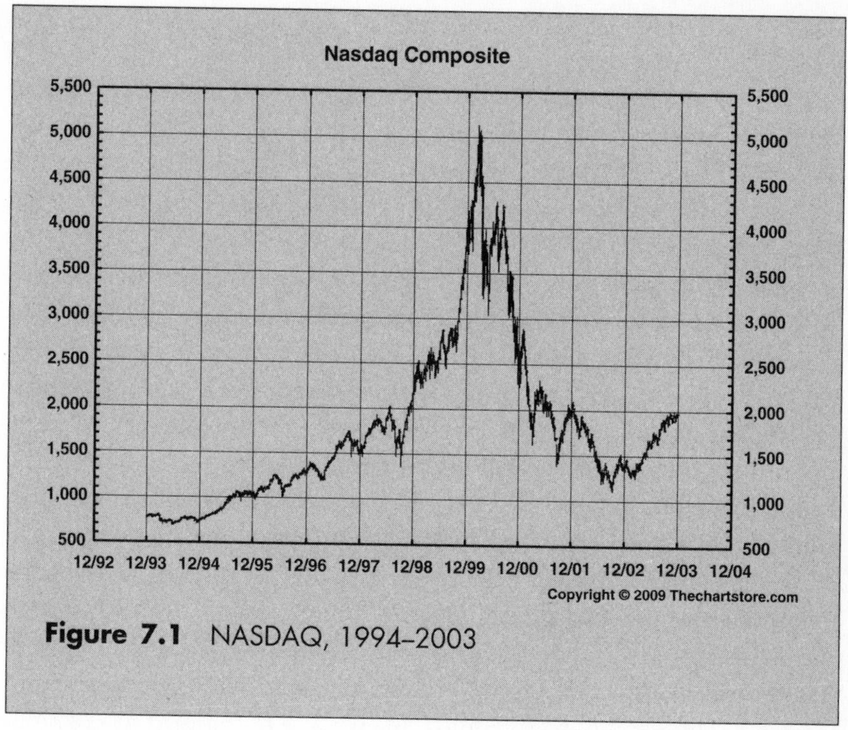

Figure 7.1 NASDAQ, 1994–2003

■ ■ ■

By 1999, stock trading had become the national pastime. People followed publicly traded companies the way they used to root for sports teams. CNBC was on in every bar, restaurant, and gym. Initial public offerings (IPOs) that merely doubled on the first day of trading were considered disappointments. Stories were rife of lawyers and dentists who gave up their practices for the more lucrative profession of day trading.

A popular discount brokerage TV advertisement of the time featured a tow-truck driver who owned his own island. He told motorists in need of aid there was no charge—he did the job only because he liked helping people. *You too, can trade your way to riches* was the not-so-subtle message.

The year 1999 began the way 1998 ended: in rally mode. The bias was to the upside, despite the fact that valuations were becoming seriously stretched. Price-earnings (P/E) ratio, a traditional measure of how expensive equities were, indicated tech stocks were wildly overvalued. The P/E of the NASDAQ was near 100, and heading higher. In the so-called new era, however, valuation mattered little. By July 1999, the Nazz was just under 2,900—up 27 percent year-to-date.

The three quick rate cuts from late 1998 were reversed. The Fed tightened a quarter point in June, in August, and again in November. But all that did was return rates to where they were in March 1997. The Wall Street warning "three hikes and a tumble"—meaning three Fed tightenings often lead to a correction—was inoperative. Markets laughed off the increases, and just powered higher.

In this environment, filled with wild speculation and overheating equities, Greenspan did . . . nothing. The Fed chief had any number of tools at his disposal to deal with the rapidly inflating bubble, but the most important was the ability to raise margin requirements for tech stocks. All those day-trading dentists, housewives, and tow-truck drivers were buying and selling stocks using mostly borrowed money. Constraining margin lending would have tamped down some of the mad speculation.

Transcripts of Fed meetings from the late 1990s—released years later—showed that Greenspan and his cohorts were concerned about excesses in the financial markets, and determined that raising margin requirements would help deflate the nation's newfound obsession with day trading dot-com stocks.

"I recognize there is a stock market bubble problem at this point," Greenspan said in a September 24, 1996, Fed meeting, and declared that raising margin requirements was a solution. "I guarantee that if you want to get rid of the bubble, whatever it is, that will do it."[1]

But the FOMC chair chose not to do so. After the famous "irrational exuberance" speech in 1996, Greenspan thereafter remained silent about speculative excesses that, by late 1999, were terribly obvious to even casual observers.

Greenspan later claimed it was impossible to know a financial bubble of immense proportions was under way.

Actually the Fed—led, of course, by its ubiquitous chairman—did something worse than nothing. Greenspan also gave explicit, intellectual support to the equity bubble by talking enthusiastically about the tech-inspired productivity miracle. The Fed chair applauded the notion that a "new economy" had emerged. It was music to traders' ears.

The New Economy

In September 1998, Greenspan gave a speech titled: "Question: Is There a New Economy?"[2]

While nuanced in its entirety, future academics will be shocked by the very idea the chairman of the Federal Reserve would contemplate such a ridiculous notion that technological innovations such as the PC and just-in-time inventories had significantly reduced, if not eliminated, the risks of future recessions.

"There is, clearly, an element of truth in this proposition," Greenspan said (reportedly with a straight face). "In the United States, for example, a technologically driven decline is evident in the average lead times on the purchase of new capital equipment that has kept capacity utilization at moderate levels and virtually eliminated most of the goods shortages and bottlenecks that were prevalent in earlier periods of sustained strong economic growth."

Furthermore, the Fed chairman "would not deny that there doubtless has been in recent years an underlying improvement in the functioning of America's markets and in the pace of development of cutting-edge technologies beyond previous expectations."

As is often the case, few people focused on the subtleties and caveats of the speech, and the media seized upon Greenspan's comments supporting the New Economy notion. This optimistic spin fit the zeitgeist of the era. Even the prevailing media coverage played along: Consider the *Wall Street Journal* capitalizing the proper noun *New Economy*—as if there was anything proper about it.

■ ■ ■

Many separate elements contributed to the boom. Cheap money was a significant factor, but it wasn't the only one. A broad

economic expansion was in its sixth year, with baby boomers in the sweet spot of their earning and spending years. Inflation appeared to be modest. New technologies had captivated the American imagination, creating instant millionaires and more than a few billionaires. Internet message boards (before they were overrun by touts and spammers) helped democratize stock research. Wall Street was flush with cash. CNBC—called "bubble vision" by noted short seller Bill Fleckenstein—was a relentless cheerleader throughout this entire era.

Credit the Y2K bug for what came next.

For the prior few years, there was increasing concern over the glitch in the software code that had been given only two digits for dates. What would happen when the calendar rolled over from 1999 to 2000? There were worries that this would wreak havoc on computer systems around the world. Companies spent huge amounts of money replacing much of their tech infrastructures. The worst of the doomsayers were survivalists who seemed to be looking forward to the American version of *Mad Max*. They advised people stock up on ammo, bottled water, and canned food, along with cash and gold.

The survivalists were a fringe group, considered paranoid loons by most thinking people. Not many took them seriously, except the Federal Reserve. It did not ignore the *Apocalypse Now* crowd. It wasn't that the Fed believed this crowd; the fear was that if enough of these paranoid loners managed to somehow convince the rest of the country that all hell was going to break loose, it could conceivably cause a run on the banks.

Greenspan's nightmare scenario was 24/7 news media coverage of long bank lines around the country, as a panicked populace withdrew their money in preparation for the end of the world.

The mad ravings of maniacs aside, the Fed figured better safe than sorry. To stave off any Y2K-related bank runs, the Federal Reserve held a bigger cash reserve than it ordinarily did. It also created a way for banks that needed any extra cash to borrow some—creating (I kid you not) the "Century Date Change Special Liquidity Facility."

But most important, the Federal Reserve injected an extra $50 billion in currency into the banking system. It's readily visible as a giant spike on a chart of U.S. currency (M1) (see Figure 7.2).

The effects of all of this extra fuel on an already "bubblicious" environment lit the market's afterburners. Stocks went from red-hot to

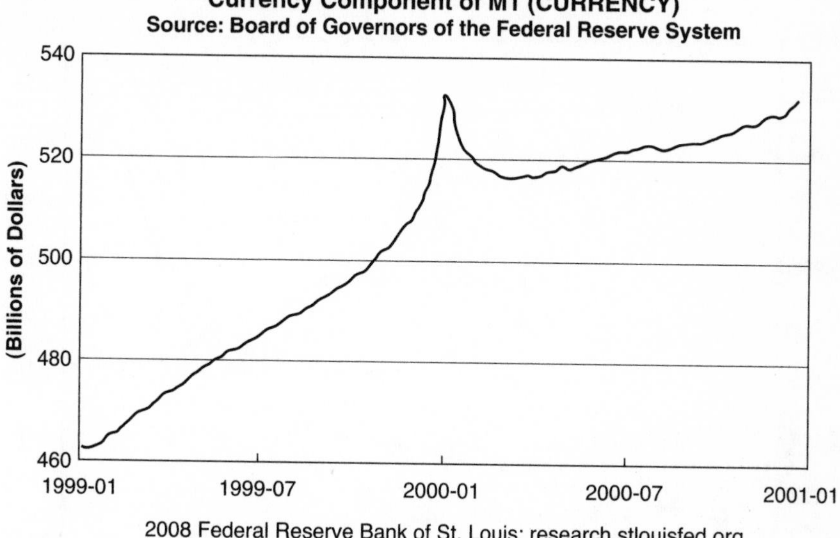

Figure 7.2 U.S. Currency (M1)

SOURCE: Board of Governors of the Federal Reserve, 2008 Federal Reserve Bank of St. Louis, http://research.stlouisfed.org.

white-hot, as all of this money found its way to the most speculatively traded issues. The NASDAQ exploded upward, despite having a P/E that was approaching 200 (a P/E of 15 is considered reasonable). For the calendar year 1999, the index gained 85.6 percent (see Figure 7.3). From the liquidity injection in late October to just six months later, the NASDAQ almost doubled, rising from 2,600 to over 5,100. It was a nearly 100 percent gain in only half a year. There simply was no precedent for anything like this in stock market history.

It was the perfect setup what came next.

The final up leg of a bull market often takes the form of a blow-off top. This occurs when the merely absurd becomes the utterly ridiculous. Blow-off tops happen when stocks (or indexes) make all-time highs, sucking in the last of those spectators who had been sitting idly on the sidelines.

In 2007, for example, China's Shanghai Stock Exchange (SSE) index had a blow-off top, rocketing from 1,200 in 2006 up to 6,400 by October 2007. The SSE had gained an unsustainable 100 percent plus year-to-date. A year later, it was back at 1,800, a tumble of 71 percent.

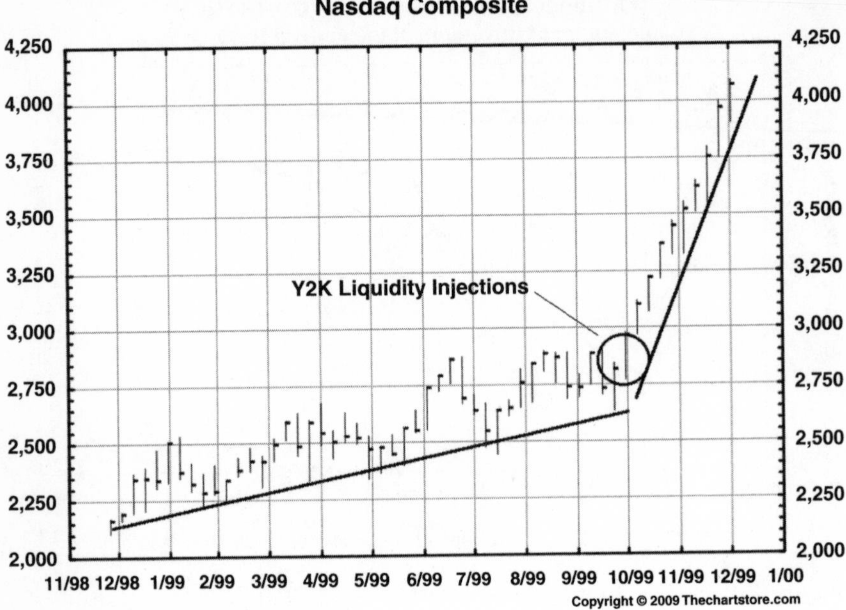

Figure 7.3 NASDAQ, 1999

In 2008, crude oil had a similar blow-off top. During the summer, crude peaked at over $147 per barrel. Before year's end, it had plummeted more than $100 a barrel, falling 69 percent to $46. Such is the nature of speculative tops.

Y2K came and went. The clocks rolled over on December 31, 1999, to January 1, 2000, virtually without incident.

Markets pulled in a bit in January—likely tax selling—then made new highs. After some backing and filling, the NASDAQ resumed its record-breaking pace in February. Thus 2000 looked to be yet another good year. From 3,600, the index gained another 35 percent over the next six weeks, breaking over 5,100.

But there were some residual effects of the Y2K bug that would soon be felt. Corporate America had just completed a massive technology upgrade. Companies had essentially rebuilt their entire information technology (IT) infrastructures over the past year or so. Hence, there was very little need to do much spending on hardware or software. The

Y2K upgrades and preparation had pulled much of the year 2000's tech spending into the 1999 fiscal year.

Preannouncement season is that period each quarter just before earnings get released. Also called "confessional season," it is when any company whose profits are below previously given public guidance to the press, investors, and analysts must fess up.

Preannouncement season was when the wheels started to come off the technology bus.

The first quarter of 2000 brought a series of warnings from Qualcomm, Intel, Dell, EMC Corporation, and a host of other stalwarts of the so-called New Economy. With stocks up enormously and valuations incredibly rich, it was sell first, ask questions later.

There is an old traders' expression: *Markets eat like a bird, but shit like a bear.* Gains accumulated over time can disappear very quickly. Momentum is a double-edged sword, and the excitement that had driven stocks higher over the prior five years quickly reversed to the downside. Barely a month after hitting its all-time peak, the NASDAQ had plummeted 37 percent, to near 3,200.

Soon after, bargain hunters appeared. The current crop of traders' only frame of reference was up, up, up! They had known nothing but a rampaging bull market, and their muscle memory had been trained to buy on the dips. This led to a reflexive bounce to 4,000, followed by another sell-off back down to 3,000.

The "buy the dip" strategy had been a successful moneymaker throughout most of the 1990s. That was good for another bounce back to 4,200 by summer's end. But the market couldn't hold on to its gains. Valuations remained too high, and earnings were falling off a cliff.

By September, stocks were back in sell-off mode again. The NASDAQ finished 2000 near 2,400; it was a brutal way to end the year.

For the calendar year 2000, the NASDAQ lost 39 percent. From its peak, it was down more than 50 percent. By October 2002, the NASDAQ Composite had traded down to 1,100, shedding 78 percent of its total value (see Figure 7.4). It was the biggest U.S. stock disaster since the 1929 Crash.

About now, you might be wondering why a book on bailouts has spilled so much ink on the U.S. stock markets. There is a good reason, in fact two good reasons why.

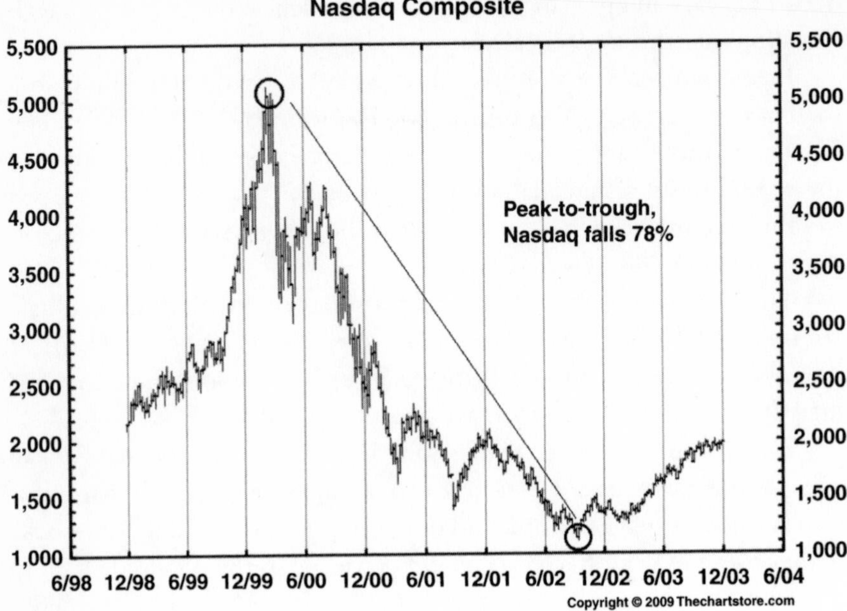

Figure 7.4 NASDAQ, 1999–2002

The first is asset prices. The Greenspan Fed had made repeated forays toward protecting asset prices from significant losses. Whether the motivation was to maintain confidence or to protect the economy is not relevant—the end results were the same. The central bankers created enormous moral hazard that resulted in ever more reckless speculation.

Second, and more important, each subsequent attempt into managing the (kinda) free markets required ever greater intervention. The capital markets are enormous, unruly beasts consisting of hundreds of trillions of dollars in value, traded by millions of people every day. They cannot be tamed or managed for very long. No, not even by a master "market whisperer" like Greenspan.

As we will soon see, the collapse of NASDAQ equities prodded the Federal Reserve into action. Greenspan began an unprecedented mop-up operation after the bubble popped. He would soon learn that the cleanup was even more expensive than anyone had imagined.

In January 2001, the Federal Reserve started an extraordinary rate-cutting process, one for which there is no comparison. On January 3, the Fed made an intermeeting cut of a half point, which was followed by another half-point cut on January 31, and then more half-point cuts on March 20, April 18, and May 15. June and August each saw quarter-point cuts. By the end of the summer, rates had been nearly halved, down to 3.5 percent (see Table 7.1).

All this rate slashing was before September 11. A recession had begun much earlier in the year, with the National Bureau of Economic Research dating its start as of March 2001. It would end shortly after 9/11, in November of that year.

There are those who have claimed that this radical rate cutting was in response to 9/11. Others have suggested that the terrorist attacks were what caused the recession. This historical revisionism is factually incorrect. As the record plainly shows, the recession had begun

Table 7.1 2001 Rate Cuts

	Federal Funds Rate	
Date 2001	**Point Change**	**New Level/Range**
January 3	$-\frac{1}{2}$	6%
January 31	$-\frac{1}{2}$	5.5%
March 20	$-\frac{1}{2}$	5%
April 18	$-\frac{1}{2}$	4.5%
May 15	$-\frac{1}{2}$	4%
June 27	$-\frac{1}{4}$	3.75%
August 21	$-\frac{1}{4}$	3.5%
September 17	$-\frac{1}{2}$	3%
October 2	$-\frac{1}{2}$	2.5%
November 6	$-\frac{1}{2}$	2%
December 11	$-\frac{1}{4}$	1.75%

one year after the market peaked, and half a year prior to the terror attacks.

On September 10, 2001, the NASDAQ was at 1,700. If you for a moment ever doubted that Greenspan specifically targeted the stock market and not the economy, consider his actions after the 9/11 al-Qaeda attack. That Tuesday saw the nation in shock. By the terrorists' design, the entire event played out live on television. That day, the Fed did . . . nothing, except for releasing a two-sentence statement: "The Federal Reserve System is open and operating. The discount window is available to meet liquidity needs."

My firm's office was headquartered on the 29th floor of 2 World Trade (I was in the Long Island office that day), so I admittedly have little in the way of objectivity about what happened on September 11. But I vividly recall wondering when the Fed was going to do something. The attacks kept markets closed for the rest of the week—the first time the NYSE had been closed since the Kennedy assassination and funeral.

With the World Trade Center smoldering in ruins, the Fed sat around and waited. Wednesday, Thursday, Friday—nothing. It wasn't until right before the markets reopened—when it would matter most to asset prices—that it finally did something. On September 17, 2001, almost one week after the attack, and precisely one hour before markets reopened, the Fed slashed rates another half point.

Whatever doubts there were that Greenspan was supporting asset prices disappeared forever that morning.

When the markets finally reopened, selling pressure was immediate. Prior to the attacks, the NASDAQ had already suffered losses of 66 percent. That week, it would lose another 17 percent. From that deeply oversold condition, a 50 percent snapback rally would have the index kissing 2,100 by January 2002. The gains were merely technical, a reaction to the massively oversold condition the postattack trading created. The downtrend soon reasserted itself.

By the summer of 2002, the post-9/11 lows of 1,400 were reached, then breached. The NASDAQ would trade down to 1,300 in July, then 1,200. By October, it would reach its ultimate bottom at 1,100.

The total NASDAQ fall from its peak was 78 percent, with losses measured in the trillions of dollars.

Greenspan Time Line

1987	Appointed FOMC chair by Ronald Reagan
1988	Working Group formed
1989	Real estate peaks, slump begins
1990	Invasion of Kuwait; oil skyrockets
1991	Recession
1992	Bill Clinton elected (reappoints Easy Al)
1993	No change in interest rates (only year of Greenspan's career)
1994	Orange County California bankruptcy
1994/95	Mexico devalued the peso
1996	"Irrational exuberance" speech
1997	Thai baht crisis (Asian contagion)
1998	LTCM bailout
1999	Dot-coms boom
2000	Crash
2001	Rate cuts begin
2002	Market bottoms in October 2002; retested in March 2003
2003	Federal funds rate is at 1 percent; housing, oil, and gold prices start moving upward
2004	Credit bubble begins to inflate
2005	Housing boom peaks
2006	Greenspan retires
2007	Credit crisis begins; U.S. stock market tops out
2008	Worst year in market history global markets cut in half
2009	Federal Reserve Chair Ben Bernanke takes rates to 0.00 percent; begins "quantitative easing"

It was in this environment that the Fed continued the most significant rate-cutting cycle in its history. From the precrash high of 6.5 percent, the Fed gradually took rates lower and lower still.

By the end of 2001, the federal funds rate was at 1.75 percent—a level not seen since John F. Kennedy was president in 1962. During previous recessions in 1954, 1958, and 1960, rates had been below 2 percent—but only for a few weeks or months at a time. Incredibly, the

Greenspan Fed maintained a 1.75 percent cap on the fed funds rate from December 2001 to September 2004. That was a total of 33 months at these ultralow levels. To people who have made a career out of watching the Fed, this was inconceivable.

And it was not quite done yet. A cut in November 2002 took rates down to 1.25 percent; they were kept there for 21 months (November 2002 to August 2004). The coup de grace was one last 25 basis point cut to a 1 percent fed funds rate in June 2003. Incredibly, the Fed left the rate this low for over 12 months, (June 2003 to June 2004). While the fed funds rate had been as low as 1 percent some 46 years earlier, it had never been allowed to stay that low for more than a year!

At this point, it's worth asking why the Fed took rates to such ridiculous extremes. The 2001 recession was fairly mild. The consumer barely paused spending. It was primarily a business capital expenditure (capex) recession. Even that was largely a one-off Y2K-related issue. And the September 11 tragedy, while horrific in its human toll, had only a minor impact on the U.S. economy.

The only plausible explanation for the radical rate cuts was asset prices. Greenspan was hell-bent on bailing out stock investors.

It is the very first rule of economics: *There is no free lunch.* If you drop rates down to ultralow levels, there will be significant repercussions. There was a reason these actions had never been done before by any prior Fed chief. There are costs associated with supposedly free money. Rates this low were incredibly inflationary. More than a few economists warned that this would lead to a massive surge in dollar devaluation, inflation, even speculation and other unintended consequences.

Someone at the Fed should have listened to them.

Chapter 8

The Backwards, Rate-Driven Economy

There are some frauds so well conducted that it would be stupidity not to be deceived by them.

—Charles Caleb Colton (*Lacon*, 1825)

In the mid-2000s, news of the housing boom and bust was omnipresent. There was no one in the United States unaware of the huge run-up in home prices during 2002–2006, or of the subsequent bust that followed.

What most people did not realize, however, was just how disproportionate the role the so-called real estate–industrial complex played during the 2002–2007 economic cycle. Few investors at the time were aware of the impact the housing boom had—not just for the real estate market, but for the stock market as well. Even today, most people do not really comprehend the full impact the real estate market had on the rest of the economy.

In order to understand how the United States ended up a Bailout Nation, it is crucial to put the extraordinary surge of housing into broader context.

In most business cycles, it is the economy that drives real estate. Job creation and wage growth are the key drivers of home purchases. Buyers save for a down payment, get approved for a mortgage, and then go shopping to buy a home. While interest rates are an important factor, in the typical cycle it's the economy that matters most.

But that's not how it happened this time.

The 2002–2007 housing cycle was historically unique. The combination of ultralow rates, new types of exotic mortgages, changes in lending standards, and massive securitization created the perfect storm for a housing boom. Consider for a moment a normal economy, with robust job creation and healthy wage gains. Under those circumstances, high-risk subprime loans and innovative mortgages would have been totally unnecessary. Without the very low rates or the new exotic debt instruments, the biggest growth in housing since World War II would not have occurred. It was that dangerous combination—and not job or income gains—that led to the unprecedented U.S. housing boom.

■ ■ ■

Let's go back to the end of the last recession: The nation had suffered through a wrenching three-year stock market crash (2000 to 2003). NASDAQ, where the hottest stocks had been listed, plummeted 78 percent from peak to trough. The losses were nearly identical to those of the 1929 crash and subsequent bear market. After the crash came the 2001 recession. Companies cut back their hiring and spending. It was unusual for a recession that consumers barely paused (consumer spending accounts for nearly 70 percent of the U.S. economy). The official National Bureau of Economic Research (NBER) dates for the economic contraction were March to November 2001—when 9/11 and its economic aftershocks hit, the recession was actually near its end.

With the U.S. economy under the weather, the government prescribed the usual medicine: big tax cuts in 2001, lots of deficit spending, increased money supply, military spending for two wars, and significant interest rate cuts. This tried-and-true treatment is usually effective in jump-starting economic growth. Some theorists argue that left alone, any economy subjected to a run of the mill recession would eventually self-correct anyway, but that's a discussion best saved for another day.

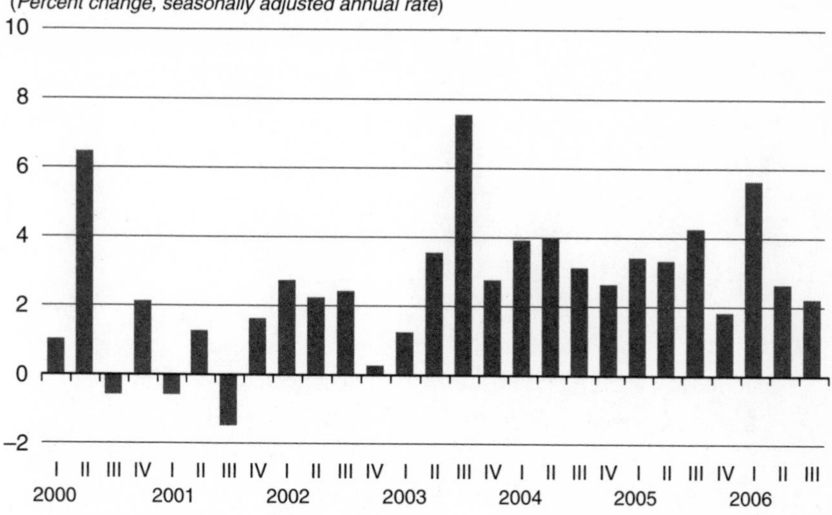

Figure 8.1 Real Gross Domestic Product
SOURCE: U.S. Bureau of Economic Analysis

A funny thing happened on the way to the recovery: *Nothing*. Despite the massive stimulus, the economy failed to respond. Following the Tax Relief Act of 2001, plenty of deficit spending in 2002, lower rates (and even more tax cuts in 2003), the economy was barely limping along. Real gross domestic product (GDP) was nearly flat in Q4 of 2002 (see Figure 8.1). The possibility of a double-dip recession was real, and that was making the Federal Reserve very nervous.

In the aftermath of the 2000–2001 recession, nonfarm payroll growth was anemic. With the exception of only one quarter (Q4 2006) real (i.e., after-inflation) wage growth was flat or negative. As of the third quarter of 2006, there were only 3.5 percent more jobs than there had been at the end of the recession. This compares very unfavorably with prior recoveries.

(*continued*)

(*continued*)

Consider the 1953–1954 period, which was followed by the worst of the nine recession recoveries since World War II. Yet even that recovery period had job gains more than double the current cycle: Following the 1953–1954 recession, total employment gained 7.6 percent over the ensuing five years. Even more astounding, that relatively poor showing was actually held down by the recession of 1957–1958.

To put this into context, five years after each of the previous nine recessions, "there were an average of 11.9 percent more jobs in the economy than there had been at the end of the recession."[1]

New job creation during the 2002–2007 recovery cycle was the worst on record since World War II. And income fared no better: Wage gains failed to even keep up with inflation for most of this period even as home prices and asset prices soared.

The Federal Open Market Committee (FOMC) had watched Japan get caught in a decade-long recession, compounded by a nasty case of deflation. After Japan's own real estate and stock bubbles burst in 1989, consumers there had become increasingly cautious. While the Japanese are culturally much more likely to save than Americans are, they had taken frugality to new extremes. And the less the Japanese spent, the more manufacturers and retailers slashed prices, hoping to draw them back to a consumptive mood. The longer consumers waited, the cheaper goods got. This vicious deflationary cycle, once started, is difficult to break.

On November 21, 2002, then Fed Governor Ben Bernanke gave a speech entitled "Deflation: Making Sure 'It' Doesn't Happen Here." Bernanke made reference to the government's not-so-secret antideflation weapon:

> The U.S. government has a technology, called a printing press (or, today, its electronic equivalent), that allows it to produce as many U.S. dollars as it wishes at essentially no cost. By increasing the number of U.S. dollars in circulation, or even by credibly threatening to do so, the U.S. government can also reduce the value of a dollar in terms of

> goods and services, which is equivalent to raising the prices in dollars of those goods and services. We conclude that, under a paper-money system, a determined government can always generate higher spending and hence positive inflation.[2]

That antideflation speech turned out to be quite prophetic: Bernanke eventually became Fed chair, and he put those printing presses to good use. Bond desks would nickname him "Helicopter Ben," thanks to his speech that threatened a metaphorical money drop as a way to stave off deflation.

But that nickname was still off in the future. Circa 2001, the Federal Reserve was getting increasingly nervous. Under the leadership of then Chair Alan Greenspan, the Fed began the most significant rate-cutting cycle in its history (see Figure 8.2). From precrash highs of 6.5 percent, the Fed took rates all the way down to 1.75 percent. As discussed in Chapter 7, the Greenspan Fed maintained a 1.75 percent federal funds rate for 33 months (December 2001 to September 2004), a 1.25 percent rate for 21 months (November 2002 to August 2004), and last, a 1 percent fed funds rate for over 12 months (June 2003 to June 2004). While the fed funds rate had been as low as

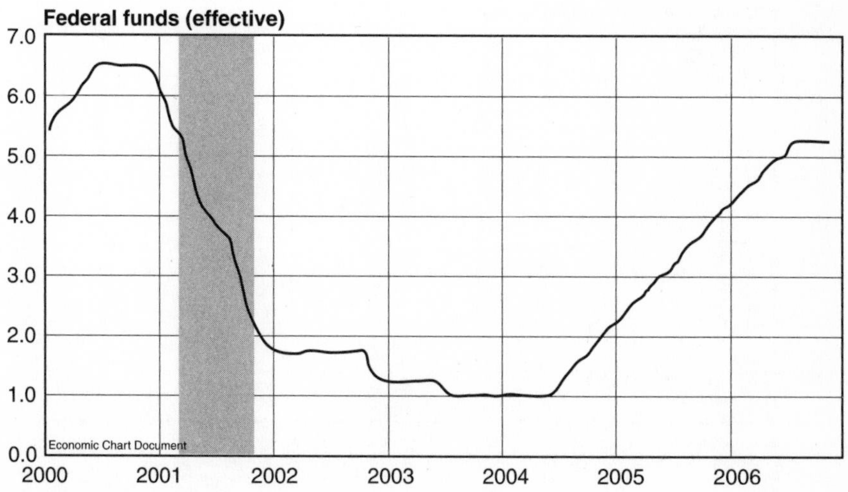

Figure 8.2 Federal Fund Rates, 2000–2006
SOURCE: Economagic

1 percent some 46 years earlier, it had never been allowed to stay that low for more than a year! This was simply unprecedented.

Money is often described as "cheap" or "expensive," depending on how costly it is to borrow. This money wasn't cheap—it was *ultra*-cheap. That fueled the housing fire, sending prices skyward.

As Figure 8.3 shows, this degree of stimulus—and for such an extended period—had never occurred before.

The global reaction was a boom in dollar-denominated assets. Consumers responded with a new round of cheap debt-funded spending. Residential real estate prices soared, and automobile sales spiked. Industrial metals reached all-time highs. And corporate profitability, as a percentage of GDP, reached never-before-seen heights. All thanks to the Fed's easy money prescription.

The Maestro had apparently done it again. Greenspan turned a market collapse into a full-blown recovery. If the tech boom and crash were caused by low rates and easy money, then a hair of the dog that bit you was just the hangover cure for the economy.

Or so it seemed.

Beneath the surface, the economy was much less rosy than it appeared. Inflation was starting to heat up. Commodity prices exploded,

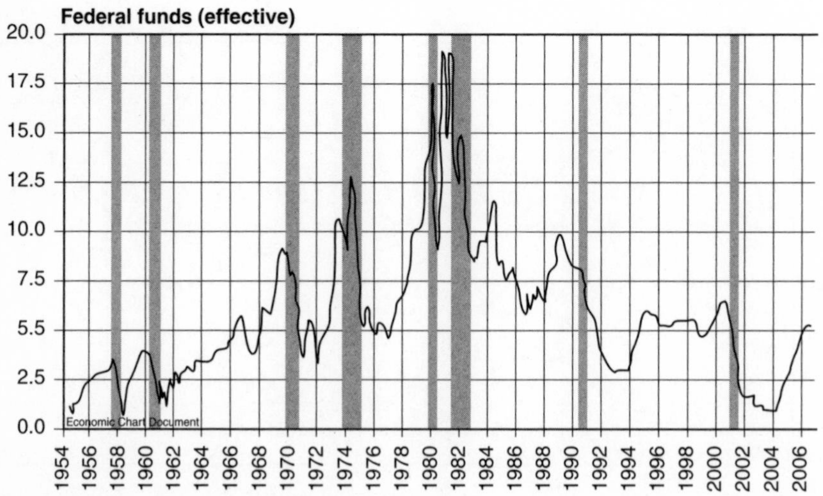

Figure 8.3 Federal Fund Rates, 1954–2006

SOURCE: Economagic

and oil broke out to record highs. That old inflation standby, gold, reached levels not seen in decades. At the same time, salaries remained flat, and compensation as a percentage of GDP dropped to multidecade lows. This was very unusual for the recovery period following a recession. It was not typically seen in healthy economies.

Also anomalous was the housing boom's outsized impact on jobs. According to a 2005 study by Asha Bangalore of Northern Trust Company, 43 percent of all new job creation between November 2001 and April 2005 was real estate related:

> Residential investment outlays have made a sizable contribution to the growth of real GDP in the current business expansion and sales of new and existing homes have soared to set new records. The future of the housing market is tied to employment conditions in the economy. The sluggish performance of payroll employment is the primary reason for the FOMC to take a measured path toward bringing the federal funds rate to a neutral level. At the same time, the performance of the housing market has played a visible role in payroll growth. Employment in housing and related industries (sum of employment in the establishment survey under various categories related to housing industry) accounted for about 43.0% of the increase in private sector payrolls since the economic recovery began in November 2001.[3]

The housing boom was creating jobs for builders, contractors, real estate agents, mortgage brokers, and even employees at Home Depot and Lowe's. But the most significant impact to the economy came from home equity lines of credit (HELOCs) and cash-out mortgage refinancings. With wages stagnant, Americans turned to home equity withdrawals in order to maintain their standard of living.

This was one of the single biggest and most unexpected elements of the debt-driven economic expansion. Outside of real estate, employment gains were modest and real wage gains flat. It was debt that drove the increase in consumer spending. Mortgage equity withdrawals (MEWs)—normally a small portion of consumer debt—exploded. The accelerating borrowing against their homes allowed consumers to keep on spending, even as their savings rate went negative for the first time since the 1930s.

Without this home equity–based consumption, the nation would have been in recession territory, with GDP flat to 1 percent. At least, according to an unofficial Fed study by none other than Alan Greenspan (see Figures 8.4 and 8.5).

Since rates hit their lows in 2003, the impact of mortgage equity withdrawal has been nothing short of breathtaking: MEW was responsible for more than 75 percent of GDP growth from 2003 to 2006.

It's helpful to consider what MEW had been like in the past: For most of the 1990s, the net equity pulled out by homeowners—either through sales or through home equity refinancing—was fairly modest: about $25 billion per quarter, or about 1 percent of disposable personal income.

The impact of MEW began to accelerate once the Fed cut rates so spectacularly. By mid-2002, the quarterly average MEW was north of $100 billion, up nearly 400 percent since 1997 and greater than 4 percent of disposable income. By 2003, those quarterly numbers were $150 billion and 6 percent.

Then, things exploded: MEW hit a peak in 2004, as quarterly withdrawals were almost a quarter of a trillion dollars—over 10 percent of disposable personal income. To put that into context, that was a 1,000 percent gain in the 10 years since 1995.

In addition to the actual dollars extracted from housing, the psychological impact that feeling financially flush has on spending cannot be underestimated. The wealth effect, as it is known, shows that every $100 gain in a stock portfolio creates $4 in additional consumer spending. But this wealth effect is even more significant for homes. A recent study found that an increase in owned housing value of $100 will boost spending by $9—more than twice the impact on spending of stock market wealth effect gains.[4]

Considering how widespread home ownership is in the United States, this is quite significant: About 68.5 percent of American families live in their own homes (it was as high as 70 percent recently). While

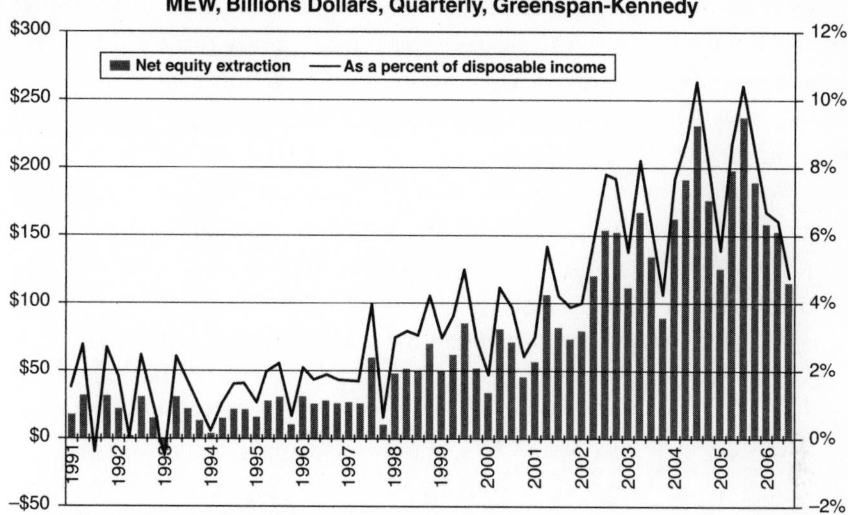

Figure 8.4 Mortgage Equity Withdrawal, Net Extraction, and Percentage of Disposable Personal Income

SOURCE: Calculated Risk, www.calculatedriskblog.com

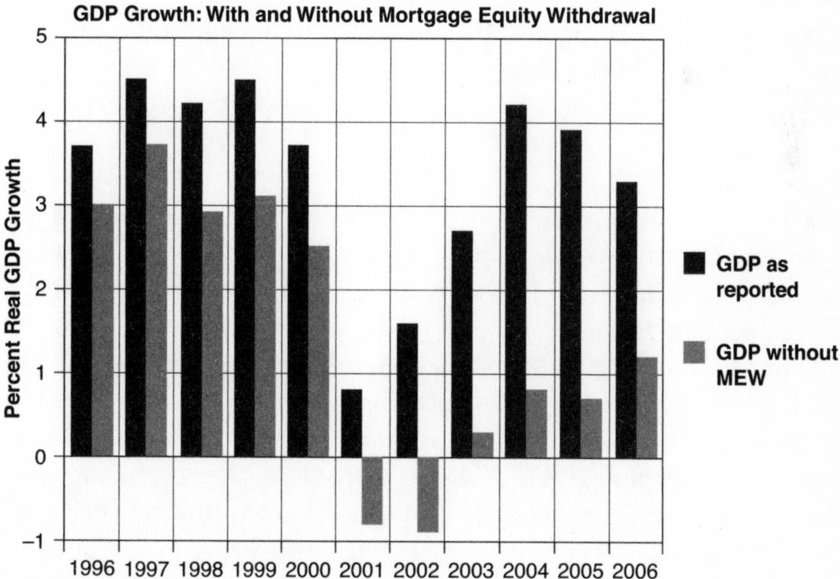

Figure 8.5 GDP Growth: With and Without Mortgage Equity Withdrawal

SOURCE: Calculated Risk, www.calculatedriskblog.com

ownership of stocks is widespread—studies put market participation at near 50 percent of all Americans—the typical family has a rather small percentage of their net worth in equities. Indeed, in most cases, stocks are their second- or third-largest asset. For the vast majority of Americans, their home is their largest asset.

Now factor that into family wealth: Increases in home price provided 70 percent of the gains in household net worth since 2001.

The wealth effect of home price appreciation is much more widely distributed than stocks. This made the generational-low interest rates the single largest factor that resuscitated the economy. Sure, tax cuts, deficit spending, increased money supply, war spending, and the like all played a role—but it was the ultralow rates and the mortgage equity withdrawal they allowed that dominated U.S. economic activity.

Even China's explosive growth was indirectly related to FOMC actions. Chinese apparel, electronics, and durable goods manufacturers were prime beneficiaries of America's debt-fueled spending binge. Beijing returned the favor, buying a trillion dollars' worth of U.S. Treasuries. This helped to keep rates relatively low, even as the Fed shifted into tightening mode, raising rates from 1 percent to over 5 percent. This "conundrum," as Fed Chief Greenspan called it, reinforced the virtuous real estate cycle, extending it even further.

■ ■ ■

The first rule of economics is that there is no free lunch, and the massive ultralow rate stimulus came at a price: Cheap money led to inflation, fueled American's worst consumption habits, and added a ton to consumers' total debt.

But it was not just Main Street that binged on easy money. On Wall Street, cheap money would become even more addictive. Leverage (borrowing capital to invest) fueled investment banks, while liquidity powered hedge funds. Private equity gorged on cheap cash and used it to go on a buying spree. How else can one explain the ridiculous purchase of Chrysler in the spring of 2007 by the hedge fund Cerberus, if not for the nearly free cost of capital used to make this bone-headed investment? It wasn't the only dumb acquisition of the time; plenty of other ill-advised mergers and acquisitions (M&A) were funded via easy money.

Corporate America also rushed to grab cheap cash; many companies increased their dividend issuance, and quite a few borrowed heavily to do so. Others used the money to make stock buybacks as markets rallied higher. Most of these share repurchases have since proven to be horrific investments.

In the age of Sarbanes-Oxley, earnings manipulation via accounting trickery was out. What was in was the simple form of financial engineering enabled by easy money: reducing share count via stock repurchases.

TrimTabs Investment Research estimated that $456 billion worth of stock repurchases—nearly half a trillion dollars!—took place in 2005. A study by David Rosenberg, Merrill Lynch's chief economist, discovered that in Q3 2006, nearly a third of earnings gains were due to share repurchases.[5]

With so much cheap money liquefying the system, the new mantra seemed to be to borrow freely. There was no need to worry about the debt or leverage—the day of reckoning was far, far off in the future.

Or so it seemed.

INTERMEZZO

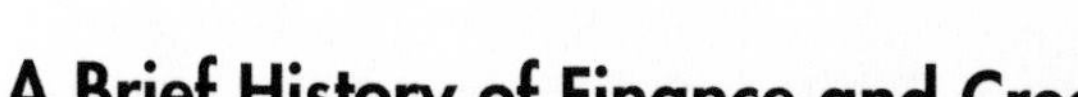

A Brief History of Finance and Credit

The great credit boom-and-bust cycle of the early twenty-first century was a typical bubble. It had its supporters and early detractors; there were the usual tortured rationales to explain what was unusual economic behavior; and there was a land rush to grab short-term profits despite increasingly obvious risks. As is often the case, it went on much longer than one would have reasonably expected.

One aspect of this credit boom, however, stands out as particularly unusual: the astonishing shift in the fundamental basis of credit transactions.

Throughout the history of human finance, the underlying premise of any lending, credit, or financing—indeed, all loans, mortgages, and debt instruments—has always been the borrower's ability to repay the loan. It is the most basic aspect of all finance.

This system of economic transactions goes as far back as when Og lent the guy in the next cave a dozen clamshells so he could purchase that newfangled wheel. If Og didn't have a reasonable basis to expect his neighbor would be able to service that debt—*Is he a good hunter? Is he trustworthy? Will he be able to repay those clamshells?*—he never would've entered into what was the first commercial loan.

From 1 million B.C. up until the present day, the ability to repay the debt has always been the dominant factor—except, however, for a brief five-year period starting around 2002. During that short era, the fundamental basis of all credit transactions was turned on its head. It was no longer the borrower's ability to repay the loan that was of paramount importance. Rather, the basis of lending money shifted to the lender's ability to sell the debt for securitization purposes.

As the world soon discovered, this was enormously important, and was the basis for what came afterward: credit bubble, housing boom and bust, derivatives explosion, economic chaos. It can all be traced back to that shift in making a lending decision.

Since the crisis began with real estate loans, let's use the typical mortgage as an example of how these earth-shattering changes occurred.

The basis for making a mortgage loan to a potential home buyer has relied on several simple factors: Banks looked at the home buyer's employment history and income, the size of the down payment, and the person's credit rating to determine the borrower's ability to service the debt. They also considered the loan-to-value ratio of the property, as well as other assets the borrower might own, to ensure that the loan was secured by the property.

Those factors went away during the early 2000s housing boom when the basis for mortgage lending was no longer the borrower's ability to pay—it was the lender's ability to securitize and repackage a mortgage.

This was a game changer. Any loan originators that could process the paperwork and quickly ship the loan off to Wall Street stood to make a lot of money from this process.

If we were to sum up the entire history of finance on a time line, it would look something like this, with the five-year period—the paradigm shift—as an unusual aberration relative to the prior million years:

|--1 million B.C.----------------------------//---[2002-07]---2009-->

It is the duty of the Federal Reserve to supervise credit and lending. We have since discovered that numerous people, including (now deceased) Fed Governor Ed Gramlich, tried to bring the problems of this lending to the attention of then Fed Chairman Alan Greenspan. You will be astonished to learn that the Federal Reserve of the United States did nothing about this shift. Indeed, the change in lending standards was praised by Greenspan as an important innovation.

I call this "nonfeasance"—failure to carry out an official charge or duty.

The so-called innovation turned out to be nothing of the sort. It was a deeply flawed lending process camouflaged, at first, by strongly rising home prices. Once prices peaked, the fault lines became clearly visible. Since late 2006, 306 major U.S. lending operations have imploded and over two million U.S. homes have been foreclosed (and rising).[3]

Allowing banks to give money to people regardless of their ability to pay it back is at the heart of the current situation. That factor, combined with the ultralow interest rates created by the Fed to bail out the prior market crash, sent the credit market cascading toward disaster.

As we will see, this isn't the first time one crisis bailout led to another.

Chapter 9

The Mad Scramble for Yield

[The option ARM is] like the neutron bomb. It's going to kill all the people but leave the houses standing.

—George McCarthy, housing economist, Ford Foundation

As we saw in prior chapters, Alan Greenspan's rate-cutting regime after the tech bubble burst was a radical departure from usual Federal Reserve policy. Starting in January 2001, the Fed began cutting rates—and kept cutting until they were at generational lows. The FOMC kept the federal fund rate at 1.75 percent or below from December 2001 to September 2004—nearly three years! This was unprecedented in FOMC history. Rates had never been kept so low for such an extended period of time.

Not only had this never happened before, it was previously unthinkable. And with good reason: Ultralow rates are an enormously irresponsible action on the part of a central bank. When money becomes that cheap, there are all manner of dire consequences. Rate cuts "reflated," then inflated the economy. But it did so at a horrific cost:

- The U.S. dollar plummeted in value. From 2001 to 2008, the greenback lost nearly 40 percent of its purchasing power.
- As the dollar tumbled, anything that was globally priced in U.S. dollars, including oil, gold, industrial metals, foodstuffs—in fact, most commodities—rallied dramatically in price. It still cost the same amount to produce/grow/mine these items, only the money used to buy 'em was worth only half as much.
- The sole exception to this massive inflation trade was labor (this becomes important later on). With wages flat and inflation rising, Americans' savings rate dropped below zero for the first time since the 1930s.
- Consumers aggressively used cheap financing to buy *everything*, especially big-ticket items such as appliances, automobiles, and homes.
- As rates plummeted, fixed-income managers desperately scrambled for yield.

This last point is critical. If you want to know how home foreclosures in the United States led to massive economic disruptions worldwide, you need to understand the relationship between ultralow rates and the bond buyers. The Greenspan Fed's radical rate policies tossed the arcane world of bond fund management into turmoil, and the net result was all sorts of unexpected consequences that continue to be felt to the present day.

■ ■ ■

Before proceeding much further, here are a few brief words about how fund managers handle capital. There is an enormous amount of money run on behalf of large foundations, endowments, pension funds, and charitable trusts. The professionals who manage money for these institutions are constrained by some basic money management principles. Foremost among these is the payout requirement—the minimum distribution of money that these organizations must pay out each year. Each fiscal year, trusts and foundations must spend or give away 5 percent of the average market value of their assets. Failing to do so leads to heavy penalties (2 percent of assets), and the possible loss of their advantageous tax status.

This is why any professional money manager who is handling capital for these organizations wants to *safely* generate sufficient income to cover the 5 percent payout obligation. Foundations want to leave the trust corpus untouched, spending or giving away only their income. A well-managed trust should last a very long time, if not forever.

I will spare you the gory details, but it is accepted asset management theory—backed up by mathematical analysis—that over the long run, market returns eventually revert to their historic means. This basic assumption is built into models that fund managers use as the basis for their asset management plans. For stocks, expected returns are 8 to 10 percent per year. For fixed income, it's about half of that—between 4 and 5 percent returns from long-dated Treasuries. These are reasonable long-term goals, based on a century of inflation, interest rates, market returns, and other factors.

Hence, ultralow rates caused tremendous angst and consternation among fixed-income managers. They simply could not generate the needed returns when the Fed had driven rates so absurdly low.

Without some other higher-yielding, yet safe fixed-income option, the trust corpus was likely to be breached.

While market shocks occur from time to time, they tend to be within a certain measure of normal variance (mathematicians call them standard deviations). Major events that are a few standard deviations from the mean cause markets to briefly wobble, but they invariably return back to their prior trend. We saw this during such significant events as World War II, the Bay of Pigs invasion, the Kennedy assassination, the 1987 crash, the 1990 Iraq invasion of Kuwait, and the September 11, 2001, terror attacks. These were all very significant *human* events, but in terms of markets, they were actually rather minor.

Indeed, these earth-shattering events barely register as a squiggle on the long-term stock charts.

None of these events were as fundamental to the bond markets as what Greenspan did. When the Fed took rates down further and held them lower for longer than ever before, bond markets rallied and yields were decimated. (Bond yields move in the opposite direction of bond prices.)

Hence, Greenspan induced a mad scramble among the bond crowd. The housing boom played right into this dash for fixed-income returns.

■ ■ ■

While fund managers were scrambling for yield, the ultralow rates simultaneously set off the biggest housing surge since World War II. In the 1980s, annual home sales averaged about three million units. That rose in the 1990s to between four and five million transactions, thanks to both population growth and declining interest rates. The 1990s bull market in stocks created plenty of paper wealth, and that too soon found its way into the real estate market. Housing prices had been in a bit of slump from the 1987 crash to the mid-1990s. Once rates fell after the 2000 tech-stock crash, however, the real estate market exploded: Prices nearly doubled from 10 years earlier, and total units sold went from under four million in 1995 to over seven million houses in 2005 (see Figure 9.1).

That meant lots and lots of mortgage financing.

The rate cuts that were fueling the real estate boom were wreaking havoc on pension fund managers' portfolios.

If they could not find additional rate of return (*and quick!*), their clients would have to tap the permanent fund corpus—meaning use some of the principal to make annual payments. To any trustee, that was unacceptable.

Figure 9.1 Housing Sales

SOURCE: www.calculatedrisk.blog.com/

The answer to bond fund managers' prayers was found in an innovative structured product: securitized debt. Wall Street could take all manner of debt—credit cards, auto loans, mortgages, student loans—and repackage them into new bundles of new paper. Collateralized debt obligations (CDOs) paid out *significantly higher interest rates* than either U.S. Treasuries or blue-chip corporate bonds. And thanks to some Wall Street razzle-dazzle, they were *all triple-A rated*.

From Low Rates to Exotic Derivatives

A mortgage-backed security (MBS) is the process by which thousands of mortgages are packaged together into bondlike financial products. Holders of these instruments are actually the folks who end up getting most of the interest and principal payments homeowners make each month.

As the graphic shows, MBS buyers can select a variety of ratings—each with a different potential risk and expected return. This is a huge liquid market: Between $1 trillion and $2 trillion in new MBSs were issued in the United States each year from 2002 to 2007.

That's just the first step. There are all sorts of different types of mortgage paper; some are backed by residential mortgages (RMBSs), and some by commercial property lending (CMBSs). These various flavors are then sliced and diced into various categories, each rated, and each with a different potential risk and return to the buyer.

If that sounds complicated, well, that's just the start: These MBSs get sliced and diced into an alphabet soup of instruments and their derivatives: collateralized mortgage obligations (CMOs), collateralized debt obligations (CDOs), and collateralized loan obligations (CLOs). You can even insure the interest payments on these—or just make bets either way—via credit default swaps (CDSs).

My personal favorite is CDO^n—a generic term for CDO^3 (CDO-cubed) and higher. These are CDOs backed by other CDOs, ranging from CDO^2 (CDO-squared) to CDO^3 to CDO^4 and so on.

(*continued*)

(continued)

Each of these is a more complicated instrument derived from another product (hence the term *derivatives*). Each new item is engineered with an increasing degree of complexity and a less transparent amount of risk. They get packaged and repackaged and repackaged further still. By the time the whole unholy mess is done, the final instrument is many, many times removed from the original paper, a simple mortgage.

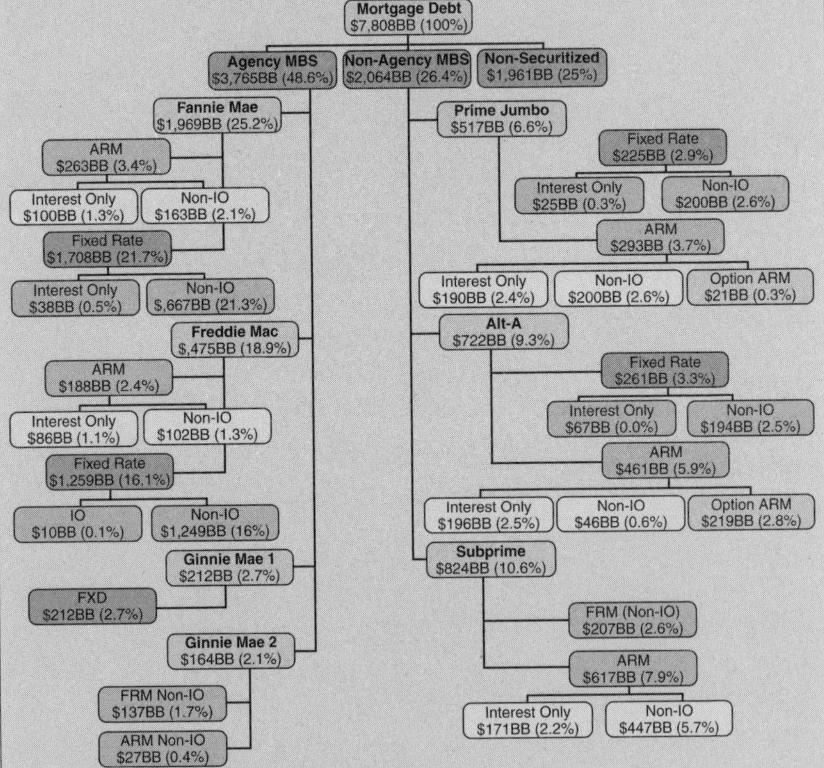

First Lien: Residential Mortgage Debt

ASSUMPTIONS: Securitization rate 75 percent; loan performance reporting rate: prime and Alt-A: 75 percent, subprime: 65 percent.

SOURCE: http://bigpicture.typepad.com/comments/files/RMBS.gif; courtesy of Credit Suisse

Most fixed-income products come with a grade from one of three major rating agencies, Moody's Investors Service, Standard & Poor's, and Fitch Ratings (more on them later). Investment-grade ratings include AAA, AA, A, and BBB. Non-investment-grade debt—also known as junk bonds—are ratings given to debt that is more economically sensitive, or whose finances are less stable, or that is highly speculative.

Triple-A is the most creditworthy rating; this grade is only given (in theory) to the highest-quality borrowers, such as the U.S. government and top companies like Johnson & Johnson, Northwestern Mutual, Berkshire Hathaway, and Exxon Mobil.

About now, you might want to ask yourself how this was possible: How could U.S. Treasuries be rated triple-A, and these CDOs also be triple-A rated? How could there be such a significant spread between the yields of the two assets? Doesn't the higher-yielding product involve more risk? If yes, why did CDOs have the same credit rating—essentially, a measure of a debt issuers' ability to pay its obligations—as bonds backed by the full faith and credit of the U.S. government (and 86th Airborne, if push really comes to shove)?

If not, isn't this a free lunch?

There really are only two possibilities: Either this was a brilliant heretofore unrealized insight or it was a massive fraud.

Rating Agencies: Moody's, S&P, and Fitch

Far from being objective arbiters of the creditworthiness of debt instruments, the three major rating agencies—Standard & Poor's, Moody's, and Fitch Ratings—engaged in a form of payola. They were willing to play along with the investment banks, putting triple-A ratings on paper that turned out to be junk—if the price was right. Call it "pay for play."

Working closely with underwriters, they frequently rated paper AA and AAA that eventually was revealed to be junk paper.

Jesse Eisinger of *Portfolio* magazine was the first mainstream reporter to call the rating agencies out in a substantive way. He noted that this collaboration, not surprisingly, led to "benign ratings

(*continued*)

(*continued*)

of securities based on subprime mortgages."[1] Not only did the initial ratings prove to be too generous, but the agencies were much too slow in downgrading housing-related bonds when mortgage defaults and foreclosures started to rise.

The *Wall Street Journal* soon followed:

"Helping spur the boom was a less-recognized role of the rating companies: their collaboration, behind the scenes, with the underwriters that were putting those securities together."

This error—placing AAA ratings on subprime-based loans and the structured products built on top of them—wasn't merely the function of bad ratings judgment; rather, it was a conscious business decision. The *Wall Street Journal* noted rating agencies were active participants in the creation of structured products—not objective third-party arbiters who merely *misunderestimated* their creditworthiness, as the companies claimed after the boom went bust.

"Underwriters don't just assemble a security out of home loans and ship it off to the credit raters to see what grade it gets," the *Journal* reported. "Instead, they work with rating companies while designing a mortgage bond or other security, making sure it gets high-enough ratings to be marketable."[2]

Not surprisingly, the rating agencies charged fees on crappy AAA-rated paper that were twice as big on subprime paper versus prime-based loans.[3] And Bloomberg estimated that from 2002 to 2007, the agencies garnered fees on $3.2 trillion in subprime-based mortgages.

If that sounds like it was an enormous amount of work requiring a highly skilled pool of analysts, well, not so much. Regulators found that Moody's and S&P didn't have nearly enough people to review all of these mortgages closely, and they didn't adequately monitor the thousands of fixed-income securities they were grading.[4]

The triple-A ratings on mortgage-backed securities were a crucial factor in the credit collapse of 2007–2008. If not for the triple-A approval of the rating agencies, much of the toxic paper that subsequently went bust could never have been bought; literally, many bond investors are prohibited from buying securities with credit ratings below a certain threshold. So the rating agencies' triple-A seal of approval was critical to the ability of Wall Street firms to package and resell subprime mortgages and other securities now euphemistically described as "toxic."

■ ■ ■

It's plain to see how historically low rates led to a housing boom. But how did something as seemingly innocent as rising home prices lead to a subprime mortgage crisis and create the great Bailout Nation circa 2008–2009?

We've seen how these mortgage-backed securities were rated triple-A, the highest designation, by the top credit rating agencies. The paper was based on mortgages originated by legitimate Main Street banks. The RMBSs were securitized by the top Wall Street firms. The underlying mortgages were frequently funded and purchased by government-sponsored enterprises (GSEs), such as Fannie Mae and Freddie Mac.

Buyers of these securities should have paused a moment to consider one simple fact: These CDOs rewrote the laws of economics. They promised to be as safe as U.S. Treasuries, but paid out a significantly higher yield. In other words, for the same exact risk, the reward was much greater. This should have been recognized as an impossibility. In the markets, greater reward always means greater risk. Someone would either be winning a Nobel Prize in economics—or going to jail.

It was the financial equivalent of cold fusion. Managers were getting something (increased yield) for nothing (identical low risk). That this was not clearly recognized immediately was a function of both *selective perception* and *cognitive dissonance.* Managers wanted, *needed* to believe these securities could solve their yield problem. Rather than challenge the fundamental economic flaw of CDO math—greater performance for the same amount of risk was impossible—they instead simply bought into the scheme.

Over the past few years, a variety of techniques have been employed to get more yield without taking on *considerably* more risk: Some managers crept further and further down the quality scale in exchange for higher interest rates. Some took on just a little more risk, hoping no one would really notice. Others borrowed money in nations with low interest rates and invested it in countries with higher rates (aka the carry trade). Some used leverage, although that has a variety of inherent problems. Some clever folks tried complexity, which hides the additional risk you are taking on from the view of most observers.

One particular group of folks checked the box marked "All of the above": hedge funds.

Aggressive fund managers borrowed lots and lots of money from their prime brokers and, suitably leveraged up, went out and dove into the alphabet soup of RMBSs, CMBSs, CDOs, CLOs, and CMOs.

Under normal circumstances, that might not matter much. However, these were not normal circumstances. The demand for these securitized products created a land rush for mortgage-backed securities. From 2003 to 2007, there was an enormous creation of credit:

- In 2000 the total annual issuance of mortgage-backed securities, including CDOs, had risen to more than $1 trillion. The volume of derivatives—including contracts such as options and swaps—grew even faster, so that by the end of 2006 their notional value was just over $400 trillion. Before the 1980s, these were virtually unknown.[5]
- In 1990 there were just 610 hedge funds, with $38.9 billion under management. At the end of 2006 there were 9,462, with $1.5 trillion under management.[6]
- Between 1980 and 2007, the volume of GSE-backed mortgage-backed securities grew from less than $200 billion to more than $4 trillion. In 1980 only 10 percent of the home mortgage market was securitized; by 2007, 56 percent of it was.[7]
- According to the Bank for International Settlements (BIS), the total notional amounts outstanding of over-the-counter (OTC) derivative contracts—arranged on an ad hoc basis between two parties—as of December 2007 had a gross market value of over $14.5 trillion.[8]

- Between December 2005 and December 2007, the notional amounts outstanding for all derivatives increased from $298 trillion to $596 trillion. Credit default swaps quadrupled, from $14 trillion to $58 trillion.[9]

■ ■ ■

In hindsight, it's clear this "more yield, same risk" scheme was a house of securitized cards destined to come tumbling down. But in the early part of the aughts, fund managers wandering in the desert created by Greenspan's radical rate cutting were just discovering securitized mortgage products. To many, they seemed a reasonable way to capture the higher yields their clients were demanding. From 2002 until 2006, AAA-rated CDOs seemed like manna from heaven.

The housing boom was the ideal environment for these products, and residential mortgage-backed securities (RMBSs) were especially popular. Bundling thousands of mortgages together, Wall Street wizard's created CDOs composed of a series of tranches of underlying mortgages of varying quality. Each tranche had a different risk level, and offered higher (or lower) yield levels. This allowed fixed-income managers to choose exactly the returns they needed. Those seeking greater returns had to take on more risk—but AAA or AA was still investment grade, right?

Note that this wasn't a U.S.-only phenomenon: Mortgage-based paper was repackaged as CDOs and purchased en masse by fixed-income managers around the world. Global fund managers—in Europe, in the Middle East, but especially in Asia—were big buyers of mortgage-backed securities. This is how the U.S. housing bust became a global issue. It explains how subprime borrowers in Southern California could default on their mortgages, setting off a chain reaction that ended with the collapse of Iceland.

This was the financial bedrock upon which our modern Bailout Nation was built. When that bedrock was found faulty, the entire economic edifice built atop it crumbled.

Part III

MARKET FAILURE

Source: By permission of John Sherffius and Creators Syndicate, Inc.

Chapter 10

The Machinery of Subprime

The superior man understands what is right; the inferior man understands what will sell.

—Confucius

How did all manner of exotic subprime mortgages and their derivatives wind up festooned all over the global financial system? To understand that question, we need to put on our detective caps and do some digging.

In the old days, traditional lenders—depository banks—accounted for the lion's share of mortgage writing. They are fairly well regulated by both the Federal Reserve and the Federal Deposit Insurance Corporation (FDIC). These banks typically are run in a very conservative, purposeful fashion. Banks have a funny way of looking at lending: *It's not the loans you reject; it's the ones you approve that get you into trouble.*

Hence, traditional lending tended toward borrowers who could put down a large down payment, had good income and credit histories, and could service the debt easily. These were the prime borrowers, and they tended to make safe bets for lenders.

Over time, other nonthrift participants got increasingly involved in the home loan industry. Independent mortgage brokers were able to steer loans to *any* bank. The savvy ones developed a reputation for knowing which bank offered the best rates at any given time.

Some developed an expertise in home buyers who did not quite meet the high standards of the major banks. Borrowers with lesser bona fides were considered subprime. Perhaps their credit scores were not as strong, their down payments smaller, or their incomes not as great. This was a small niche market that was serviced by a handful of firms. Given the inability of subprime borrowers to get a prime loan, along with the increased risk of default due to the weaker ratios, these lenders were able to charge a premium for their services.

Most large, reputable banks steered clear of subprime. It was too messy, with too many defaults. It simply didn't fit in with their risk-averse model.

Starting in the early 2000s, conservative lending became unfashionable and aggressive risk taking appeared. Fiscal prudence was replaced with weakened (and eventually, irresponsible) lending standards. It soon reached a point where much of the industry tossed out the garden-variety mortgages that had served them so well, and replaced them with jungle-variety loans.

In the new era of banking, "lend to securitize" became the industry's standard operating procedure, and the subprime mortgage machinery's assault on suburban America began.

■ ■ ■

One of banking's major changes in the latter part of the twentieth century was the rise of the nondepository mortgage originator. Often located in California, these lenders used an army of independent brokers to push their products. Like so many mushrooms in cow dung after a summer rain, these brokers sprouted up in the early 2000s. They were the prime salespeople of the subprime adjustable-rate mortgage (ARM).

These firms were not like traditional banks. They had no depositors to provide them with a capital base. They started with seed money, but once that grubstake was exhausted, they could not write more loans. To do more business, they had to move the existing paper off their balance sheets and replace it with fresh capital. Hence, they had little choice but to sell the mortgages they underwrote just as soon as they could. They found a willing buyer in Wall Street, which was all too happy to purchase these loans for securitization purposes.

Wall Street's insatiable demand for mortgages to securitize led originators to completely abdicate all lending standards. If you could fog a mirror, you qualified for a mortgage. The best example of this was found in California. Anthony Ha reported in the *Hollister Free Lance* that Alberto Ramirez, a strawberry picker earning just $14,000 a year, was able to obtain a mortgage to buy a home for $720,000.[1]

That was just the most egregious example. Anyone with a modicum of experience in the mortgage industry will confirm the rampant disregard for lending standards during the boom years. This was very different from the way traditional banks operated. To your local banker, a mortgage is a reliable and secured form of lending. With few notable exceptions, lending standards by banks had always been rigorous. When a traditional depository bank originated a mortgage, it assumed it would hold on to the loan for the full 15- or 30-year term; depository banks felt no compulsion to resell them. Guarding against default over the life of that loan was the key to not only being profitable, but staying in business.

That wasn't how the newfangled lend-to-securitize originators worked. In one of many examples of misplaced compensation schemes we have seen, they were paid on the volume, not the quality, of their loans. Besides, they didn't need to find a buyer who was a good risk for 30 years—they needed only to find someone who wouldn't default before the securitization process was complete. Thus, they had very different standards from the traditional lenders. The sellers of these mortgages made warranties to the Wall Street buyers of this paper that the borrowers would not default for 90 days—enough time for the loans to be sold off and repackaged as residential mortgage-backed securities (RMBSs).

This was a radical change in lending standards.

In the past, lenders had to make sure the borrower was good for the full 30 years of a mortgage. In the old days, a bank would make a mortgage loan and hold on to it until the home was either paid off or sold. If there was a default—even 20 years later—it was the original lender

(the mortgage originator) that was on the hook. Some securitization took place, but it was a small percentage of outstanding mortgages. That was why the borrower's ability to repay the loan was the primary basis of all lending.

What happened in the recent housing bubble—it's more accurate to describe it as a credit bubble—represented an enormous paradigm shift. Mortgage originators no longer had to find someone who could carry the debt for three decades—they had only three months to worry about! Hell, practically anyone could meet those requirements!

That alone was enough to guarantee trouble. However, for the most part, the industry itself was lightly regulated or, in some cases, not regulated at all. It was ripe for lots of abuse. By the middle of the decade, the mortgage lenders had become the new boiler rooms.[2]

The many sleazy mortgage brokers and originators who sold loans they knew were likely to default were most definitely the inferior men Confucius warned of. And the banks that underwrote these loans certainly weren't superior.

Fraud in Real Estate, Mortgages, and Home Building

Minor amounts of real estate–related fraud have always existed. During the housing boom years of 2002 to 2007, it became a pandemic. These various fraudulent actions helped make the housing boom much bigger—and the bust that much more painful:

- **Appraisal fraud:** Historically, there was no incentive to inflate appraisals. But with the rise of the mortgage brokers—many working closely with real estate agents—the business of steering appraisals to the most generous rose rapidly. By inflating appraisals, many appraisers found they could attract more referral business; some even managed to always hit the target prices given by real estate agents, which contributed significantly to the huge run-up in home prices.

  In 2005, more than 8,000 appraisers—roughly 10 percent of the industry—petitioned the federal government to take action against such abuses. But both Congress and the White

House did nothing, allowing this rampant fraud to continue unabated.[3]

- **Referral fraud:** Complicit in appraisal fraud were mortgage brokers and real estate agents who knowingly steered referrals to appraisers they knew would give them the valuation they sought. These people were co-conspirators, as they paid for, aided, and abetted the actual fraud. And they did so for personal gain—higher prices and more transactions meant bigger commissions for all.
- **Application fraud:** It's an open secret that mortgage applications were usually completed by mortgage brokers, rather than by the borrowers themselves. "Just leave those lines blank; we'll take care of them" was a common refrain. Savvy brokers knew how to meet the requirements of each bank in order to get loans approved.

  That banks knew what was going on and looked the other way does not make this deception any less a felony.
- **Mortgage fraud:** Anyone who filled out a mortgage application and put false information on it committed fraud. Borrowers who overstated assets or income, or understated debt or financial obligations, to obtain a mortgage committed fraud.

  Ultimately, lenders are responsible to be proactive against all forms of deception. That they so willingly looked the other way was one factor that made this era such an aberration.
- **Predatory lending:** There are numerous examples of lenders deceptively convincing borrowers to agree to loan terms that are abusive. One of the most common versions in recent years was representing an adjustable-rate loan as a 30-year fixed-rate loan. Other mortgage brokers placed qualified prime and Alt-A applicants into more expensive subprime loans for the sole purpose of generating greater commissions. A significant percentage of subprime loans appear to have been a form of predatory lending.

(*continued*)

(*continued*)

As of this writing, the FBI has arrested nearly 1,000 people in connection with this form of fraud.

- **Home builder incentive fraud:** With their houses dropping in value, many builders became creative with incentives. By August 2008, the FBI was investigating cases where disclosure of incentives wasn't made to the lender (i.e., the builder misrepresented the true price of the sale).

When false statements are occasionally made in the course of business, you have potential trouble. Once they become the norm, it has turned into systemic fraud.

■ ■ ■

Banks that were originating mortgages for securitization found that their manual processes—humans pushing paper around—could not keep up with the now insatiable demand. So they did what other industries throughout time have done: They automated.

Ultralow rates drove the initial demand for mortgages, but it took new a technology—evaluation software—to allow mortgage applications to be processed in numbers never before possible. Computers replaced what was previously a human judgment process.

The nearly insatiable assembly line Wall Street was running for mortgage-backed securities drove the demand for bundling mortgages; home price appreciation kept even poor credit risks from defaulting for some years. These factors are what led to the huge spike in real estate sales from 2002 to 2007 and the accompanying explosion in issuance of mortgage-backed securities. It was a vicious, self-reinforcing cycle, but a highly profitable one as long as the real estate sector kept growing.

Farmers say you have to "make hay while the sun is shining." Bankers saw the nearly unquenchable demand for mortgages, and they knew it was time to make hay.

The automation systems permitted rapid processing of bad credit risks, but it was the outstanding sloppiness and violation of the banks' own internal procedures that allowed even more bad loans to get written. Hard as this may be to imagine, some loan documentation was so incomplete that federally mandated Truth-in-Lending Disclosure Statements were omitted. Without the proper disclosures, a mortgage could become unsecured—meaning the bank no longer has a first priority lien on the mortgaged property.

Across the mortgage industry, corner cutting and shortcuts were official corporate policy. There was headlong rush to originate, process, and securitize mortgages—and the wherewithal to repay the mortgages be damned. Loans were written to people with low FICO scores, on properties with very high loan-to-value (LTV) ratios; documentation was often poorly filled out. An entirely new category was created: so-called no-doc (no-documentation) loans. Today, we know these products as "liar loans," thanks to the commission-driven mortgage brokers who encouraged borrowers to get creative when filling out the no-doc applications.

Funky Loans

As the securitization process heated up, mortgage originators came up with increasingly exotic loans. Alan Greenspan had applauded these as "innovations." We subsequently found out that they were merely clever ways to get home buyers to borrow the most amount of money possible, with no regard to their ability to repay these loans, in order to generate the highest commissions. *Predatory lending* was the term used to describe the most egregious of these loans.

Mortgage Types

30-year fixed: The traditional mortgage; fixed rate, no gimmicks.

2/28 ARM: An adjustable-rate mortgage that came with a fixed, two-year teaser rate. After the two years had elapsed, the mortgage would reset, as much as 300

(*continued*)

(*continued*)

basis points above the prior teaser rate. The 2/28s were mostly offered to subprime borrowers—those with weak FICO scores and modest incomes. This allowed even bigger mortgages to be written, since the first 24 payments were artificially low. The sales pitch was: "Buy as much house as you can get. Refinance before the reset."

Interest only: Mortgage payments were reduced dramatically by not paying back any of the principal.

Piggyback loan: This loan let a borrower take out an equity loan against the property to be used for the down payment; it was on top of a primary mortgage.

Reverse amortization: Each month, the total outstanding amount owed went up.

Liar loan: No income verification was required.

"No money down": A mortgage that required 0 percent down payment.

High loan to value: A mortgage loan of up to 120 percent of the property's value, versus the traditional 80 percent.

NINJA loan: No income, no job or assets.

For one of the most astounding examples of the industry's grotesque role in the housing boom, consider this JPMorgan internal memo, titled "Zippy Cheats & Tricks." Zippy was the name of JPMorgan's automated loan processing software. The memo taught loan officers how to "cheat" the firm's own system. It offered some "handy steps"—workarounds, really—for getting questionable loans approved:

Zippy Cheats & Tricks

If you get a "refer" or if you DO NOT get Stated Income/Stated Asset findings . . . Never Fear!! ZiPPY can be adjusted (just ever so slightly).

Try these steps next time you use Zippy! You just might get the findings you need!!

Always select "ALTERNATE DOCS" in the documentation drop down.
Borrower(s) MUST have a mid credit score of 700.
First time homebuyers require a 720 credit score.
NO! BK's OR Foreclosures, EVER!! Regardless of time!
Salaried borrowers must have 2 years time on job with current employer.
Self employed must be in existence for 2 years. (verified with biz license)
NO non-occupant co borrowers.
Max LTV/CLTV is 100%.

Try these handy steps to get SISA findings . . .

1. In the income section of your 1003, make sure you input all income in base income. DO NOT break it down by overtime, commissions or bonus.
2. NO GIFT FUNDS! If your borrower is getting a gift, add it to a bank account along with the rest of the assets. Be sure to remove any mention of gift funds on the rest of your 1003.
3. If you do not get Stated/Stated, try resubmitting with slightly higher income. Inch it up $500 to see if you can get the findings you want. Do the same for assets.

It's super easy! Give it a try! If you get stuck, call me . . . I am happy to help!

Tammy Lish
(503) 307-7079
tammy.d.lish@chase.com

Let me point out this was not some little fly-by-night outfit; it was JPMorgan Chase bank. This internal Chase memo accidentally found its way into the hands of Jeff Manning, a journalist with the *Oregonian*. It was the basis for an article titled, "Chase Mortgage Memo Pushes 'Cheats & Tricks.'"[4]

Tammy Lish was subsequently fired from Chase for releasing the memo publicly. Before then, it had been circulated only internally within the firm.

■ ■ ■

Indiscriminate lending by mortgage originators helped inflate the housing boom. While housing was an extended asset class, it was not a true bubble. To be sure, it was frothy as all hell, and some areas—namely California, Southern Florida, Arizona, and Las Vegas—were bubblicious. But the actual bubble was found in credit. As of Q1 2009, house prices have corrected on a national basis about 25 percent, according to the Case-Shiller index.

Credit, however, has absolutely collapsed.

At the center of it all was subprime lending, especially among the nonbank mortgage originators. They lent to unqualified borrowers, fed the derivatives market, and ultimately helped bring about a disaster—in housing, in subprime mortgages, and in mortgage-backed securities. This was the epicenter of the credit crisis.

What was their impact on lending? In 2004, 2/28 adjustable-rate mortgages (ARMs) accounted for almost 46 percent of new loans in dollar value and were about a third of total mortgages made, according to the Mortgage Bankers Association (MBA). That was up from 29 percent and 19 percent, respectively, in 2003. Subprime mortgage lending was one out of five mortgage loans in 2004, up from less than one out of 10 the year before.

Why would ARMs make up so much lending when mortgage rates were at their lowest levels in 50 years? The only possible answer was to sell more—and bigger—loans. Getting people into teaser-rate mortgages, regardless of suitability, would get them past that default period covered by the initial warranty. This was the sub-prime mortgage industry's primary raison d'être.

Ivy Zelman, the well-regarded housing analyst at Credit Suisse First Boston, noted the absurdity as early as 2006:

- In 2005, 32.6 percent of new mortgages and home equity loans were interest only, up from 0.6 percent in 2000.

- Forty-three percent of first-time home buyers in 2005 put no money down.
- In 2006, 15.2 percent of 2005 buyers owed at least 10 percent more than their home was worth (negative equity).
- Ten percent of all homeowners with mortgages had no equity in their homes (zero equity).
- Fully $2.7 trillion in loans were scheduled to adjust to higher rates in 2006 and 2007.

And those borrowers who convinced themselves an ARM would help them get into a bigger house until they could refinance (or flip the house) at a higher price? They were lying to themselves as they financially engineered their way into homes they couldn't afford.

■ ■ ■

Mortgage brokers were big fans of refinancing. Those buyers who couldn't afford the mortgage in the first place were potential repeat customers down the road. As a house went up in value, you could always pull out the increase in equity to pay for the shortfall in monthly payments. Commission-driven real estate agents, along with the commission-driven mortgage brokers, liked to remind reluctant buyers that the longer they dithered, the higher prices were going. *Best to get in now before the next leg up in real estate values!*

It is no surprise that these were the first mortgages to default. Disproportionately, subprime adjustable-rate mortgages have had the highest foreclosure rates of all mortgages. Rather than being "contained," as Ben Bernanke and Henry Paulson (among other so-called experts) claimed throughout 2007, the subprime mortgage caused a cascade reaction all the way through the entire financial system.

And the mortgage-based fun was only just beginning.

INTERMEZZO

A Memo Found in the Street: Uncle Sam the Enabler

To: Washington, D.C.
From: Wall Street
Re: Credit Crisis

Dear D.C.,

Wow, we've made quite a mess of things here on Wall Street: Fannie and Freddie in conservatorship, investment banks in the tank, AIG nationalized. Thanks for sending us your new trillion-dollar bailout.

We on Wall Street feel somewhat compelled to take at least some responsibility. We used excessive leverage, failed to maintain adequate capital, engaged in reckless speculation, and created new complex derivatives. We focused on short-term profits at the expense of sustainability. We not only undermined our own firms, we destabilized the financial sector and roiled the global economy, to boot. And we got huge bonuses.

But here's a news flash for you, D.C.: We could not have done it without you. We may be drunks, but you were our enablers. Your legislative, executive, and administrative decisions made possible all that we did. Our recklessness would not have reached its soaring heights but for your governmental incompetence.

This memo provides a brief history of your actions that helped create this crisis.

1997: Federal Reserve Chairman Alan Greenspan's famous "irrational exuberance" speech in 1996 was somehow ignored by, um, Fed Chairman Greenspan. The Fed missed the opportunity to change margin requirements. Had the Fed acted, the bubble would not have inflated as much, and the subsequent crash would not have been as severe.

1998: Long-Term Capital Management was undercapitalized, and used enormous amounts of leverage to purchase all manner of thinly traded, hard-to-value paper. It failed, and under the authority of the Federal Reserve a private-sector rescue plan by banks was cobbled together. Had these bankers suffered big losses from LTCM, they might have thought twice before jumping into the exact same business model of undercapitalized, overleveraged, thinly traded, hard-to-value paper. Instead, they reaffirmed Benjamin Disraeli's famous aphorism: "What we learn from history is that we do not learn from history."

1999: The Financial Services Modernization Act repealed Glass-Steagall, a law that had separated the commercial banking industry from Wall Street, and the two industries, plus insurance, came together again. Banks became bigger, clumsier, and harder to manage. Apparently, risk management became all but impossible, even as banks had greater access to larger pools of capital.

2000: The Commodity Futures Modernization Act defined financial commodities such as "interest rates, currency prices, and stock indexes" as "excluded commodities." They could trade off the futures exchanges, with minimal oversight by the Commodity Futures Trading Commission. Neither the Securities and Exchange Commission (SEC) nor the Federal Reserve, nor any state insurance regulators, had the ability to supervise or regulate the writing of credit default swaps by hedge funds, investment banks, or insurance companies.

2001–2003: Alan Greenspan's Fed dropped federal funds rates to 1 percent. Lulled into a false belief that inflation was not a problem, the Fed then kept rates at 1 percent for more than a year. This set off an inflationary spiral in housing, as well as a desperate hunt for yield by fixed-income managers.

2003–2007: The Federal Reserve failed to use its supervisory and regulatory authority over banks, mortgage underwriters, and other lenders, who abandoned such standards as employment history, income, down payments, credit rating, assets, property loan-to-value ratio, and debt-servicing ability. The borrower's

ability to repay these mortgages was replaced with the lender's ability to securitize and repackage them.

2004: The SEC waived its leverage rules. Previously, broker-dealer net capital rules limited firms to a maximum debt-to-net-capital ratio of 12 to 1. This 2004 exemption allowed them to exceed this leverage rule. Only five firms—Goldman Sachs, Merrill Lynch, Lehman Brothers, Bear Stearns, and Morgan Stanley—were granted this exemption; they promptly leveraged up 20, 30, and even 40 to 1.

2005–2007: Unscrupulous home appraisers found that they could attract more business by inflating appraisals. Intrinsic value was ignored, so referrals kept coming in. This helped borrowers obtain financing at prices that were increasingly unsupportable. When honest appraisers petitioned both Congress and the bureaucracy to intervene in the widespread fraud, neither branch of government acted.

There's actually a lot more we could add to these items. We could mention impotent supervision of Fannie and Freddie by the Office of Federal Housing Enterprise Oversight, the negligent oversight on rating agencies, the Boskin Commission's monkeying around with how inflation gets measured, the Greenspan put, and so on.

We could mention former Fed Governor Edward Gramlich, who warned about making home loans to people who could not afford them, and who said the runaway subprime mortgage industry would create problems in housing and the credit markets. But Gramlich was up against a Fed chairman who apparently believed that markets can regulate themselves. (Gramlich died in 2007, three months after the housing bubble started to deflate.)

We on Wall Street do not deny our part. We created these securities, we rated them triple-A, and we traded them without understanding them. Now that they have gone bad, we are really close to getting the rest of the country to take them off our hands.

Thanks, D.C. None of this would have been possible without you.

Very truly yours,
Wall Street

Chapter 11

Radical Deregulation, Nonfeasance

Those of us who have looked to the self-interest of lending institutions to protect shareholders' equity, myself included, are in a state of shocked disbelief.

—Alan Greenspan, Senate testimony, October 22, 2008

How the United States ended up a Bailout Nation is more than the work of just one man. Sure, Alan Greenspan looms large in this story, and in more ways than one. But it took the creative irresponsibility and misguided philosophy of many players to create the massive debacle that has enveloped the global economy. Presidents, senators, Securities and Exchange Commission (SEC) chairmen, Treasury secretaries, and members of Congress all contributed.

A brief review of modern U.S. regulatory history shows where the United States made its wrong turn, and the consequences of those errors.

Following World War II, the world set about righting itself. The Marshall Plan was helping to rebuild Europe; Japan became a cheap source of industrial manufacturing. Millions of GIs returned home to

the land of opportunity. Returning veterans had the benefit of the GI Bill, which meant free college or vocational school and low-cost loans to buy homes or start businesses. The nascent growth of suburbia also contributed to economic activity. The U.S. economy was expanding, and it led the rest of the world into a period of rapid growth.

Along the way, the government's bureaucracy also began expanding. Twenty years after the war, complying with U.S. regulatory oversight was increasingly complex, time-consuming, and expensive for American businesses. By the late 1960s, the many rules and regulations were a costly part of doing business. It wasn't too much later when politicians seized on the concept of reducing costly regulations. It soon became a political rallying cry.

Deregulation found an enthusiastic advocate in President Ronald Reagan. In many ways, Reagan is the intellectual father of the modern radical deregulatory movement. At first, expensive, onerous provisions were targeted. But it wasn't long before all regulation became viewed as inherently evil. In this worldview, government was the source of problems, not possible solutions. Reagan famously quipped: "The nine most terrifying words in the English language are, 'I'm from the government and I'm here to help.' " Reducing not only regulations, but the entire size of the government became a goal of this ideology.

Of course, that was before the entire banking system fell apart, and Uncle Sam began writing checks for trillions of dollars. Today, the most terrifying words might be more along the lines of "I run a highly leveraged, unregulated financial institution that owns lots of derivatives."

But that was yet to occur. Adherents of a strict free market philosophy wanted to remove the decision-making oversight from the bureaucracy and replace it with the "relentless efficiency" of the markets. This was a hopelessly idealistic view of markets, naively premised on false assumptions of market efficiency and human rationality.

Eventually, deregulation became an end unto itself, rather than a means to an end. Along with the costly, unnecessary regulations that were targeted for elimination, effective and necessary safeguards were also removed. Pragmatic decision making was replaced with rigid ideology.

In the ensuing decades, the United States morphed from an overly regulated economy to an absurdly deregulated one. What started as a reasonable pushback against excessive government regulations was soon taken to all sorts of irrational extremes. Any supervision was soon viewed as suspect.

This was especially true when it came to the regulation of commercial and investment banks. Under President Bill Clinton, several key legislative proposals were passed that reduced oversight and supervision. Key Depression-era legislation was overturned.

While Clinton was a Southern Democrat who believed in both government and markets, President George W. Bush took this a huge step further. Like his predecessor, he believed in markets; but when it came to government, he was far less enthusiastic. His appointments to key administrative positions—SEC chairman, Treasury secretary, and most infamously the Federal Emergency Management Agency (FEMA)—were lackluster at best.

Thus, the United States moved from a state of aggressive, post-Depression financial oversight to one of negligent supervision. The potential for disaster increased rapidly. It was this massive philosophical and regulatory shift that set the table for the current financial crisis.

■ ■ ■

The first major regulatory changes came about in 1999. That's when a significant Depression-era banking regulation, the Glass-Steagall Act, was repealed. The Gramm-Leach-Bliley Act reversed the rules that prohibited bank holding companies from owning other financial firms. This allowed insurers, banks, and brokerage firms to merge into giant financial centers. Had it not been for Gramm-Leach-Bliley, Citibank could not have evolved into the unruly beast it became.

Freed from Glass-Steagall's strictures, money center banks entered into all manner of underwriting: not just initial public offerings (IPOs) and bond issuance, but structured financial products, including collateralized debt obligations (CDOs) and credit default swaps (CDSs). These derivatives are one of the prime villains in the credit crisis, and grew out of the housing debacle.

The key factor was size. In the new, deregulated environment, banks and brokers were allowed to scale up to become behemoths. What was big became huge; what was huge became enormous. With so many moving parts, too much leverage, and too much risk taking, banks

became too big to be effectively managed. In bailout terms, they were too big to fail, but in actual operation they were too big to succeed. They had become so massive that managing all the moving parts—and controlling for risk—was all but impossible. Once conservative, risk-averse banks had become giant unregulated hedge funds, disaster was all but inevitable.

More importantly, banks started adopting the "eat what you kill" compensation systems. The bonus structure, replete with short-term financial incentives, began to dominate banks. Throw in monthly performance fees and annual stock option incentives, and you end up with a skewed business model suddenly embracing quicker trading profits.

This had an enormous impact upon the ways investment banks approached business generation and risk management. Like many public companies, they became increasingly short-term focused. "Making the quarter," in Street parlance, meant pulling out all the stops to hit your quarterly profit figures, by any means necessary. Incentives became misaligned with shareholders' interests, as risky short-term performance was rewarded with huge bonuses. Not surprisingly, this worked to the detriment of long-term sustainability.

But short-termism was only part of the equation. Of greater concern was how these firms' internal risk management changed. Unlike in public corporations, partners are *personally liable* for the acts of any of the members of the partnership. If any one of a firm's partners or employees loses a trillion dollars, every last partner is on the hook for that money. As you would imagine, this creates enormous incentives to make sure that risk is managed very, very carefully. Nothing focuses the mind like the real possibility that any partner could bankrupt all the rest. It's no coincidence that partnerships like Lazard Freres and Kohlberg Kravis Roberts did not suffer the same kind of risk management failures as Bear Stearns and Lehman Brothers, among others. (Lazard went public in 2005, but too late in the credit cycle for it to get into much trouble.)

Depository banks are *supposed* to be managed in ways that limit risk. They hold the public's deposit accounts (such as checking and savings accounts), which they then use to provide credit to businesses and individuals. The Federal Deposit Insurance Corporation (FDIC) insures all of these deposits against loss, and insists (quite reasonably, I might add) the monies not be handled recklessly. In contrast, investment banks *by definition* embrace risk; their business model focuses on more speculative activities that are inherently riskier. Activities such as trading and mergers, bringing companies public, and managing investments involve a greater possibility, even likelihood, of losses.

The repeal of Glass-Steagall didn't cause the crisis—it only made the collapse worse, deeper, and more expensive. The skyrocketing costs of the bailouts are in part due to disasters in the riskier investment banking sector spilling over into the risk-averse commercial (depository) banking sector. Glass-Steagall was adopted in 1933 *expressly to prevent this from occurring.* Repealing the act allowed the commercial banks to operate investment bank units. Both ends of the risk spectrum ended up festooned with all manner of junk paper. If Glass-Steagall were still in effect, the banks would have had little incentive to buy the junk from the brokers.

It also meant financial carnage at investment banks was no longer quarantined from commercial banks. Hence, the ugly financial impact at Citibank and others can be traced directly to the Gramm-Leach-Bliley act. The repeal of Glass-Stengall could very well end up being the single most costly legislative repeal in the nation's history.

Gramm-Leach-Bliley may not have been the proximate cause of the disaster, but it is precisely why the overall problem was not "contained."

■ ■ ■

> *The rapidly growing trade in derivatives poses a "mega-catastrophic risk." . . . [F]or the economy, derivatives are financial weapons of mass destruction that could harm not only their buyers and sellers, but the whole economic system.*
>
> —Warren Buffett, Berkshire Hathaway 2002 Annual Report

Allowing banks and brokers to merge was only one factor that led to the credit crisis. After repealing Glass-Steagall, the following year Congress passed the Commodity Futures Modernization Act of 2000 (CFMA). This legislation allowed derivatives such as credit default swaps (CDSs) to become an enormous, unregulated shadow insurance industry. Many of the horrific losses suffered by AIG, Lehman Brothers, and Bear Stearns trace their paternity to this act.

Glass-Steagall may have set the table, but the Commodity Futures Modernization Act was the poison in the wine.

The CFMA removed derivatives and credit default swaps from *any and all state and federal regulatory oversight*. There were no reserve requirements, as were required in insurance policies. There were no audit mandates, so parties were not assured that their counterparties could make payment when a CDS was supposed to pay off. And there was no central clearing firm, so nobody knew precisely how many CDSs there were or who owned them. Until recently, even the dollar value these derivatives totaled was unknown.

Since the crisis has broken into the open, we now have a few reasonable, if imprecise, estimates on the value of derivatives contracts at various bailout banks. Prior to the passage of the CFMA, unregulated credit default swaps were under $100 billion—a sizable, if manageable, amount of derivatives contracts. By 2008, they had grown to over $50 trillion. To put this in context, that's four times the size of the annual gross domestic product (GDP) of the United States.

Alan Greenspan had "fiercely objected whenever derivatives have come under scrutiny"[1] in either Congress or on Wall Street. In 2003, Greenspan told the Senate Banking Committee:

> What we have found over the years in the marketplace is that derivatives have been an extraordinarily useful vehicle to transfer risk from those who shouldn't be taking it to those who are willing to and are capable of doing so. We think it would be a mistake to more deeply regulate the contracts.[2]

Critics had been warning about derivatives for years, but they made no headway against Greenspan. In 2008, Peter Goodman took a hard new look at the Greenspan legacy. Writing in the *New York Times*, he observed, "Time and again, Mr. Greenspan—a revered figure affectionately nicknamed the Oracle—proclaimed that risks could be handled by the markets themselves."[3] Former Federal Reserve board member and Princeton economist Alan S. Blinder was less generous. "I think of him as consistently cheerleading on derivatives."[4]

Why was Greenie so opposed to any oversight of derivatives trading? Former SEC chair Arthur Levitt said it was a fundamental disdain for government. It was part of an ideological shift away from government—from Reagan to Greenspan to Clinton to Bush—and toward markets.

Kenny Boy and the Gramms

The Commodity Futures Modernization Act is one of the most egregious examples of private enterprise dictating public policy via a combination of sophisticated lobbying and old-fashioned nepotism. The bill was introduced on December 15, 2000, the last day before the Christmas recess. The bill was never debated in either the House or the Senate and was discreetly attached as a rider to the 11,000-page-long omnibus budget bill signed into law by (then) lame-duck President Bill Clinton on December 21, 2000.

But that's just the half of it.

Among the over-the-counter derivatives freed from any federal jurisdiction by the CFMA were energy futures. The bill also included "language advocated by Enron that largely exempted the company from regulation of its energy trading on electronic commodity markets, like its once-popular Enron Online."[5]

This became known as the "Enron loophole" and was designed to help the Houston-based firm pursue its goal of becoming the dominant player in the trading of energy futures, which it saw as having much more profit potential than actually producing energy had.

A key sponsor of the CFMA was Texas Senator Phil Gramm, whose wife, Dr. Wendy Gramm, was a member of Enron's board, which she joined in 1992 after providing the company with some regulatory relief in her prior role as chair of the Commodity Futures Trading Commission.

According to Public Citizen, a national, nonprofit consumer advocacy organization:[6]

- Enron paid Dr. Gramm between $915,000 and $1.85 million in salary, attendance fees, stock option sales, and dividends from 1993 to 2001. The value of Wendy Gramm's Enron stock options swelled from no more than $15,000 in 1995 to as much as $500,000 by 2000.

(*continued*)

(continued)

- Days before her attorneys informed Enron in December 1998 that Wendy Gramm's control of Enron stock might pose a conflict of interest with her husband's work, she sold $276,912 worth of Enron stock.
- Enron spent $3.45 million in lobbying expenses in 1999 and 2000 to deregulate the trading of energy futures, among other issues.

In 2002, internal Enron documents revealed the company helped write the Commodity Futures Modernization Act. Senator Gramm later claimed he was not responsible for inserting the "Enron loophole" into the legislation. "But once the Commodity Futures Modernization measure—with this provision included—reached the Senate floor, Mr. Gramm led the debate, urging his fellow senators to pass it into law," the *New York Times* reported.[7]

After failed efforts in 2002, 2003, and 2006, Congress finally closed the "Enron loophole" in 2008 with the passage of the Farm Bill that included an amendment to have the energy futures contracts regulated by the CFTC "with the same key standards ('core principles') that apply to futures exchanges, like NYMEX, to prevent price manipulation and excessive speculation."[8]

Enron's scam had long since come unraveled by 2008, but it still had powerful friends in Washington: Congress had to override President Bush's veto to get the bill passed and the loophole closed.

Immediately after the CFMA legislation was passed, a few observers raised concerns. Frank Partnoy, a former derivatives trader at Morgan Stanley (now a law professor at the University of San Diego), is the author of *F.I.A.S.C.O.: Blood in the Water on Wall Street*, a 1997 book warning about the danger of derivatives. In 2000, referring to CFMA, he noted:

> The new bill's second impact, in the swaps market, is less direct but still worrisome. The act ends an argument about whether swaps qualify for regulation by making it clear that they are not regulated if a participating company or individual has $10 million in assets. That means that the swaps activities of most companies and mutual funds

> are not regulated. Yet few investors know what swaps are. And there's almost no publicly available information about specific trades in this market, now bigger than many stock or bond markets. By contrast, futures trading takes place on exchanges; an investor can find closing quotes for futures in a newspaper's financial section.[9]

Even Partnoy's prescient fears failed to anticipate exactly how devastating the results of the legislation would be. The potential for financial Armageddon was unconscionably enormous (see Figure 11.1). The CFMA allowed unregulated, unsupervised, unreserved derivatives trades that were ultimately responsible for the biggest bankruptcies in American history. It created the monster that brought down several important companies.

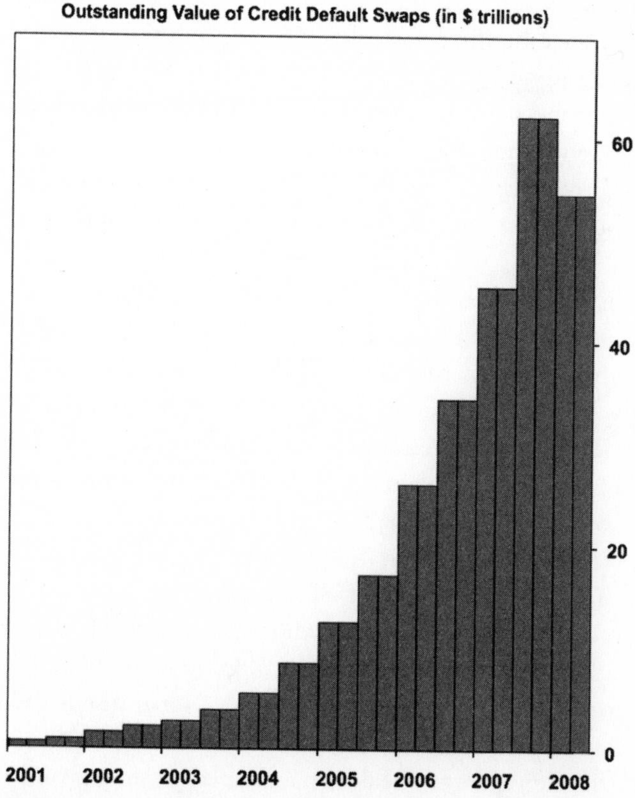

Figure 11.1 Outstanding Value of Credit Default Swaps
SOURCE: International Swaps and Derivatives Association

First came Bear Stearns, which collapsed in March 2008. Bear's total derivatives holdings were estimated at $9 trillion; JPMorgan Chase was believed to have had about 40 percent of Bear's exposure, leading numerous wags to surmise that was why JPMorgan bought Bear.

Lehman Brothers also had a decent-sized derivatives book, estimated at between $2 trillion and $4 trillion when it collapsed into bankruptcy in September 2008. The Lehman failure triggered waves of disruption in the CDS market.

Shortly after Lehman fell, AIG, the world's largest insurance company, followed. AIG was nationalized by Treasury and the Fed (in exchange for 79.9 percent of its stock) in October 2008. The $68 billion bailout was only the first of four U.S. government bailouts totaling over $175 billion as of March 2009.

Then there were the monoline insurers—Ambac, Financial Guaranty Insurance Company (FGIC), and MBIA Insurance Corporation. These were once highly profitable, low-risk, municipal bond insurance firms. Their businesses were demolished once they started dabbling in derivative products. Ambac lost 99 percent of its market cap. MBIA is marginally better, but still trading far below its former $25 billion peak valuation. Private bond insurer FGIC, once partly owned by General Electric and Blackstone, has long since given up any hopes of going public.

The thought process behind the CFMA—really more of a religious belief—was that self-interested, rational market participants would not endanger themselves or their firms. No one, went the thinking, would knowingly engage in self-destructive, reckless behavior. Markets are perfectly efficient, humans are rational (not emotional), and financial firms and markets can self-regulate. In theory, Adam Smith's invisible hand keeps the worst impulses of bad players in check.

In the real world, however, things operated quite differently. Perfectly rational humans and perfectly efficient markets exist only in economics textbooks. In reality, this belief system is sheer, unadulterated nonsense. Compensation systems can get out of alignment with shareholder interests. Short-term profits often trump longer-term sustainability. Complexity is often ignored; risk is poorly understood.

What the deregulatory zealots have failed to understand is that we don't regulate markets; what we do is regulate the behaviors of the human beings who *work in those markets*. And humans need to know what is acceptable and allowable behavior. Without rules and guidelines, people misbehave—and even more so when large sums of money are involved.

The way markets manage to self-regulate companies that make bad decisions is by annihilating them. The theory that self-regulating markets would prevent these poor decisions from occurring in the first place is wrong; the market instead brutally punishes those who made bad risk management decisions. But prevention? Humans simply aren't that clever.

The belief that markets self-regulate reads like a bad joke: Two economists are walking across campus. The younger one points out a $20 bill on the ground. "Nonsense," says the senior, tenured professor. "If there was $20 on the ground, someone would have picked it up."

Self-regulating markets differ from our two economists in one major way: Bad jokes don't destroy economies.

■ ■ ■

The last six months have made it abundantly clear that voluntary regulation does not work.

—Christopher Cox, former chairman of the Securities and Exchange Commission, September 26, 2008

Not only are market participants not always rational, they often act inadvertently against their own best interests.

My favorite example: To ensure that Wall Street firms maintained adequate capital levels, the Securities and Exchange Commission employed what became known as the "net capital rule." From 1975 to 2004, this was the primary tool used to prevent investment banks from taking on too much leverage. The rule limited their ratio of debt to net capital to 12 to 1; in other words, $12 was the maximum they could borrow for every $1 in capital.

For the most part, it worked fine. Firms maintained sufficient liquidity to meet their needs; banking disasters were few and far between. But bankers were agitating for a less restrictive leverage rule. They were complaining to the SEC that this excessive regulation was costly. To them, the rules were limiting their return on equity. Loosening the net cap rules would let them leverage their capital further, and therefore earn

greater profits. Sure, it would increase their risks—significantly so—but "Hey, we're a bunch of smart guys—we can handle it."

Or so the investment banks argued.

In 2004, the five biggest investment banks—Goldman Sachs, Merrill Lynch, Lehman Brothers, Bear Stearns, and Morgan Stanley—got their wish. Led by Goldman Sachs CEO Hank Paulson—the future Treasury Secretary/bailout king—the SEC acquiesced to grant them (and only them) a special exemption. At the time, it was (ironically) called "the Bear Stearns rule." The firms with a market capitalization over $5 billion would no longer be governed by 12-to-1 net cap rules.

As soon as this exemption was passed, the collection of brainiacs that ran the five big firms promptly levered up 30, 35, even 40 to 1. You read that right—after 30 years of effective risk management, at the first opportunity they whacked up the leverage as far as they could.

Thus we learn that the tragic financial events of 2008 and 2009 are not an unfortunate accident. Rather, they are the results of a conscious SEC decision to allow these firms to legally violate net capital rules that had existed for decades, limiting broker-dealers' debt-to-net-capital ratio to 12-to-1. You couldn't make this stuff up if you tried.

Writing in the *American Banker*, Lee A. Pickard, former director of SEC's trading and markets division and an author of the original net capital rule in 1975, declared:

> The SEC's basic net capital rule, one of the prominent successes in federal financial regulatory oversight, had an excellent track record in preserving the securities markets' financial integrity and protecting customer assets. There have been very few liquidations of broker-dealers and virtually no customer or interdealer losses due to broker-dealer insolvency during the past 33 years.
>
> Under an alternative approach adopted by the SEC in 2004, broker-dealers with, in practice, at least $5 billion of capital (such as Bear Stearns) were permitted to avoid the haircuts on securities positions and the limitations on indebtedness contained in the basic net capital rule. Instead, the alternative net capital program relies heavily on a risk management control system, mathematical models to price positions, value-at-risk models, and close SEC oversight.[10]

In Latin, we call that *Res ipsa loquitur*— "the thing speaks for itself." All five exempt brokers no longer exist in their prior forms. As a result of the Bear Stearns rule, Bear Stearns was the first to go belly-up. Lehman became the largest bankruptcy in American history, and Merrill Lynch, on the verge of blowing up, scrambled to sell itself on the cheap to Bank of America. Morgan Stanley and Goldman Sachs received capital injections from the Feds, and had to change their status to commercial banks—to make it easier to obtain even more government bailout money.

Relying on the self-interest of individuals and firms to prevent egregiously reckless and irresponsible behavior only served to enrich senior management at the expense of shareholders, taxpayers, and employees.

So much for *that* idea.

■ ■ ■

The newfangled lend-to-securitize mortgage originators discussed previously were covered by a patchwork of state regulations. They should also have been supervised by the Federal Reserve.

Only they weren't.

At the Fed, Chairman Alan Greenspan *purposefully* chose not to supervise these new mortgage makers. This was yet another example of Greenspan's free-market beliefs blinding him to the simple realities of the real world. One of the duties of the Federal Reserve is to supervise banking and lending. However, the Fed chief did not believe these lenders needed any supervision. Remember, he believed that market forces would make these lenders police themselves.

Not only did the Fed do nothing about these changes in lending standards, they were actually praised by Greenspan. Here is what he said in 2005:

> Innovation has brought about a multitude of new products, such as subprime loans and niche credit programs for immigrants. . . . With these advances in technology, lenders have taken advantage of credit-scoring models and other techniques for efficiently extending credit to a broader spectrum of consumers. . . . Where once more-marginal applicants would simply have been denied credit, lenders are now able to quite efficiently judge the risk posed by individual applicants and to price that risk appropriately. These improvements have led to rapid growth in subprime mortgage lending . . . fostering constructive innovation that is both responsive to market demand and beneficial to consumers.[11]

There was a reason why some people in the past had been denied credit: They simply could not afford the homes they tried to purchase. Any mortgage structure that ignores the borrower's ability to service the loan is destined for failure.

Greenspan's encouraging remarks about the benefits of ARMs in February 2004 are another tale of woe (and woeful misjudgment).

"American consumers might benefit if lenders provided greater mortgage product alternatives to the traditional fixed-rate mortgage," Greenspan said in a speech before the Credit Union National Association. "To the degree that households are driven by fears of payment shocks but are willing to manage their own interest rate risks, the traditional fixed-rate mortgage may be an expensive method of financing a home."[12]

Meanwhile, at the Office of Thrift Supervision, former chief James Gilleran took a chainsaw to a stack of regulations to symbolize how his agency was going to "cut red tape" for thrifts (aka S&Ls), which are heavily involved in mortgage lending. "Our goal is to allow thrifts to operate with a wide breadth of freedom from regulatory intrusion," Gilleran said in a 2004 speech.[13]

This wasn't malfeasance by Greenspan and Gilleran; rather, it was nonfeasance, the intentional failure to perform a required legal duty or obligation. Even the FBI got into the deregulatory act: In 2004, the FBI warned that "fraud in the mortgage industry has increased so sharply that an 'epidemic' of financial crimes could become 'the next S&L crisis.'" Subsequently, the FBI(!) made a "strategic alliance" in 2007 with the Mortgage Bankers Association (MBA), the trade association for (then) major industry players like IndyMac and Countrywide Financial.[14]

Truly, the foxes were guarding the henhouse.

When we look into the details of these lenders, we see they were especially enamored of risk. In a fatal twist on traditional banking, their employees got paid on the volume, not the quality, of their loans. Besides, they didn't need to find a buyer who was a good risk for 30 years—they only needed to find someone who wouldn't default before the securitization process was complete, as detailed in Chapter 10.

This was an unbelievably enormous change in lending standards. So what did federal bank regulators have to say about this paradigm shift?

Various government agencies did nothing about this shift, even though the FBI warned of an "epidemic" of mortgage fraud in 2004.[15]

Not surprisingly, the abdication of lending standards—and the trillions in subsequent resets—resulted in skyrocketing mortgage default rates. As of December 2008, a record 10 percent of all homeowners with mortgages were behind in their payments, up from 7.3 percent in 2007. According to the MBA, among subprime borrowers, the rate was 33 percent. (In the United States, 70 percent of homes carry a mortgage.)

Tragically, this was avoidable. Former Fed Governor Edward Gramlich was an expert on subprime lending and became increasingly concerned about predatory lending in the early part of this decade. His 2007 book, *Subprime Mortgages: America's Latest Boom and Bust* (Urban Institute Press), presciently warned of the dangers these loans presented to the credit and housing industry, and the economy as a whole.

In 2007, the *Wall Street Journal* reported that Gramlich "said he proposed to Mr. Greenspan in or around 2000, when [predatory lending] was a growing concern, that the Fed use its discretionary authority to send examiners into the offices of consumer-finance lenders that were units of Fed-regulated bank holding companies."[16]

"I would have liked the Fed to be a leader" in cracking down, Gramlich, who retired from the Fed in 2005, told the *Wall Street Journal* shortly before his death in 2007. The *Journal* noted, "Knowing it would be controversial with Mr. Greenspan, whose deregulatory philosophy is well known, Mr. Gramlich broached it to him personally rather than take it to the full board."[17]

If only Greenspan had heeded Gramlich's warnings. Instead, he chose to dismiss them. As we have since learned, this turned out to be an enormous error on Greenspan's part.

Credit Ben Bernanke for having the good sense to close the barn door after all the horses had escaped. In December 2007, Bernanke reversed his predecessor's antiregulatory fervor:

> The Federal Reserve, acknowledging that home mortgage lenders aggressively sold deceptive loans to borrowers who had little chance of repaying them, proposed a broad set of restrictions Tuesday on exotic mortgages and high-cost loans for people with weak credit. The new rules would force mortgage companies to show that customers can

> realistically afford their mortgages. They would also require lenders to disclose the hidden sales fees often rolled into interest payments, and they would prohibit certain types of advertising. Borrowers would be able to sue their lenders if they violated the new rules, though home buyers would be allowed to seek only a limited amount in compensation.[18]

Ahhh, a return to lending money only to people who could "realistically afford their mortgages." What a quaint and charming notion.

Chapter 12

Strange Connections, Unintended Consequences

There is only one difference between a bad economist and a good one: the bad economist confines himself to the visible effect; the good economist takes into account both the effect that can be seen and those effects that must be foreseen.

—Frédéric Bastiat[1]

One of the great risks of human endeavors is that all actions, however well intended, have unintended consequences. This is especially true when governments are involved.

History shows that government actions—as well as inaction—have repercussions that are rarely anticipated. This is the case of legislation, tax policy, and most especially of bailouts. Legislative policy pursued at the request of a given company or industry often ends up harming that industry immeasurably. That it was pursued *by friend rather than foe* makes it only ironic, not untrue.

For the Bailout Nation, this critical issue is well worth pondering, especially now that we have written some rather enormous checks. Our collective actions and omissions will leave an onerous legacy to future generations, often manifesting themselves in unanticipated ways.

As examples of how unintended consequences can be felt far in the future, consider two legislative acts wholly unrelated to the current financial crisis.

The 1996 Telecommunications Reform Act amended the Communications Act of 1934 and eliminated media ownership regulations. This led to an enormous degree of media consolidation, especially in radio. Prior to the 1996 Act, broadcasters could own just 40 stations nationally. After the Act became law, 10,000 radio stations were bought up or merged.

The biggest of the buyers was Clear Channel Communications, acquiring over 1,200 channels. They fired local talent—DJs, program managers, music directors—and on many of these stations, ran a homogenized playlist feed from a central bunker in Texas. Call it Hamburger Helper for radio. Replace tasty, expensive meat with cheap filler and hope no one notices.

For a while, it worked. Clear Channel became enormously profitable. It had the costs of a small radio network, but an audience 100 times the size.

And then, that audience . . . left. They didn't even change the channel; they simply abandoned radio in droves. Ask a radio executive what broadcasters sell, and most will tell you "Advertising." That is actually wrong; what radio sells is *an audience to advertisers*. Once the listeners figured out they were getting filler instead of steak, they went elsewhere. Between satellite radio, iPods, and streaming Internet audio, the terrestrial music business model of radio was thoroughly damaged—mostly, at the request of the industry.

Clear Channel once had a stock price over $70 and a market cap near $40 billion; now it trades for pennies. What's left is an outdoor billboard company, with an under $1 billion market cap.

Next, consider the Securities Litigation Reform Act of 1995. This legislation was supposed to be a way to eliminate class action lawsuits that were the bane of public companies' existence. Buried in the legislation was a little-noticed clause that eliminated "joint and several liability" for those who contribute to securities fraud. The consequences of the change were significant. It removed liability for fraud from the accountants who audited quarterly statements for public companies.

What do you think happened once accountants were no longer liable? *An explosion of accounting fraud!* The accounting scandals of the late 1990s and early 2000s were directly attributable to this small legal change. So too was the collapse of Enron, which led to the corporate death penalty for Arthur Andersen. We can probably pin the subsequent enactment of Sarbanes-Oxley, which is undoubtedly having all sorts of its own unintended consequences, on that same clause. These all trace back to what the industry itself had requested.

As the saying goes: *Be careful what you wish for; you may get it.*

■ ■ ■

The repercussions of current Treasury Department bailouts and Federal Reserve rescue plans may not be realized for years or even decades. The unintended consequences of these bailouts fester beneath the surface, slowly working their mischief.

It turns out that many different prior actions contributed to the great unraveling of the U.S. financial system. The old cliché is "success has many fathers, but failure is an orphan." Let's do some DNA testing to see if we can identify the ancestry of the modern financial system collapse.

One of the oddest connections is the direct line one can draw from the Boskin Commission, a Senate-appointed board charged with reviewing the consumer price index (CPI) in 1995, to the collapse of Bear Stearns in 2008.

When Alan Greenspan brought interest rates down to such ultralow levels, he did not in all likelihood think he was being reckless. We will deal with the inherent contradiction of a free market economist's constant intervention in the economy in a later chapter (and perhaps on the couch of Alan's shrink). The Fed might have been panicked over the state of the economy, but a fair reading of Greenspan's public testimony shows the Fed chairman was convinced inflation was "contained." He did what he felt was necessary to revive the economy.

Yet home prices doubled in a short period of time, crude oil increased ninefold from its 2001 lows of $16 to $147, and food prices skyrocketed. There was also enormous inflation in medical costs, education, insurance, and other services.

During most of this 2003–2007 run-up in prices, the consumer price index (CPI), the official measure of inflation, hardly budged. Credit the Boskin Commission for contributing to this illusion of low inflation. The Boskin reforms changed not only the basket of goods measured for inflation, but how we measure them. It allowed "hedonic adjustments" for the improvement of quality. Forget what the window sticker says; your new car isn't really more expensive—*it's better*.

Then there was "substitution"—for example, when the price of steak rises, consumers can replace it with chicken at the previous low prices. In the topsy-turvy world of Boskin, substituted prices remained the same. In the real world, inflation just drove steak out of your price range.

Convened by President George Bush Sr. and signed into law by President Bill Clinton, the 1996 report of this Advisory Commission to Study the Consumer Price Index concluded that CPI overstated inflation by 1.1 percent. It was through tricks like substitution, hedonic adjustments, and other intellectually dishonest methods that the Boskin Commission made their disingenuous claims.

It was as dishonest a study of inflation as has ever been published. The government's keeper of all things statistical is the Bureau of Labor Statistics (BLS). Some of the absurdities foisted upon the BLS by the Boskin Commission made it clear that accurately measuring inflation was not remotely their concern.

In reality, the Boskin Commission was formed to lower the reported inflation rate as a backdoor method of reducing the cost of living adjustment (COLA) paid by Social Security and many other government programs, including benefits for veterans and their dependents. These payments are linked to CPI inflation.

Rather than accurately measuring inflation, the commission's apparent goal was to avoid bankrupting the U.S. Treasury. Unfunded entitlement programs (Medicaid, Social Security, and now Medicare Prescription Drug Plans) have been the so-called third rail of American politics—and lacking the will or courage to deal with them directly, politicians of both parities simply kicked the can down the road for future policymakers to deal with (or not).

The Boskin study was an exercise in tortured logic that is itself worthy of another book—try Kevin Phillips' *Bad Money* (Viking, 2008). If the CPI was overstated by 1.1 percent annually for 10 years starting in 1996, the Congressional Budget Office estimated the error would add about $148 billion to the federal deficit in 2006 and $691 billion to the national debt.[2]

As it turned out, the true cost of the Boskin Commission was immeasurably higher. Since the Boskin Commission's recommendations were adopted in 1999 by the Bureau of Labor Statistics, the spread between real-world inflation and official CPI the BLS reports has only grown further apart. In the current decade, the BLS has reported only modest inflation increases as actual prices of goods and services have skyrocketed.

For a while, the Boskin-influenced CPI data convinced many economists that the inflation beast really had been tamed. Soon, however, the official data became laughable. The Fed was insisting inflation was moderate as food and energy prices soared. Even more absurd was the Federal Reserve's preferred measure of inflation—the core CPI, minus food and energy costs.

Or as I prefer to call it, inflation *ex-inflation*.

What happens when we deny objective reality, purposefully misstate the economic data, and try to hide beneath a series of obfuscations and misdirection? We end up making policy based on a false view of reality. The drumbeat of bad data, and the imprimatur of legitimacy thereof, provided an undeserved credibility for the "low inflation" theme. That created a level of acceptance of elevated inflation that eventually led to several disasters. Rates were left at levels that responsible central bankers, aware of reality and concerned about inflation, would never have allowed.

The post-Boskin fantasy world made ultralow rates for extreme lengths of time more acceptable. The Boskin Commission's recommendations turned BLS data reporting into something once removed from actual inflation. Unfortunately, this gave some degree of cover to Alan

Greenspan's dramatic reduction of interest rates from 2001 to 2003 down to 1 percent.

Without the commission's changes, it's hard to imagine Greenspan could have kept rates as low—and for as long—as he did. Those ultralow rates begat the boom in housing, which fed the residential mortgage-backed security (RMBS) business.

And the single biggest player in RMBSs? Bear Stearns.

Many factors led to the credit crisis—but we can draw a straight line from the silliness of the Boskin Commission to Greenspan's 1 percent federal funds rate to a surge in derivatives trading, and on to the collapse of many financial firms. Bear Stearns was the first—but it wouldn't be the last.

■ ■ ■

From Boskin to Bear Stearns on to Lehman: Perhaps the most obvious of our strange connections is the number of repercussions that the Fed-engineered rescue of Bear Stearns had on other investment banks' managements, most notably Lehman Brothers.

Larger and better diversified than Bear, the 158-year-old Lehman was the second-biggest player in the RMBS market. Following the Bear bailout in March 2008, Lehman management may have assumed that the Fed and Treasury would come to its rescue if it ran into real trouble.

That misplaced reliance was a fatal mistake. But it may have begotten the strangest, least-intended consequence of all: Lehman turning down a rescue offer from Warren Buffett's Berkshire Hathaway. To date, this marks the single biggest missed opportunity of the bailout era.

After the Bear collapse, Lehman CEO Dick Fuld reached out to a few sources to round up some extra capital. Somewhat surprisingly, Buffett was receptive to taking a stake in Lehman. In 1987, Buffett had successfully rescued Salomon Brothers, but the experience had soured him on Wall Street. It was widely believed that he had sworn off owning any investment banks unless they could be had for a song.

Fuld must have been singing Buffett's tune. According to Bloomberg, Berkshire Hathaway offered to buy preferred shares that would pay a dividend of 9 percent and could be converted to common at the then-market price of $40.30.

Buffett's money was costlier than other potential investors, but it came with the imprimatur of the world's best-loved investor. That alone probably would have guaranteed Lehman's survival.

Surprisingly, Fuld spurned Buffett's offer, choosing instead to sell $4 billion in convertible preferred (7.25 percent rate, 32 percent conversion premium) on April Fool's Day; the buyers of those preferreds turned out to be quite the fools indeed.

By rebuffing Berkshire and, as Bloomberg described it, "corporate America's *Good Housekeeping* seal of approval," Lehman likely missed its last, best chance for survival. Ironically, Buffett got the chance to make an even tougher deal with Goldman Sachs after Lehman went belly-up—a 10 percent interest rate on a $5 billion investment.

Lehman's Fuld also had other chances to raise money before the firm's bankruptcy filing in mid-September 2008. But the deals were never consummated, most notably negotiations with Korea Development Bank, which reportedly broke down over price.[3]

One cannot help but imagine: But for the Bear Stearns bailout, would Lehman CEO Dick Fuld have been as arrogant? One has to think he expected policy makers would give Lehman the same treatment as his smaller rival.

■ ■ ■

Enron's lobbying for an energy derivatives trading exemption ultimately was what led to the Commodity Futures Modernization Act. The CFMA, we now know, created an unregulated shadow insurance industry. This led to all sorts of normally staid firms getting in way over their heads.

Consider the bond insurers. The Ambacs, MBIAs, and FGICs (formerly a GE/Blackrock company) of the world used to have a nice little business. They were called monolines, because they did only one thing: They wrote insurance on bonds issued by cities, states, and local

municipalities. Historically, muni bonds have very low default rates; state and local governments have the power to levy taxes to make principal and interest payments, and hence rarely default. With an additional guarantee on those payments from the monolines, insured munis were granted triple-A ratings, the highest possible. The monolines' fees were the "vig" on getting those top default risk ratings. The premium more than paid for itself in reduced borrowing costs for state and local governments.

This was a lovely, low-risk business, with few defaults and a steady revenue stream. At one point in time, Ambac had the highest revenue per employee on the planet.

That situation was obviously intolerable. So the muni bond insurers brought in the financial engineers, who decided that they should be issuing insurance on credit default swaps (CDSs)—*the premiums were so much bigger than those on boring old munis!*

These firms were used to heavy oversight and supervision in the municipal bond business. In their structured finance division, regulatory oversight was nonexistent; without it, they went off the rails.

Since 2007, the stock prices of Ambac and MBIA have cratered, losing more than 90 percent. Both firms faced investigations by regulators. How a highly profitable, low-risk business stumbled into the treacherous worlds of exotic derivatives is worthy of a book itself. Tens of billions of dollars would be lost by the monoline (now duoline) insurers, and chaos in the municipal bond market ensued when the credit crunch hit in 2007–2008.

The absence of bond insurance has made borrowing much more expensive for many state and local municipalities. The increased costs of financing municipal projects—sewers, bridges, roads, schools, hospitals—have put many of these projects on hold for now. The timing couldn't be worse; the slowdown started shortly before the recession began.

When the Senate unanimously passed the Commodity Futures Modernization Act, the senators could not have foreseen the impact it would have on municipal bond underwriting and local government activity in just a few short years. That's to say nothing of the impact unregulated derivatives had on AIG.

■ ■ ■

The Lockheed bailout of 1971 led directly to the Chrysler bailout nine years later in 1980. Both took the form of guaranteed loans; both were in sectors and industries deemed to be indispensable.

What made the Chrysler bailout have such significant repercussions in the future was that it forestalled dealing with a ruinous employment agreement, originally signed by the major automakers and the United Auto Workers (UAW) in the 1950s. It also failed to address rising guaranteed pensions and expensive health care costs. That contract eventually would cost the Big Three hundreds of billions of dollars in both areas. The Chrysler bailout effectively kicked that can further down the road, and by 2008 GM, Chrysler, and Ford were all in shambles. And it allowed Toyota to become the world's largest automaker, employing over 300,000 people around the globe.

Had the Chrysler bailout not occurred in 1979, it is very likely the Detroit automakers would look quite different than they currently do: The UAW contract, health care and pension provisions, company management, and even the cars they design and sell would likely be very different today. In a bizarre way, we can trace Lockheed's $250 million bailout to the potential $34 billion (at least) bailout of General Motors, Ford, and Chrysler in 2008 and 2009.

▪ ▪ ▪

In Chapter 11, we reviewed how a 2004 exemption to a 1975 rule governing banks' net capital ratios paved the way for the excessive risk taking at major Wall Street firms. But even that 1975 rule, which ultimately earned an "excellent track record in preserving the securities markets' financial integrity and protecting customer assets," contained seeds of future bailouts.[4]

The original net capital ratio rule said the value of broker-dealers' assets should be based on the credit ratings of nationally recognized statistical rating organizations (NRSROs). This ruling imparted tremendous power to firms deemed NRSROs—a designation process controversial to this day—and effectively gave the two largest firms, Moody's and Standard & Poor's, a duopoly on the rating of financial securities. (Fitch was also granted NRSRO status in 1975 but has historically played Chrysler to Moody's GM and S&P's Ford.)

As Wall Street's dependence on the NRSROs grew, so too did the power of the rating agencies. As Pulitzer Prize–winning journalist and author Thomas Friedman famously declared in 1996:

> There are two superpowers in the world today in my opinion. There's the United States and there's Moody's bond rating service. The United States can destroy you by dropping bombs, and Moody's can destroy you by downgrading your bonds. And believe me, it's not clear sometimes who's more powerful.[5]

Friedman was exaggerating, but only by a little bit. As the power of Moody's, S&P, and their smaller rival Fitch continued to grow, it attracted the attention of federal regulators.

As SEC Commissioner Paul Atkins said in a 2008 speech:

> Subsequently, NRSRO ratings were incorporated into additional SEC regulations, gaining momentum with Rule 2a-7, which governs which assets may be held in a money-market mutual fund. Rule 2a-7 was promulgated in the early 1990s when some funds came close to breaking a dollar of net asset value because of declining values of certain riskier securities that they held in their portfolios. The new rule looked to *high-rated debt instruments* as suitable investments for money-market funds.[6] (emphasis added)

In essence, a ruling that began in 1975 with good intentions (measure and limit the risk taken by investment banks) granted tremendous power to a small number of credit rating agencies. Those firms became the ultimate arbiters of what mutual funds, money market funds, banks, brokers, and a whole host of other investors could or could not own. Not content with their "superpower" status, the rating agencies ultimately sought "super profits." They were one of the great enablers of the derivatives mania of this decade.

Although the rating agencies had been feckless in accurately assessing the credit quality of Enron (Aaa until just prior to its bankruptcy), investors around the world deluded themselves into believing all manner of CDOs, CMOs, RMBSs, and other toxic securities were really of triple-A quality because rating agencies said so. These NRSROs had been blessed by the government to have the official word on such matters, so very few people questioned the veracity of the process.

"You have legitimized these things, leading people into dangerous risk," an executive with Fortis Investments, a money management firm, wrote in a July 2007 e-mail message to Moody's.[7]

■ ■ ■

Actions have consequences. Denying reality, falsifying data, gaming the numbers, cooking the books, making believe inflation is more modest than it really is, or pretending toxic assets deserve the highest credit ratings all have real-world consequences, intended and otherwise.

Chapter 13

Moral Hazard: Why Bailouts Cause Future Problems

To be sure, some moral hazard, however slight, may have been created by the Federal Reserve's involvement. [Such negatives were outweighed by the risk of] serious distortions to market prices had Long-Term [Capital Management] been pushed suddenly into bankruptcy.

—Alan Greenspan[1]

What is moral hazard? During this past year of our bailout, the phrase has been bandied about haphazardly. Let's define this important term before proceeding further.

Moral hazard is "the prospect that a party insulated from risk may behave differently from the way they would if they were otherwise fully exposed to that risk. It arises when an individual or institution does not bear the full consequences of its actions, and therefore tends to act less carefully than they otherwise would, leaving a third party to bear the responsibility for the consequences of those actions."[2]

That's the formal definition. E. S. Browning, writing in the *Wall Street Journal*, used this less complicated description:

> Moral hazard is an old economic concept with its roots in the insurance business. The idea goes like this: If you protect someone too well against an unwanted outcome, that person may behave recklessly. Someone who buys extensive liability insurance for his car may drive too fast because he feels financially protected.[3]

Hence, there is very real concern that the many bailouts of 2008 and 2009 are creating moral hazard, encouraging more reckless behavior in the future.

Consider the Greenspan quote at the beginning of this chapter; I first came across it in Roger Lowenstein's *When Genius Failed: The Rise and Fall of Long-Term Capital Management*. Rest assured that LTCM did not present, as Greenspan claimed after LTCM's rescue, only "slight" moral hazard. The collapse of that hedge fund in 1998 and its subsequent Fed-orchestrated rescue plan provided one of the greatest—and most terrible—examples of moral hazard ever known.

As noted in Chapter 6, LTCM used enormous amounts of leverage. The fund's traders applied complex quantitative strategies, using over $100 billion in borrowed capital to buy thinly traded assets that were hard to value. Overall, the entire operation was highly dependent on global liquidity.

Gee, that sounds vaguely familiar.

Leverage, complexity, thin trading, difficult-to-value, liquidity dependent—it's as if the trading gods are mocking those managers who came after LTCM and managed to lose billions upon billions of dollars anyway. How on earth could the lessons of LTCM be missed? One can imagine the booming voice of the Almighty, both amused by and annoyed at these traders: "You want a sign? How much more of a sign do you idiots need? I never should have taught you primates to wear pants. There are smarter chimpanzees running naked in Africa than you morons."

At least, that's how I imagine it.

Contrary to what Greenspan claimed, the Federal Reserve's involvement did not create "slight" moral hazard. Rather, the 1998

Fed-orchestrated rescue was moral hazard writ humongous. Lowenstein presciently wrote the following in 2000:

> If one looks at the Long-Term episode in isolation, one would tend to agree that the Fed was right to intervene, just as, if confronted with a suddenly mentally unstable patient, most doctors would willingly prescribe a tranquilizer. The risks of a breakdown are immediate; those of addiction are long term.
>
> But the Long-Term Capital case must be seen for what it is: not an isolated instance but the latest in a series in which an agency of the government has come to the rescue of private speculators. . . . It is true that the Fed's involvement was limited and that no government money was used. But the banks would not have come together without the enormous power and influence of the Fed behind them, and without a joint effort, Long-Term surely would have collapsed. Presumably, the banks and others would have suffered more severe losses—though not, one thinks, as great as some suggested. Long-Term's exposure was huge, but, spread over all of Wall Street, it was hardly of apocalyptic proportions. . . .
>
> Permitting such losses to occur is what deters most other people and institutions from taking imprudent risks. Now especially, after a decade of prosperity and buoyant financial markets, a reminder that foolishness carries a price would be no bad thing. Will investors in the next problem-child-to-be, having been lulled by the soft landing engineered for Long-Term, be counting on the Fed, too? On balance, the Fed's decision to get involved—though understandable given the panicky conditions of September 1998—regrettably squandered a choice opportunity to send the markets a needed dose of discipline.[4]

We now know the answers to Lowenstein's rhetorical question: Yes, they most certainly were counting on the Fed. And, we know precisely what that next problem child was—the many mortgage-backed bonds and credit default swap bets upon them. Further, we have witnessed investors lulled from 2005 to 2007 into what I have described elsewhere as a "stupefying complacency."

To be certain, the management of large investment banks missed the obvious lesson here; as soon as they were able to, they willingly leveraged up nearly as much as LTCM had. When one considers the astonishing parallels between that past crisis and the current one, the

missed opportunity for a "dose of [market] discipline" is all the more regrettable.

Had Long-Term Capital Management been allowed to fail, it's quite possible the worst of the current credit crisis, regulatory fecklessness, and speculator recklessness could have been avoided. Instead, there was a massive, cascading systemwide failure. At every point along the way, from home purchases in Stockton, California, to Iceland's fiscal demise, things went awry.

So much for the lessons learned.

■ ■ ■

LTCM was not the only missed opportunity to teach a lesson about moral hazard. Other bailouts continue to leave lasting, negative effects on future behaviors, including a lack of discipline across many industries.

Recall the original 1980 Chrysler bailout. Since then, the Detroit automakers have seen their market share tumble from 74 percent of autos sold in the United States to 47 percent; the UAW has since lost over two-thirds of the 1.5 million members the union had back in 1980. That was *with* a bailout. Would they really have fared much worse had circumstances been allowed to run their natural course (i.e., without government interference)? Perhaps this is why the first bailout proposal for Detroit automakers was defeated at the behest of Senate Republicans in December 2008.

The moral hazard of the original Chrysler bailout showed up in subsequent actions by the automakers, as detailed in Chapter 4. The impetus to make more reliable, attractive, fuel-efficient cars seemed to have been forgotten until it was way too late. For many years, innovative designs and automotive technologies were the sole province of Japanese and German auto designers. Making ever less expensive cars became the province of the Koreans.

Meanwhile, the Big Three spent much of the intervening decades since the bailout—and millions upon millions of dollars—lobbying Congress. Rather than innovate the way other manufacturers did, they fought for exemptions from Corporate Average Fuel Economy (CAFE) standards, or litigated against emission standards from states such as California.

As a car guy, I can say without hesitation that General Motors hasn't designed a dashboard that wasn't ugly as shit since the 1950s (the early 1960s Corvettes were the sole exception, but they were a special project). The biggest automotive accomplishment out of Detroit during recent decades was getting SUVs exempt from various car safety and fuel efficiency rules. Is it any wonder that Toyota has royally kicked GM's ass since then, bypassing the still-bloated manufacturer for the number one slot in auto sales in the United States? Toyota is now the world's biggest automaker. I am hard-pressed to name any nonfinancial American company that *deserves* bankruptcy more than GM.

■ ■ ■

There is yet another reason to be wary of broad government interventions: Vast amounts of money up for grabs have a tendency to corrupt anything they come near. The pork attached to the original Troubled Assets Relief Program (TARP) plan was a disgraceful showing. It was an embarrassing spectacle of business as usual from a Congress with the lowest approval rating of any political organ in America. To merely witness it made one rethink the wisdom of poll taxes, and reconsider one's belief in democracy.

Once the auto bailout lost in the Senate, the White House said the government was likely to make an emergency loan to GM, Ford, and Chrysler out of TARP. Well, I guess if you think about it, the automakers *are* "troubled assets"—but that's hardly what was contemplated by the term when Congress originally approved the $700 billion emergency fund.[5]

How typically corrosive and corrupting a big pile of money can be. This is yet another downside of bailouts: It brings the leeches and vultures, mostly in the form of lobbyists, seeking to grab a slice of that sweet pork pie.

And that's before we even consider what other, worthwhile programs will be squeezed out by the bailouts' terrible financial costs.

How to Pay for National Health Insurance

Since the government has spent such an inordinate amount of taxpayer money cleaning up after Wall Street's so-called best and brightest and the mess they made, there is not a whole lot of money left over for other new programs.

Once such legislative work was national health insurance. Surveys have shown that a significant majority of Americans support it. It was one of the key planks of Barack Obama's presidential campaign.

Well, no worries over the lack of funding for health care. There is a simple way to ensure that every man, woman, and child in the United States is covered by health care insurance. Taking a page from the cleverest of Wall Street's financial engineers, all it takes is a little of that Street magic and derivative-based hocus-pocus in seven steps:

1. Set up a large, well-capitalized hedge fund. About $5 billion should do it.
2. The prospectus of the fund should note its purpose is to "seek out profit opportunities via arbitraging inefficiencies in the markets and health care system of the United States." Include standard socially conscious fund language with clauses such as "We plan to do well by doing good."
3. Launch the fund—and promptly max out your leverage. The credit crisis makes it difficult to go 50 to 1, but 10 or 20 to 1 should not be much of a problem.
4. Use the money to write credit default swaps with a notional value of $3 trillion. The premiums on these CDSs should be about 10 percent to 15 percent or so.
5. Roll over the cash premiums—about $350 billion worth—into a national fund. Use it to buy health care insurance for all U.S. citizens!
6. Send certified letters to your counterparties, declaring that due to the unfortunate current credit conditions, you will be

defaulting on these CDSs. Be sure to mention that a significant amount of your CDS paper is held by JPMorgan and Citigroup. Another trillion is held by China and Japan, with other sovereign wealth funds owning the rest.

7. Send out a press release announcing "systemic risk." Tell the Treasury secretary and the Federal Reserve chair that your imminent collapse will wreak global havoc. Apply for bailout.

Congratulations! You have national health care!

Repeat for any major government program: alternative energy research, school vouchers, Mars mission, global warming, or missile defense shield.

In the future, this is how all government spending programs will be funded.

■ ■ ■

The other danger that moral hazard presents is to allow investors to mistakenly believe a paternal Fed will always be there to bail them out of any jams. Some evidence of this can be seen in the behavior of several well-known funds and famous investors. In 2007 and 2008, they placed a series of large bets in the financial sector. Some purchased investment banks with long, storied histories and pedigreed founders. Others jumped into the mortgage business, buying firms that specialized in underwriting, origination, or securitization. Still others have scooped up bank shares at prices that were perceived to be on the cheap.

What were originally thought to be bargains turned out instead to be quite pricey. Losses have ranged from the merely enormous to the utterly devastating. Of the approximately $57.3 billion in high-profile investments tallied in Table 13.1, an international group of presumably savvy investors had suffered a collective loss of about 75 percent as of December 2008.

Note: These devastating losses are ongoing—and seemingly getting worse all the time.

Table 13.1 You Call That "Smart Money"?

Investor	Company	Investment (Date)	Loss (%)*
Various (stock sale)	Lehman Brothers	$4B (April 2008)	$4B (100%)
Warburg Pincus	MBIA	$1B (Dec. 2007)	$836M (84%)
Citic Securities	Bear Stearns	$1B (Oct. 2007)	$925M (93%)
Joseph Lewis	Bear Stearns	$1.2B (2007)	$1.1B (91%)
Citadel	E*Trade	$2.55B (Nov. 2007)	$2.170B (85%)
Various (FDIC-backed debt sale)	Wachovia	$6B (Dec. 2008)	$4.5B (75%)†
Govt. of Singapore Investment Corp.	UBS	$9.75B (Dec. 2007)	$7.7B (79%)
Bank of America	Countrywide Financial	$2B (Aug. 2007)	$1.48B (74%)
Korea Investment Corp./Kuwait Investment Authority/ Mizuho Bank	Merrill Lynch	$6.6B (Jan. 2008)	$2.9B (45%)
Abu Dhabi	Citigroup	$7.5B (Aug. 2007)	$6.74B (89%)
China Investment Corp.	Morgan Stanley	$5B (Dec. 2007)	$2.6B (52%)
Temasek Holdings	Merrill Lynch	$4.4B (Dec. 2007)	$1.7B (40%)
Christopher Davis	Merrill Lynch	$1.2B (Dec. 2007)	$475M (40%)
Various (stock + debt sale)	Ambac	$3B (Feb. 2008)	$2.7B (90%)
Bank of America	Countrywide	$2.1B (Jan. 2008)	$626M (30%)

*Loss as of March 2009.

†Wachovia shares valued at $7 when bought by Wells Fargo in $15.4B transaction.

NOTE: Merrill shares valued at $29 when bought by BoA in $50B all-stock transaction.

SOURCE: Published reports, Yahoo! Finance

How did otherwise intelligent, experienced investors find themselves on the wrong side of these trades? These were not mere stock-picking foibles of the "win some, lose some" variety. Rather, they were catastrophes that had nothing to do with these investors' ability to read complex balance sheets, or assess financial leverage, or recognize counterparty risks. These investment losses did not come about based on some unforeseen macroeconomic challenge to a company's business model.

No, the problem that these investors encountered was one of misplaced confidence. It's yet another risk that is run when investors perceive that the government is there to rescue them. These fund managers made the simple mistake of placing their faith in the central bank of the United States of America. Inspired at first by the Federal Reserve, and then subsequently by the Treasury, these formerly savvy traders rushed headlong into the U.S. financial sector, regardless of what proved to be readily apparent risks.

These turned out to be exquisitely expensive mistakes.

Indeed, one of the more fascinating aspects of the Fed's intervention in the financial markets has been the impact it has had on the psyches of some of its largest players.

This is another consequence of moral hazard. By creating a perceived readiness to bail out markets and speculators, central banks run the risk that they can perversely end up encouraging even more risk taking by other market participants. The bravado and false confidence the Fed's intervention engendered led quite a few funds down the wrong path. This rise in false confidence among those who should otherwise know better is merely another aspect of moral hazard.

It can be argued that these misguided rescue operations made the financial system *more* unstable by encouraging greater recklessness and additional risk taking (see Figure 13.1). All the while, the speculators' profits remain their own, while the risks are born by the taxpayers.

The smart money was proven in 2008 to be not so smart after all. The very expensive costs were summed up by an anonymous trader who e-mailed a colleague: "This has been even worse than my first divorce. I've lost half my net worth but I still have my wife."

Wall Street gallows humor being what it is, the e-mail circulated far and wide among trading desks. But that's a wholly different kind of moral hazard.

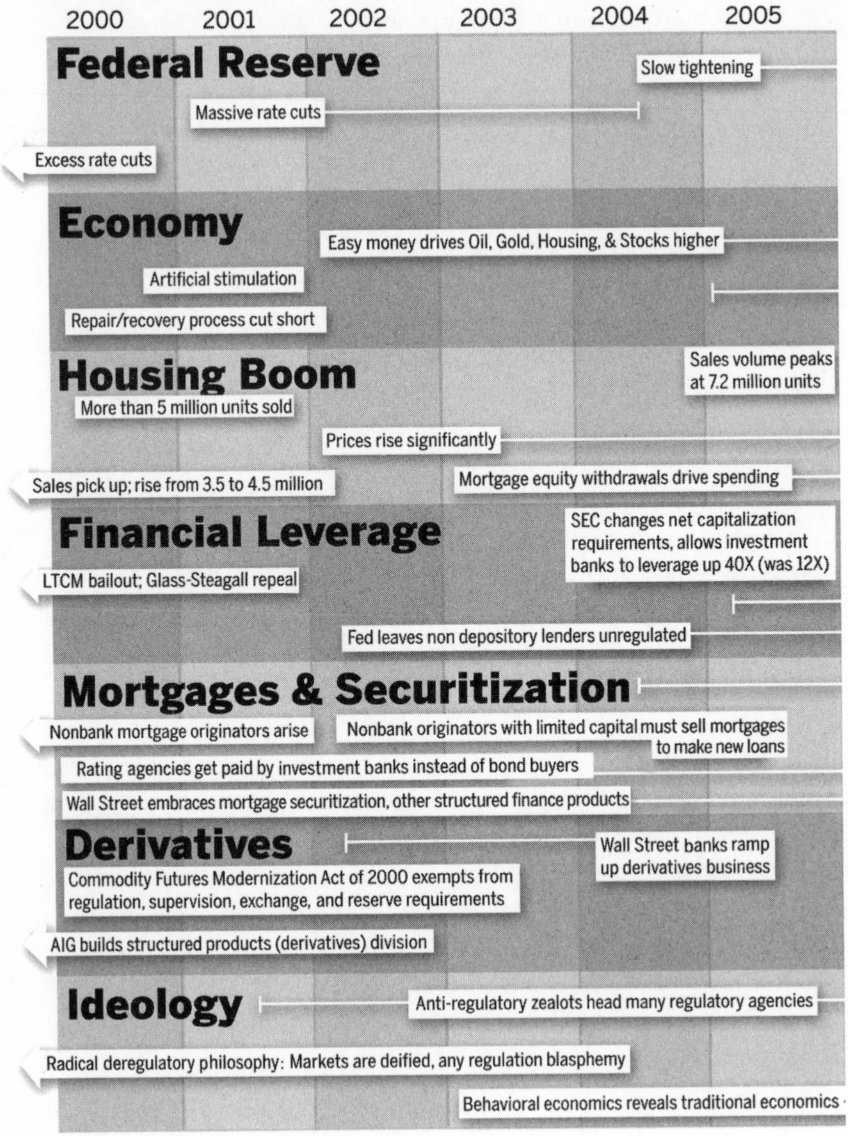

2000 2001 2002 2003 2004 2005

Federal Reserve

Slow tightening

Massive rate cuts

Excess rate cuts

Economy

Easy money drives Oil, Gold, Housing, & Stocks higher

Artificial stimulation

Repair/recovery process cut short

Housing Boom

Sales volume peaks at 7.2 million units

More than 5 million units sold

Prices rise significantly

Sales pick up; rise from 3.5 to 4.5 million

Mortgage equity withdrawals drive spending

Financial Leverage

SEC changes net capitalization requirements, allows investment banks to leverage up 40X (was 12X)

LTCM bailout; Glass-Steagall repeal

Fed leaves non depository lenders unregulated

Mortgages & Securitization

Nonbank mortgage originators arise

Nonbank originators with limited capital must sell mortgages to make new loans

Rating agencies get paid by investment banks instead of bond buyers

Wall Street embraces mortgage securitization, other structured finance products

Derivatives

Wall Street banks ramp up derivatives business

Commodity Futures Modernization Act of 2000 exempts from regulation, supervision, exchange, and reserve requirements

AIG builds structured products (derivatives) division

Ideology

Anti-regulatory zealots head many regulatory agencies

Radical deregulatory philosophy: Markets are deified, any regulation blasphemy

Behavioral economics reveals traditional economics

Figure 13.1 The Anatomy of a Collapse

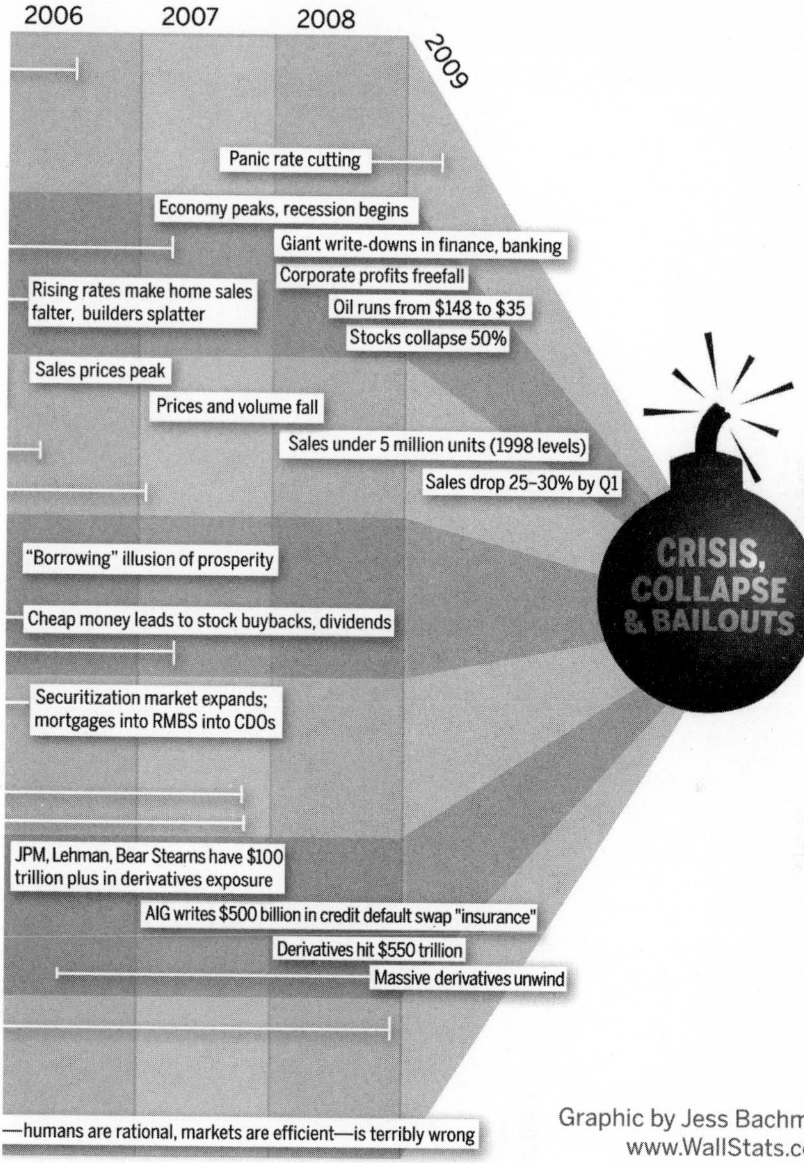

2006 2007 2008 2009

Panic rate cutting

Economy peaks, recession begins

Giant write-downs in finance, banking

Corporate profits freefall

Rising rates make home sales falter, builders splatter

Oil runs from $148 to $35

Stocks collapse 50%

Sales prices peak

Prices and volume fall

Sales under 5 million units (1998 levels)

Sales drop 25–30% by Q1

"Borrowing" illusion of prosperity

Cheap money leads to stock buybacks, dividends

Securitization market expands; mortgages into RMBS into CDOs

JPM, Lehman, Bear Stearns have $100 trillion plus in derivatives exposure

AIG writes $500 billion in credit default swap "insurance"

Derivatives hit $550 trillion

Massive derivatives unwind

—humans are rational, markets are efficient—is terribly wrong

CRISIS, COLLAPSE & BAILOUTS

Graphic by Jess Bachman
www.WallStats.com

Part IV

BAILOUT NATION

"I have found a flaw."

– Alan Greenspan

Source: By permission of John Sherffius and Creators Syndicate, Inc.

Chapter 14

2008: Suicide by Democracy

Remember, democracy never lasts long. It soon wastes, exhausts, and murders itself. There never was a democracy yet that did not commit suicide.

—John Adams

How did the once proudly independent United States become a Bailout Nation?

The first modest government interventions and legislative fixes soon changed to far more insidious corporate welfare. What once was unthinkable slowly morphed into something merely undesirable on its way to becoming the least bad option facing policy makers. The cumulative effect has been a creeping paternalism, rife with moral hazard.

During the debates about earlier bailouts, be they Lockheed in 1971 or Chrysler in 1980, the language and philosophy were very different from the 2008 Troubled Assets Relief Program (TARP) debate. Historically, there was a legitimate battle between ideologies as to whether any bailout should be enacted in a market-based economy. Concern about

the negative future ramifications of these bailouts was paramount. The bailout discussion circa 2008 was long on fearmongering and short on substantive issues. Lawmakers were presented with a "Trust me" document, then hardly given a chance to read it. "Vote for this or suffer horrific consequences to the entire financial system" was the administration's approach.

How did this philosophical shift take place? Philosophically, the politics, economics, and financial analysis of bailouts have shifted dramatically since the 1970s. What makes this so ironic is the rightward political shift of the same era. Since Ronald Reagan was elected president in 1980, Republicans have ascended to power at the federal and state levels. The GOP won the White House in five of the seven elections from 1980 to 2008. The Republicans controlled Congress from 1994 to 2006. One might imagine that a conservative president and a rightward-leaning Congress would boldly object to bailout after bailout.

One would be disappointed: The TARP plan, the various 2008 bailouts of Bear Stearns, Fannie Mae/Freddie Mac, Citibank, Merrill Lynch, Bank of America, American International Group (AIG), and others all took place during a purportedly conservative Republican administration.

Maybe it was less a matter of political ideology than it was governing style. For most of the Bush administration's two terms, the GOP adhered tightly—perhaps too tightly—to Karl Rove's discipline. The Rove approach helped President Bush govern, but it stifled debate on major issues. Too much party-line groupthink and too little independent thought is the likely reason why social conservatives became conservative socialists.

Just as there are no atheists in foxholes, there were no free market capitalists in the face of a financial system collapse.

■ ■ ■

When Bear Stearns, the nation's fifth-largest investment bank, ran into trouble, the assumption among many Fed watchers was that it wasn't deemed "too big to fail." It was almost an article of faith that the marketplace would be allowed to operate unimpeded. As the crisis at Bear heated up, though, both the Federal Reserve (headed by an academic expert on the Great Depression) and Treasury (headed by a former Goldman Sachs CEO) seemed increasingly uncomfortable with the prospect of so much creative destruction.

Maybe *panicked* is a better word than *discomfort* for how Ben Bernanke and Henry Paulson reacted.

In March 2008, Bear was "liquidated in an orderly fashion" (*rescued* is far too kind a word). With Treasury Secretary Paulson concerned with moral hazard, Bear was originally sold for $2 per share. Shareholders balked, and ultimately Bear went to JPMorgan Chase for $10 per share. The bondholders were made whole, with the Federal Reserve and the U.S. Treasury backstopping $29 billion in losses for the deal to get done.

The issue of whether "too big to fail" played a role in the Bear saga is still the operative question. Bear had extensive ties with JPMorgan Chase, including a rumored 40 percent exposure by JPM to Bear Stearns' $9 trillion derivatives book. A bankrupt Bear would have significantly damaged JPM, which by all accounts *was* considered too big to fail. The best explanation I've seen as to why Bear was rescued in the first place was to prevent its derivatives mess from dragging down JPMorgan Chase with it.

Thus began a 12-month period that would see bailout after bailout, all funded by the American taxpayer.

Then there were the government-sponsored enterprises (GSEs): It's hard to say why Fannie and Freddie were bailed out on September 7, 2008. Certainly the reason wasn't insolvency, for as former St. Louis Federal Reserve President William Poole had said in July 2008, they had been technically insolvent for years.[1] And it wasn't cash flow, as the GSEs had enough operating capital to keep going for another 8 to 12 months. Politics during an election year? Saving the next president from making a tough decision? Influencing mortgage rates? These were some of the reasons given, and they are all questionable.

Then came Lehman Brothers. It wasn't deemed too big to fail, but its September 14, 2008, bankruptcy helped force the thundering herd of Merrill Lynch into the waiting arms of Bank of America. Curiously, we'll never find out if Merrill was too big to fail. More important, Lehman's demise impacted lots of the credit default swaps (CDSs) written in the shadow banking system, including hundreds of billion of dollars' worth insured by AIG. The same factors that caused Lehman's bankruptcy also triggered AIG's crash and contributed to the Reserve Primary Fund "breaking the buck."

Soon Uncle Sam was scrambling for his checkbook again.

Size and interconnections were no longer the sole factors that mattered; side bets—such as the credit default swaps placed on Lehman's debt—became a key factor, also.

Bear wasn't allowed to fail for fear of damaging JPM; Lehman was allowed to fail, but no one considered letting AIG fend for itself. Rather than wait for Citigroup to fail, Treasury acted preemptively, rescuing the giant money center bank before it was on the verge of collapse.

Discern any pattern here? Me neither.

Bailing out banks one at time wasn't working, so on October 14, 2008, the U.S. Treasury injected $125 billion of capital into the nine largest banks and another $125 billion into other, smaller banks. Were the bailout architects using these other banks as cover—a smokescreen to conceal an attempt to shore up Citigroup? Perhaps Citi was closer to collapse than previously realized. Using the authority granted to him by Congress when it passed the controversial $700 billion TARP package (in another of Congress's finest moments, the original bill was defeated in the House but then approved after Wall Street freaked out and $150 billion in pork was added), Paulson literally made the banks an offer they couldn't refuse. Any fan of *The Godfather* or *The Sopranos* knows the term for someone who forces you to take money you don't want and might not need.

On top of the $25 billion Citigroup got in October, regulators decided the firm needed more money and protection from its own bad trades. Outrageous though it seems, the U.S. government gave Citi another $20 billion on November 24, 2008. And that wasn't all. Uncle Sam guaranteed $306 billion of troubled home loans, commercial mortgages, subprime bonds, and low-grade corporate loans the firm had made.

Why was there more than $300 billion for Citigroup, but General Motors and Chrysler had to beg and plead for $13.4 billion to stave off their imminent collapse in late 2008? Damned if I know why.

There is a pattern here, but it's one of randomness, not predictability. There seem to be no operative governing rules. Every event is a one-off; the response to each company was not part of any well-planned strategy or grand overview. James Montier of Société Générale called it an *adhocracy*. There has been no broad strategy and apparently no architects to the trillions in bailout dollars so far.

Battles are won with tactics, but in war victory is achieved via strategy.

■ ■ ■

The bailout decision-making process has been dominated by two very different minds and disparate personalities. At the Fed, there is Chairman Ben Bernanke. An academic, he has proven to be a quick study of the ways of Wall Street. His crosstown compatriot at the Treasury, Hank Paulson, was the former deal-making CEO of Goldman Sachs. They are intelligent men of very differing styles and approaches. The government's initial response to the crisis seems to be a hybrid of their two different approaches. We have yet to see if the dynamic will be any different with President Obama's Treasury secretary, Tim Geithner, who had a hand in many of the 2008 bailouts as president of the New York Federal Reserve Bank.

Saving the U.S. financial system bound Paulson and Bernanke together in common purpose. That neither man saw it coming further ties them together. There is a third factor they had in common: They each saw a leadership void as things progressed into crisis.

Indeed, about now you should be asking yourself why a cabinet department and a central bank were running the greatest government rescue operation in history. And you may be wondering, "Where is the man at the top of the organization chart?" It is a fair question. Why did George Bush go AWOL during this crisis period?

Indeed, during the second half of 2008, one got the sense that the Bush White House had no stomach for the entire affair. The bailouts were a repudiation of everything the president believed in; perhaps he simply couldn't bear to take the lead on something he found so philosophically distasteful. Bush's approval ratings were at record lows, his legacy and reputation in tatters. In the latter half of 2008, the sense was that the Bush White House was running out the clock. As Bush's last term was ending, the wheels came off the bus. Then the bus caught fire, rolled down a ravine, and ended up at the bottom of the sea. Running out the clock may have seemed easier than the alternative.

During the interregnum between the November 4th election day and the January 20th inauguration, the void became even more

pronounced. Democratic Congressman Barney Frank criticized president-elect Barack Obama for not being more "assertive" during the crisis. "Part of the problem now is that this presidential transition has come at the very worst possible time," Frank told *60 Minutes*. "You know, Senator Obama has said, 'We only have one president at a time.' Well, that overstates the number of presidents we have at this time."[2]

Bernanke and Paulson soldiered on. To be fair to our D.C. twosome, this has been the crisis that keeps on changing. It started out as a real estate boom and bust, driven by ultralow interest rates and a bubble in credit and lending. That alone would have been difficult to resolve. It then slowly morphed into a full-blown credit crunch, where commercial lending ceased. Then it changed into a Wall Street crash as stocks crumbled globally and yields dramatically fell. Ultimately, it became a U.S., then global, economic recession, with deflation driving the prices of most commodities into the ground.

This has been an unprecedented period in American history.

All the while, the government's response has always been at least one step—and one crisis—behind the curve.

As the government dithered, flailed blindly, and generally meandered aimlessly, casting about for a suitable response to these many crises, the tally grew.

And grew.

And grew.

Until the total commitment hit an astronomical figure: $15 trillion.

That is how much Uncle Sam has spent, promised, lent, guaranteed, or assumed in liabilities thus far on its way to becoming Bailout Nation's government in residence. (See Table 14.1.)

The year 2008 has long since passed any other year—indeed, any other century—in terms of government expenditures directed toward rescuing damaged companies. As this book went to print, the total outlay of government monies and credit from the Treasury Department, the Federal Deposit Insurance Corporation (FDIC), and the Federal Reserve was nearing $9.5 trillion. Add in the $5.5 trillion in Fannie Mae/Freddie Mac mortgage portfolios that the U.S. taxpayer assumed responsibility for when the GSEs were placed into conservatorship, and you get an astonishing total.

Table 14.1 Bailout Tally

	Maximum Amount	Current Amount
Federal Reserve - $5.255 trillion - 62%		
Commercial Paper Funding Facility LLC (CPFF)	1,800,000,000,000	270,879,000,000
Term Auction Facility (TAF)	900,000,000,000	415,302,000,000
Other Assets	601,963,000,000	601,963,000,000
Money Market Investor Funding Facility (MMIFF)	540,000,000,000	0
Unnamed MBS Program Announced 11/25/08	500,000,000,000	0
Term Securities Lending Facility (TSLF)	250,000,000,000	190,200,000,000
Term Asset-Backed Securities Loan Facility (TALF)	200,000,000,000	0
Other Credit Extensions (AIG)	122,800,000,000	122,800,000,000
Unnamed GSE Program Announced 11/25/08	100,000,000,000	0
Primary Credit Discount	92,600,000,000	92,600,000,000
ABCP Money Market Fund Liquidity Facility (AMLF)	61,900,000,000	61,900,000,000
Primary Dealer and Others (PDCF)*	46,611,000,000	46,611,000,000
Net Portfolio Maiden Lane LLC (Bear Sterns)	28,800,000,000	26,900,000,000
Securities Lending Overnight	10,300,000,000	10,300,000,000
Secondary Credit	118,000,000	118,000,000
Longer-Term Treasury Purchase (3/18/09)	300,000,000,000	300,000,000,000
Agency mortgage-backed securities (3/18/09)	750,000,000,000	750,000,000,000
Agency debt purchase (3/18/09)	100,000,000,000	100,000,000,000
Federal Deposit Insurance Corporation - $1.788 trillion - 21%		
FDIC Liquidity Guarantees	1,400,000,000,000	0
Loan Guarantee to Citigroup**	249,300,000,000	249,300,000,000
Loan Guarantee to Lending Arm of General Electric	139,000,000,000	139,000,000,000
Treasury Department - $1.15 trillion - 13.5%		
Troubled Asset Relief Program (TARP)	700,000,000,000	350,000,000,000

(Continued)

Table 14.1 Bailout Tally (*Continued*)

	Maximum Amount	Current Amount
Fannie Mae/Freddie Mac Bailout	200,000,000,000	0
Stimulus Package	168,000,000,000	168,000,000,000
Treasury Exchange Stabilization Fund (ESF)	50,000,000,000	50,000,000,000
Tax Breaks for Banks	29,000,000,000	29,000,000,000
Stimulus Program (2009)	787,000,000,000	0
Homeowner Affordability and Stability Plan (2009)	75,000,000,000	0
Federal Housing Administration - $300 billion - 3.5%		
Hope for Homeowners	300,000,000,000	300,000,000,000
Total - 100%	10,502,392,000,000	4,274,873,000,000

*Purchase an additional $100 billion of agency debt, which would bring their total purchases up to $200 billion.

**$306 billion in guarantees, with Citigroup absorbing the first $29 billion in losses. Additional losses are split 90% U.S. gvt., 10% Citigroup.

The math is 306 − 29 = 277 × .90 = 249.3.

The good news is the final bill should be considerably smaller than $15 trillion. Many of the loans will be repaid, and the vast majority of the Fannie/Freddie portfolio is sound. My best guess is the final costs for the cleanup of Wall Street's worst excesses bill should total somewhere between 10 and 20 percent of that number. But that is merely an operating assumption. It is certainly conceivable that circumstances, and the final bill, may change.

But even so, that is a lot of money.

Trying to explain a trillion dollars to most humans is difficult. Indeed, a trillion is a lot of anything. It is a nearly impossible number to conceive of, and it is much larger than most people's conception of time and space. Consider these comparables. The average lifetime is a little longer than two billion seconds (72 years = 2,270,592,000 seconds). One trillion seconds is 31,546 years. In astronomical terms, the universe is believed to be 15 billion years old—that is just shy of 5.5 trillion days old (5,475,000,000,000 days). Suffice to say a trillion is a big number.

The only event in American history that even comes close to matching the cost of the credit crisis is World War II: In 1940 dollars, it cost the Treasury $288 billion. Adjust that for inflation, and it is $3.6 trillion.

That's a fair guess as to what the net cost of the 2008 bailouts will be to the taxpayers in terms of actual expenditures; $15 trillion is the gross cost. Perhaps the United States will show a profit, or maybe the monetary cost will be much greater than that of World War II. Your guess is as good as mine. No one knows.

Let's take a closer look at all of the bailouts from March 2008 to March 2009 in the next chapters. Perhaps we might discern if there is some method to the madness.

Chapter 15

The Fall of Bear Stearns

Buying a house is not the same as buying a house on fire.

—Jamie Dimon, CEO of JPMorgan Chase, on his \$2-per-share offer for Bear Stearns

When Bear Stearns fell apart, few suspected a cascading collapse across the entire financial firmament. Yet that is precisely what occurred as the house of cards built atop residential mortgages wavered, then crumbled.

The first signs of the mess to come burst into view in the early summer of 2007. That was when Bear Stearns reported heavy losses at two of its internal hedge funds. The announcement would prove to be the tip of the iceberg for the coming global financial crisis and the beginning of the end for the firm that had survived the Great Depression, two world wars, the 1987 crash, the Long-Term Capital Management implosion, and the 2000 dot-com tech wreck.

The culture at Bear was unique. The firm was heavily focused on fixed-income trading and institutional clients, as opposed to equity trading and retail clients. It was considerably smaller than rivals such as Merrill Lynch and Morgan Stanley. The firm had a history of hiring traders with street smarts, rather than the best pedigrees. This was a

polite way to say Bear Stearns didn't hire only WASPs when that was the de rigueur on Wall Street. You could be Jewish with a degree from Brooklyn College, or (later) from India or Pakistan, but it didn't matter as long as your trading made money for the firm.

Bear was different from most other Wall Street firms in one other crucial way as well: It was the only primary dealer of Treasury securities that refused to participate in the 1998 bailout of Long-Term Capital Management. This, despite the fact that Bear was LTCM's prime broker. It was an act of selfish defiance that many on Wall Street never forgot—or, apparently, forgave.

Oh, and one last thing: Bear was the biggest underwriter and trader of mortgage-backed bonds.

■ ■ ■

The firm's 14,000 employees and its many shareholders were victims of Bear Stearns' management. Bonuses included stock and options, so many of Bear's employees were stung twice when the firm failed and the stock crashed. Management allowed (and indeed encouraged) the investment bank to become overexposed to mortgage-backed securities. This alone was a significant factor in its demise. When the firm didn't seek additional liquidity when it was available, its fate was sealed.

JPMorgan-Bear Finalized Deal

- JPMorgan Chase agreed to pay $10 per share in stock and to purchase an additional 92 million shares for an immediate stake of 39 percent.
- JPMorgan Chase assumed the risk of the first billion dollars of the $30 billion of Bear Stearns' most risky assets. The Federal Reserve Bank of New York guaranteed the remaining $29 billion but will reap any gains on the portfolio. (As of October 2008, the Federal Reserve stated it had suffered a $2.7 billion paper loss on the $29 billion portfolio of toxic assets.)

In part, the vagaries of the prime brokerage business, where hedge funds park capital with a prime broker in exchange for broker services, further exacerbated conditions at Bear Stearns. The lucrative business of facilitating trades for hedge funds became a millstone for Bear in 2008: As the firm's problems became public, many of its prime brokerage clients—Jim Simon's Renaissance Technology, Citadel Investment Group, and PIMCO—sought to protect themselves from a messy collapse, pulling their capital out of the firm. Each departing client depleted the company's capital base; each led to more Wall Street rumors of a possible bankruptcy. Each rumor prompted more prime brokerage clients to pull capital, and so on.[1]

Plummeting almost 90 percent, Bear Stearns' liquidity pool went from $18.1 billion on March 10, 2008, to $2 billion by March 13, 2008. It was evidence of how quickly fortunes can change on Wall Street, especially at highly leveraged firms.

"A lot of people, it seemed, wanted to protect themselves from the possibility of rumors being true and act later to learn the facts," Bear Stearns President and Chief Executive Alan Schwartz said in a March 14, 2008, conference call.

Was it a self-fulfilling prophecy? Funds fled Bear because they feared it might become insolvent; hedge funds shorting Bear Stearns' stock passed along rumors that others were doing as much. Others bet on credit default swaps linked to the company, and were none too shy about e-mailing negative analysis to their peers and colleagues.

Is that what did Bear Stearns in?

Hardly.

Bear was a highly leveraged firm that bought lots and lots of bad assets with mostly borrowed money. The assets these products were based on—namely, subprime and Alt-A mortgages—were going bad at an increasingly rapid pace. It was readily apparent to the analysts and short sellers who crunched the numbers that Bear Stearns' days were numbered.

That was the factor Wall Street CEOs like Dick Fuld, Hank Paulson, and Jimmy Cayne failed to consider: When you are a bank, your existence depends on the confidence of your clients, investors, and counterparties. "A company is only as solvent as the perception of its solvency," said noted analyst Meredith Whitney, formerly of CIBC Oppenheimer.

Anything you do that puts that perception at risk is extremely dangerous. If you want to run lots of leverage and push the envelope, well, then, you'd better hope nothing else goes wrong. At 35:1 leverage, you do not leave a lot of room for error. If your business model is highly dependent upon access to cheap capital, what happens when that access to liquidity disappears?

Which raises this question: Why aren't there ever runs on semiconductor firms or software companies? Why don't the integrated oil companies or railroads suffer from similar bear raids? The short answer is their business model does not depend on a belief system—of solvency, liquidity, deleveraging, or risk management. All these firms have to do is not go bankrupt.

If you run a major investment bank, however, you *also* have to make sure you don't appear to be *remotely close* to going bankrupt. You needed a bigger margin of safety. Such is the fate of those who depend on the confidence of others.

Bear was perhaps the most colorful example, but it wasn't only a crisis of confidence that did in the investment banks; it was a crisis of *competence.*

And yet, somehow, the investment bank CEOs all failed to realize this. It is inexcusable that this much leverage was applied to firms that relied on others' favorable belief in their solvency. It was unconscionable these firms had been purposefully put into a risk-taking position in extremis. That the CEOs blamed short sellers and rumors—but tried to exonerate their own horrific actions—serves only to emphasize not only their own failures, but their lack of comprehension of what *they themselves had done to their firms.* It was their own incompetent stewardship that purposefully and unknowingly placed these firms at such grave danger of destruction.

Imagine a patient being treated for a particularly aggressive form of cancer. The chemotherapy makes the patient's hair fall out, so he buys himself a Yankee baseball cap to wear. Unfortunately, the cancer is too far progressed, and patient succumbs to the illness. If you were the management of Bear Stearns, you would blame the Yankees for the death of this patient.

■ ■ ■

Bear's failure contained harbingers of what other management teams would soon do also:

- Executives kept an upbeat public persona in the face of corporate disaster. "We don't see any pressure on our liquidity, let alone a liquidity crisis," Schwartz said on March 12, 2008. Four days later, when JPMorgan Chase announced its takeover of Bear for about \$2 per share, he said: "The past week has been an incredibly difficult time for Bear Stearns. This transaction represents the best outcome for all of our constituencies based upon the current circumstances."
- Executives failed to raise capital, or raised too little: "At least six efforts to raise billions of dollars—including selling a stake to leveraged-buyout titan Kohlberg Kravis Roberts & Co.—fizzled as either Bear Stearns or the suitors turned skittish," the *Wall Street Journal* reported. Lehman Brothers, most notably, failed to heed this warning.
- Executives failed to see the folly of their ways. Former CEO James Cayne said Bear "ran into a hurricane," which is a variation of the "act of God" and "100-year flood" excuses used by many a floundering CEO. There are reasons why buildings are made to withstand hurricanes and/or people buy hurricane insurance. CEOs reaping huge salaries can't take all the credit for the good times and then blame so-called acts of God when things go bad—as they inevitably do.

Schwartz was in many ways the fall guy for the failures of his predecessor, Jimmy Cayne, who famously spent much of 2007 and 2008 playing golf and bridge. Infamously, the *Wall Street Journal* reported Cayne also favored marijuana.[2] As Bear careened toward disaster, Schwartz got burned for Cayne's fiddling.

An investment banker by training, Schwartz was admittedly not an expert in the complex mortgage-backed securities that were crippling the firm. That was the purview of co-president Warren Spector. In the years leading up to Bear's fall, Cayne had reportedly given Spector free rein to run that side of the business (and it was a big side at Bear). Spector became the fall guy after those internal hedge funds blew

up in the summer of 2007, and he was unceremoniously fired shortly thereafter.

When the crisis intensified in late 2007 and on into early 2008, Bear was being run by one executive who was in over his head, and another who had figuratively (and possibly literally) checked out. The *Wall Street Journal* reported that "repeated warnings from experienced traders, including 59-year Bear Stearns veteran Alan 'Ace' Greenberg, to unload mortgages went unheeded." Schwartz, most notably, "didn't want to unload tens of billions of dollars' worth of valuable mortgages and related bonds at distressed prices, creating steeper losses."[3] Any experienced trader will tell you to "cut your losers short and let your winners run." That the corner office at Bear failed to grasp this is telling.

■ ■ ■

After Bear's bailout, the question of who might be next was on all of Wall Street's minds. What other overleveraged firm might also be in trouble?

The obvious answer was Lehman Brothers. Just two months after Bear's demise, hedge fund manager David Einhorn explained at the Ira Sohn Investment Research Conference, an annual charity event, why he believed Lehman Brothers was the next candidate for problems. Einhorn questioned Lehman's accounting, its Level 3 ("mark-to-make-believe") assets, and its solvency. There were suggestions the firm was being evasive in terms of hard numbers for its liabilities.[4]

Why was Lehman Brothers allowed to fail when Bear Stearns was rescued? Why the nonbailout? Lehman was both older and larger than Bear Stearns. It had 25,000 employees at its peak, and the two firms were involved in similar businesses.

Unfortunately for Lehman, it seemed as if the team of Paulson and Bernanke were desperately hoping to avoid moral hazard. Bear was a one-off, they noted. Referring to the Fed's funding of JPMorgan Chase's takeover of Bear, Ben Bernanke said: "That was an extraordinary thing to do. I thought about it long and hard. . . . I hope this is a rare event. I hope this is something we never have to do again."[5]

Rare? Hardly. History would repeat itself again and again as the year unfolded.

■ ■ ■

After Bear's implosion, Lehman's management considered their options. Its senior team—longtime, entrenched employees—were contemplating raising capital. Unfortunately, their loyalty and closeness to the company prevented them from fully grasping the firm's dire circumstances—at least, not until it was too late. Selling a few billion dollars in preferred stock was the plan. By engineering JPMorgan's takeover of Bear Stearns, the Fed may have lulled Lehman's executives into a false sense of bravado regarding the urgency of their need to raise capital. Similarly, Lehman's prime brokerage clients kept more funds with the struggling firm than they surely would have if they had seriously thought the Fed would let Lehman go under.[6]

In April 2008, less than a month after Bear Stearns' demise, Lehman's annual meeting took place. CEO Richard Fuld was pugnacious, and seemed not at all worried about the situation. He was rumored to have told Lehman Brothers employees: "I will hurt the shorts, and that is my goal."

Talk about your misplaced efforts. Six months later, Lehman Brothers filed the biggest bankruptcy in American history. (Full disclosure: My firm was one of the shorts that was decidedly unhurt by Fuld's efforts.)

Warren Buffett made an offer to Lehman, one that turned out to be more generous than the offer later accepted by Goldman Sachs.[7] As noted in our discussion of moral hazard, one can surmise Lehman's rejection of Buffett's bid was the last straw as far as the Fed and Treasury were concerned. *If they were unwilling to help themselves,* went the thinking, *then we'll be damned if we'll write another $30 billion check.*

With Buffett spurned and an irritated Fed and Treasury, there were fewer and fewer options. Potential suitors kicked the tires at Lehman, but there were simply too many toxic assets on the books to attract a serious buyer.

Once Lehman filed for bankruptcy, Barclays scooped up most of the U.S. and U.K. operations—without any troubling bad paper to worry about. Neuberger Berman's management—who had sold to Lehman Brothers a decade earlier—bought the wealth management unit post bankruptcy. They essentially bought themselves back. Nomura Securities took over Lehman's Asian operations.

After 158 years, Lehman Brothers was no more.

The Terrible Lessons of Bear Stearns

Bear Stearns was rescued, but Lehman Brothers was forced to declare bankruptcy. Why?

These are the terrible lessons of Bear Stearns:

- **Go big:** Don't risk just your company; risk the entire world of finance. Modest incompetence is insufficient—if you destroy merely your own company, you won't get rescued. You have to threaten to bring down the entire global financial system. The fear and disruption caused by a Bear collapse were why it was saved. (AIG had the right idea about size.)
- **If you can't go big, go first:** Had Lehman collapsed before Bear, then the same fear and loathing over the impact to the system might have worked to its advantage. But the Fed having been through this once before, the sting was somewhat lessened—especially for an apparently less interconnected firm like Lehman (in the dot-com days, this was called "first mover advantage").
- **Threaten your counterparties:** Bear Stearns had about $9 trillion in its derivatives book, of which 40 percent was held by JPMorgan. Some people have argued that the Bear bailout was actually a preemptive rescue of JPMorgan. That points to another good strategy, if your goal is a bailout—risk bringing down someone much bigger than yourself.
- **Risk an important part of the economy:** If your book of derivatives is limited to some obscure and irrelevant portion of the economy, you will not get saved. In contrast, AIG's

$40 trillion in credit default swaps (CDSs) might threaten much of the financial system. Mortgages are important, credit cards and auto loans less so—but securitized widget inventory is completely unimportant. To use a dirty word, Lehman's exposure was "contained"—Bear's and AIG's were not.

- **Incompetence is more tolerable than arrogance:** Play bridge. Roll up a fattie. Work on your handicap. All these acts of foolishness generate a tsk-tsk from the powers that be. But this bumbling also led to a $29 billion assist for the purchase of the company. Pride, hubris, and a lack of humility create far worse results. Reject a legitimate bid from Warren Buffett and you're really screwed.
- **Balance sheets matter:** You can focus on the media, complain about short sellers, and obsess about PR, but these are the hallmarks of a failing strategy—and a grand waste of time. Why? Insolvency. When everything is said and done, all that really matters is the firm's balance sheet. Lehman's liabilities exceeded its assets, and that meant no one wanted to buy the firm. Merrill Lynch got a lot of the junk off of its books, and was taken over at a 70 percent premium to its recent closing price. And Credit Suisse, which dumped much of its bad paper many quarters ago, remains in a better position than most of its peers.
- **Unintended consequences lurk everywhere:** When the Fed opened up the liquidity spigots via its alphabet soup of lending facilities, the fear was of the inflationary impacts. But the bigger issue should have been complacency. The Dick Fulds of the world said after Bear that these new facilities "put the liquidity issue to rest." Lehman got complacent once liquidity was no longer an issue—and failed to act more quickly to resolve its capital needs.

Unfortunately, these are the terrible moral hazard lessons of 2008—via Bear Stearns, Lehman Brothers, Fannie Mae, Freddie Mac, and AIG.

Chapter 16

Dot-Com Penis Envy

What you do speaks so loud that I cannot hear what you say.

—Ralph Waldo Emerson

What took down the grand financial icons of Wall Street? Why did a veritable conga line of storied names and legendary firms follow Bear Stearns and go the way of the dodo?

There are no hard-and-fast answers, but if you will indulge me, I have a theory. It may surprise and even shock you, given the stunning irresponsibility involved. But it is the only explanation that makes any logical sense, from either an economic perspective or a behavioral one.

No, it wasn't a conspiracy of short sellers. Mark-to-market accounting rules had nothing to do with it. And in the recent era of radical deregulation, you can be sure that excess supervision and regulatory compliance were not the root cause.

The question before us is simply this: Why did these profitable, well-run companies insist on embracing ever greater amounts of risk? What was it that compelled formerly conservative, low-risk business models to throw caution to the winds, and shoot the moon?

The most cogent explanation is tied to misplaced incentives and the overcompensation of senior executives, especially the C-level execs. Much of it can be traced back to the glory days of the tech boom.

I call it the "dot-com stock option penis envy" theory of financial mismanagement.

Got a better theory? I'm all ears. But before you dismiss this one, let's try it on for size:

In the bull market boom of 1982 to 2000, employees at Silicon Valley start-ups received huge pools of stock options. These were wildly risky companies whose potentials for success were quite slim. Indeed, the typical start-up eventually fails via conception or execution. Once the venture capitalist money is exhausted, it is on to the next start-up. Those few who made it really hit the big time: first Intel, then Microsoft, then Cisco, Apple, Dell, Oracle, AOL, and EMC. Each of these firms' founders became billionaires, and many of their early hires became multimillionaires.

That alone wasn't what did it. These were storied names, famously started in garages and dorm rooms. It wasn't even the second wave of technology firms that went public that caused the problem. Netscape, Rambus, Microstrategy, Global Crossing, Research in Motion, Yahoo!, and others all grew rapidly, had enormous revenue, and were real businesses (well, maybe not Netscape, but the others did).

I suspect it was the third wave of technology initial public offerings (IPOs)—whisper-thin business models, zero profitability—that really got under the bankers' skin. These were the merest wisps of companies, put together over the course of a semester or two by college kids. The bankers watched as companies like WebMD, CMGI, eToys, Investor Village, Excite, and InfoSpace went public, creating vast paper wealth; perhaps Pets.com was the last straw. When the pubescent founders/CEOs/dudes-in-chief became billionaires after their IPOs, one can only imagine what the bank executives thought.

I'd bet the East Coast CEOs turned green with envy. The big investment houses, banks, and insurers saw this from 3,000 miles away—and started losing their minds. It was going on right in the backyards of West Coast banks like Washington Mutual and IndyMac and Countrywide Financial. They witnessed this, and it got to be too much for their dopamine-addled brains. Soon they were scheming to get some of that sweet stock option lucre for themselves. They created a system of incentives that gave themselves huge stock options bonuses. Sauce for the goose is sauce for the gander indeed.

Unfortunately, there were two major flaws in the plan. When technology creates what has become known as "the killer app"—the hockey stick portion of growth—it catches a wave. These were new product lines, groundbreaking ecosystems, vast changes in consumer habits. E-mail! Mobile phones! Online retail! iPods! Game-changing booms like these were most likely to come from technology. The companies that developed these were awesome wealth producers. As these products became widely adopted, a natural sweet spot for cashing in stock options was created.

The major finance businesses—banking, lending, insurance, investing—did not lend themselves to the sort of explosive growth that created overnight billionaires. Sure, you could get wildly wealthy, but you had to be somewhat patient. But that wouldn't do; these were the sort of folks who couldn't be bothered even to wait for immediate gratification. The bankers needed some way to get to that next level *now*, to embrace the sort of models that would be game changers immediately.

They needed a Viagra.

The 100-year-old financial houses could never compete with that sort of growth. Well, at least not with their relatively staid old business models, their conservative approach to risk. Slow growth and modest profit margin was not how you got rich quick. So they leveraged up, embraced risk, and reinvented themselves as newfangled quants. *"We're engineers, too—financial engineers! We design derivatives and securitize debt! We have access to massive leverage! Hey, everybody, we're all gonna get laid!"*

How else can you explain CEOs going all in?

Financial engineering took care of the first problem, the killer app. Be it leverage or derivatives or securitization, the wizards of Wall Street had found their Viagra. At least, they thought they did. What they failed to consider was the cost of failure.

That was something that Silicon Valley had down to a science. In tech land, start-ups hit it big or fizzled. The cost of failure was minimal, and working at the right crashed-and-burned company was a badge of

honor. During the post-2000 tech wreck, FuckedCompany.com was a favorite web site among the geek crowd.

Those who work at start-ups risk thousands of dollars of money from friends and family; they roll the dice with hundreds of thousands of angel investor cash. They gamble millions of venture capital dollars on new business ideas. And when it all goes kaput, hey, it was a long shot in the first place. They all pick themselves up, dust themselves off, and move on to the next project.

Not so with the finance gurus. When you are a 100-year-old company handling hundreds of billions of dollars, there is no easy exit. Big investment banks were not playing with venture capital money, where the expectation was that 99 out of 100 projects would return nothing. They were playing with the rent money and life insurance premiums and mortgages and 401(k) cash of their clients, businesses, and individuals alike.

These weren't modest investments made by people who understood the long odds against them and allocated risk capital accordingly. This was blood money. They bet the house—and lost.

■ ■ ■

We've come a long way from the days when the man atop the organizational chart made 40 times what the person on the lowest rung earned. Over the past few decades, executive compensation has exploded, with some CEOs taking 200, 300, even 400 times the base pay at the company.

With so much of this compensation made via options-based incentives, the bosses had every reason to swing for the fences. The upside was all theirs, and the downside was the shareholders'—and taxpayers'.

But don't for a moment think their terrible track record had a negative impact on their compensation. Despite their performance, these CEOs were paid as if they were enormous successes. The compensation figures that follow are enormous; that they were paid for such abject failure is a national embarrassment.

It is also an indictment of three major corporate governance issues that have not been discussed widely enough. The first is the crony capitalism that was rife in boardrooms across the United States. The cronyism of major corporate boards, especially those in the finance area, has become legendary. Rubber-stamp directors who rarely buck the chairman or challenge the CEO are unfortunately all too common. These boards did not serve either their companies or their shareholders well.

Also enabling this festival of greed are the large institutions that held the companies' stock, most especially the big mutual funds that have been AWOL when it comes to policing the senior management. They have the time, expertise, and incentives to do so; it is beyond the capability of individual shareholders. Besides, it makes no economic sense for someone who owns 100 or 1,000 shares of stock to act as overseer and scold to corporate boards. But it was squarely in the interest of owners of 10 million shares and up to do so. Why the mutual fund complexes failed to protect their shareholders is hard to fathom. Perhaps when it comes to the finance sector, they feared missing out on syndicate deals and hot IPOs if they asked too many questions.

Then there are the so-called compensation consultants. They did a horrific disservice to the shareholders as well as the companies. The role of these primarily ethicless weasels was to give cover for these ridiculous compensation packages. I would love to see a review of the packages as written back then. If the compensation experts were members of an actual profession with standards and ethics, they would be drummed out of that profession. Instead, these people were merely tools used by the C-level execs to transfer vast sums of wealth from the shareholders to themselves.

■ ■ ■

Astonishingly, many of the corporate chieftains whose firms have been bailed out at taxpayer expense still maintain very significant net worths, courtesy of those now destroyed firms. Stan O'Neal left Merrill Lynch with $160 million. Ace Greenberg is reputed to have sold over $100 million in Bear Stearns stock. And Hank Paulson, who as both CEO of Goldman Sachs and Treasury secretary under President Bush, dumped nearly half a billion dollars' worth of his Goldman Sachs stock (thanks to his new government job, it was tax defered, too!) Had they been running partnerships when their firms collapsed, they would have been left in a rather different financial situation.

That is how incentive pay is supposed to work—upside gains and downside risks as well. But that's not at all what happened:[1,2]

- Lehman Brothers Chairman and CEO Richard Fuld Jr. made $34 million in 2007. Fuld also made nearly a half-billion—$490 million—from selling Lehman stock in the years before Lehman filed for Chapter 11 bankruptcy.
- Goldman Sachs always pays its top executives handsomely: Chairman and CEO Lloyd Blankfein got $70 million in 2007. Co-Chief Operating Officers Gary Cohn and Jon Winkereid were paid $72.5 million and $71 million, respectively.
- While Bear Stearns was rescued by a $29 billion Fed shotgun wedding to JPMorgan Chase, former chairman Jimmy Cayne received $60 million when he was replaced.
- American International Group CEO Martin Sullivan got $14 million in 2007 (he was thrown out in June that year). Robert Willumstad was handed $7 million for his three months at the helm (Edward Liddy took over as AIG's chief executive in September 2008). So far, the tab for AIG's bailout is $173 billion.
- Morgan Stanley Chairman John Mack earned $1.6 million plus stock in 2007. CFO Colin Kelleher got a $21 million paycheck in 2007. Morgan Stanley also received an expedited approval to become a banking holding company in 48 hours—a record.
- Founder and CEO Angelo Mozilo of Countrywide Financial, which was at the forefront of the subprime fiasco, cashed in $122 million in stock options in 2007; his total compensation over the years was over $400 million.
- Stan O'Neal, who steered Merrill Lynch into collapse before being deposed, was given a package of $160 million when he left his post in 2007. That package makes his successor CEO John Thain's $17 million in salary, bonuses, and stock options in 2007 look like a bargain. (That may explain why Thain used $1 million of company—and shareholder—money, rather than his own, to redecorate O'Neal's old office.)
- Bank of America CEO Kenneth Lewis brought home $25 million in 2007. Bank of America acquired Merrill and Countrywide in 2008

and has thus far received $45 billion of direct government bailout money and another $300 billion in asset guarantees.

- JPMorgan Chase & Company Chairman and CEO Jamie Dimon earned $28 million in 2007. JPM Chase acquired troubled investment house Bear Stearns in March 2008 with the Federal Reserve backstopping $29 billion in Bear assets to help get the deal done.
- Fannie Mae CEO Daniel Mudd received $11.6 million in 2007. His counterpart at Freddie Mac, Richard Syron, brought in $18 million. In 2008, the federal government took over the firms' combined $5.5 trillion mortgage portfolio, with Herbert Allison to serve as Fannie CEO and David Moffett the new CEO at Freddie.
- Wachovia Corporation Chairman and CEO G. Kennedy Thompson received $21 million in 2007. He was succeeded by Robert Steel as CEO in July 2008. Steel is slated to get a $1 million salary with an opportunity for a $12 million bonus, according to CEO Watch. Wachovia merged with Wells Fargo in late 2008 in a deal notable for its shocking lack of government involvement.
- Seattle-based Washington Mutual was scheduled to pay its new CEO, Alan Fishman, a salary and incentive package worth more than $20 million through 2009 for taking the helm of the battered bank. It was seized by the FDIC in the fall of 2008, and in October was acquired by JPMorgan Chase.

These compensation packages for miserable performance were little more than a massive wealth transfer from shareholders to C-level executives. It just goes to show you: In the world of crony capitalism, failure pays extremely well.

Chapter 17

Year of the Bailout, Part I: The Notorious AIG

Panics do not destroy capital; they merely reveal the extent to which it has been previously destroyed by its betrayal into hopelessly unproductive works.

—John Stuart Mill, 1867

September 2008 started with a bang: Fannie Mae and Freddie Mac were put into conservatorship on September 7, 2008. The following week, Lehman Brothers filed the largest bankruptcy in American history.

The repercussions of setting Lehman Brothers adrift on an ice floe were much worse than either Hank Paulson or Ben Bernanke had contemplated. The complications caromed throughout the financial world, causing panics on trading desks. The cascade quickly froze credit markets.

The month was barely under way, and it was already a September to remember. The same weekend Lehman began its long dirt nap, Bank

of America hastily purchased Merrill Lynch for $50 billion. Before the month ended, the Treasury Department would guarantee money market funds; the Securities and Exchange Commission (SEC) would ban short selling; the Troubled Assets Relief Program (TARP) would be unveiled; Goldman Sachs and Morgan Stanley would convert to commercial banks, and Washington Mutual would be taken over by JPMorgan Chase.

Then there was American International Group (AIG).

Once Bear Stearns tumbled, traders' immediate reaction was to identify analogous risk: *Who else held similarly bad assets? What other firms had equivalent risk exposure?* When Bear fell, the obvious answer was Lehman Brothers. Once Lehman went down, the next in line was AIG.

In 2000, AIG had a $217 billion market cap and was the world's largest insurer.[1] It had numerous divisions, but was in essence two companies under one roof. One was an insurer, the other a structured products firm.

AIG-the-insurer was well known to the public. It was in the Dow Jones Industrial Average, a select club with only 30 members. Regulated by each state's insurance commission, well reserved for in case of loss, the company was a model corporate citizen. It was also a member of an even more select group, one of a mere handful of firms with a triple-A credit rating. The insurance company made consistent if unspectacular profits.

Hidden among the actuarial tables and staid regulated insurance services was an entirely different company: AIG's Financial Products (FP) division, or as it came to be known, AIGFP. It was essentially a giant hedge fund, and like private investment firms, its managers kept a fat 32 percent of the profits it generated. Not surprisingly, FP made outsized bets on derivatives. Even though the firm's CEO, Hank Greenberg, had negotiated the joint-venture agreement between AIG and Financial Products, aspects of the compensation arrangement troubled him. The *Washington Post* noted that FP received "its profits upfront, even if the transactions took 30 years to play out. AIG would be on the hook if something went wrong down the road."[2]

Not, however, the Financial Products team. They were compensated immediately.

Financial Products had begun 20 years earlier with a handful of junk-bond traders from Drexel Burnham Lambert. From 1987 on, the division grew in both size and importance to AIG. From just 13 employees in 1987, FP ballooned to over 400 by 2005.[3] "The unit's revenue rose to $3.26 billion in 2005 from $737 million in 1999," Gretchen Morgenson observed in the *New York Times*. "Operating income at the unit also grew, rising to 17.5 percent of AIG's overall operating income in 2005, compared with 4.2 percent in 1999."[4]

It turns out there was no great secret to making all that money. What AIGFP did was simple: It assumed an enormous amount of risk. As of September 2008, FP had exposed AIG to over $2.7 trillion worth of swap contracts via 50,000 trades made with over 2,000 counterparties.[5] In exchange for that massive potential liability, FP took in premiums of one-tenth of 1 percent of the exposure. By the time Nassim Nicholas Taleb's book *The Black Swan: The Impact of the Highly Improbable* was published in 2007, it was already far too late for FP's mathematicians and computer geeks. They were a (highly improbable) accident about to happen.

■ ■ ■

No matter how hard you try, there are too many people who simply refuse to learn the first law of economics: *There is no free lunch.* Amazingly, AIGFP actually had a product internally called "free money." By 1998, FP was looking at a new kind of derivative contract: the credit default swap (CDS). Set all of the complexity aside, and at its heart any CDS is merely a bet as to whether a company is going to default on its bonds. According to AIGFP's computer models, the odds were 99.85 percent against ever having to make payment on a CDS.

Tom Savage, the president of FP, summed up the free lunch mantra succinctly: "The models suggested that the risk was so remote that the fees were almost *free money*. Just put it on your books and enjoy."[6] And what of that 0.15 percent risk? According to the *Washington Post*, AIGFP figured "the U.S. economy would have to disintegrate into a full-blown depression to trigger the succession of events that would require Financial Products to cover defaults."[7]

You know the rest.

■ ■ ■

Back in the markets following Lehman's demise, it was shoot first, ask questions later. The chatter among traders was that AIG's huge derivatives book must have been festooned with Lehman default swaps. Short sellers backed up the truck. The death of Lehman would be the last straw for AIG.

But that turned out not to be the case. AIG had treated Lehman debt derivatives the way any smart oddsmaker would: It had taken offsetting trading positions that canceled each other out. As far as Lehman CDS exposure was concerned, AIG was essentially flat.[8]

The greater concern was AIGFP's massive derivatives book. My firm was short AIG's stock long before Lehman collapsed. Our downside bet was motivated by its $80 billion derivative exposure related to subprime mortgages.[9] This turned out to be a much larger problem for the insurance giant than Lehman's face-plant. As AIG's rapidly devaluing mortgage assets fell, their loss potential became unmanageable.[10] The weekend before it became the next bailout recipient, Bloomberg put a dollar figure on AIG's derivative risk: "$587 billion in contracts guaranteeing home loans, corporate bonds and other investments." The more housing fell, the further these contracts plunged in value.[11] The need for putting up billions in additional collateral was what would be the final straw.

Laughably, both Standard & Poor's and Moody's warned of potential downgrades to AIG's credit ratings the further these mortgage assets fell. The absurdity of the situation appeared to be lost on the rating agencies' analysts. FP's losses were directly related to subprime mortgage securities—the ones these same agencies had previously rated AAA. Ironically, nearly everyone who relied on Moody's or S&P's ratings to invest in mortgage-backed securities (MBSs) ended up getting downgraded themselves.

The Naughty Child Index

For those who have a hard time conceptualizing the differences between Bear Stearns, Lehman Brothers, and AIG, consider the Naughty Child Index.

Lehman Brothers is like the little kid pulling the tail of a dog. You know the kid is going to get hurt eventually, so no one is surprised when the dog turns around and bites him. But the kid hurts only himself and no one else. No one really cares that much.

Bear Stearns is the little pyromaniac—the kid who is always playing with matches. He could not only harm himself, but burn the house down and indeed burn down the entire neighborhood. The Fed steps in to protect not him, but the rest of the block.

AIG is the kid who accidentally stumbles into a biotech warfare lab and finds all these unlabeled vials. He heads out to the playground with a handful of them jammed into his pockets.

■ ■ ■

The decision to allow Lehman Brothers to go belly-up has been roundly criticized by many people as a mistake that cost AIG dearly. That turns out to be an incorrect conclusion, a classic correlation-versus-causation error. It is much more accurate to observe that the same factors that drove Lehman into bankruptcy also drove AIG to the brink.

It began with rates so low that everyone in the nation decided they wanted a house (and the bigger, the better). This included many people who could not afford one. So these folk applied for mortgages from a new kind of lender, one that operated with little regulation and even less supervision. These lenders were able to give loans to these people—bad credit risks, too little income, no equity—due to their unique business model. They could ignore traditional lending standards because they did not plan on holding these mortgages very long. They could specialize in higher-commission subprime loans because they were so-called lend-to-securitize originators. They made higher-risk loans, then flipped them to Wall Street firms, which repackaged them into complex mortgage-backed securities.

These same investment banks had too little capital and used too much leverage, but that didn't stop them from buying too much of this paper from each other. It didn't matter much anyway; since it was rated triple-A by S&P and Moody's, there wasn't anything to worry about. Underlying all of these transactions was the assumption that home prices in the United States never went down.

Oh, and this entire series of events took place at a time when the dominant political philosophy was that it was impossible for this to go wrong—the self-regulating markets, you understand, would see to that.

What bad could possibly come of that?

Plenty, as you might imagine. The teetering insurance giant lost $13 billion in the first half of 2008, but the real trouble was about to hit. It wouldn't be long before AIG would need a lifeline from Uncle Sam—or, as it turned out, Uncle Ben.

When Lehman went down, there was all manner of bad mortgages on its books. Dick Fuld, Lehman's CEO, had already given these assets a substantial haircut. Lehman was carrying its subprime mortgage securities on its books at 34 cents on the dollar, and its Alt-A holdings at 39 cents. Lehman had written down about two-thirds of their value.

AIG had not had its *come-to-Jesus* moment yet—not when it came to its housing derivatives, anyway. It had over $20 billion of subprime mortgages marked at 69 cents on the dollar and more than $24 billion in Alt-A securities valued at 67 cents on the dollar.[12]

Forget "mark to market." AIG was carrying these assets at values that were double what Lehman was. You can call that bookkeeping "mark to make-believe."

The Lehman bankruptcy occurred on September 15, 2008. Two days later, the Federal Reserve stepped in. AIG was effectively nationalized on September 17, 2008, with Uncle Sam picking up 79.9 percent of the former Dow component.

■ ■ ■

To anyone who believed in the doctrine of "too big to fail," AIG was a must save: almost a century old, with tentacles reaching everywhere. When the world's largest insurer collapses, it is every Fed chairman's nightmare. Hence, the massive effort policy makers have engaged in to keep the firm quasi-solvent as it is wound down. As of March 2009, more than a $173 billion in loans, lines of credit, direct capital injections, and purchases of stock have been made by the government to AIG. No private capital was willing to step up to 70 Pine Street in lower Manhattan.

Some cockeyed optimists believe this will be a profitable transaction for taxpayers, but I find that hard to believe. Not because AIG doesn't own some fine assets. Rather, because of the extent of the damage done by the structured finance half of the firm. At the end of Q1 2009, AIG announced a staggering $61.6 billion fourth-quarter loss. Even more AIG-related risk was moved to the Federal Reserve (a private institution), and to the Treasury—which is to say you and me.

Understanding how AIG went rogue and what happened since is critical, not only because it's one of the biggest single bailout beneficiaries, but because AIG encompasses all the elements that led us to the brink of financial catastrophe. These include:

- Massive use of leverage.
- Excessive risk taking.
- Abuse of lax regulation.
- Off-balance-sheet accounting.
- Inept risk management.
- Shortsighted (and greedy) incentives.
- Interconnectedness and complexity that screams "systemic risk" to any policy maker within earshot.

Once you can wrap your head around AIG, the mess that is Bailout Nation becomes much clearer. AIG was a fearsome combination of too many bad factors converging together. As is so often the case, these risk elements came together at precisely the wrong time.

"It's a terrible situation, but we're not doing this to bail out AIG or their shareholders," Bernanke declared. "We're doing this to protect our financial system and to avoid a much more severe crisis in our global economy."[13]

Bernanke's comments about AIG were eerily similar to what former Treasury Secretary Paulson said on September 7, 2008, about Fannie Mae and Freddie Mac: "Fannie Mae and Freddie Mac are so large and so interwoven in our financial system that a failure of either of them would cause great turmoil in our financial markets here at home and around the globe."[14]

As with Bernanke's statement about AIG, Paulson statement was accurate, concise—and wholly irrelevant. Neither man specified the real reason AIG, Fannie, and Freddie were nationalized: to protect their

counterparties and debt holders, including major financial firms and foreign institutions, such as Japan's central bank, China's sovereign wealth fund, and Saudi Arabia's holdings, among others.

Why? The short answer is that foreigners have been funding the profligate ways of the American consumer for decades. Once you begin to depend on the kindness of strangers, it's best not to make those strangers too angry. We in the United States have lived beyond our means for many years. We consume far more in goods and services than we produce, and that net deficit has to be funded somehow. The global economy has come to depend on the excessive consumerism of the United States. In return, we finance our massive deficit via the constant flow of capital from foreigners. As of June 30, 2008, that capital flow was $1.65 billion per day, every day.

How much kindness would these strangers offer if we allowed our paper that they held to default? Think about the $2 trillion in Treasury securities expected to be issued in 2009—who would be the takers?[15] How about any appetite for holding the $4.25 trillion of U.S. government and agency debt already owned by foreigners as of Q3 2008?

Forget going nuclear: These foreign treasury holders could all but destroy the U.S. economy by selling this debt on the open market at once. The only thing that prevents them is the same doctrine that precluded nuclear war during the Cold War: mutually assured destruction (MAD). They'd destroy themselves as well as us.

Why bail out overseas counterparties and debt holders? One gets the sense Uncle Sam had little choice in the matter.

Chapter 18

The Year of the Bailout, Part II: Too Big to Succeed?

No private enterprise should be allowed to think of itself as "too big to fail." No taxpayer bailouts should allow executives or stockholders to relax.

—William Safire[1]

The month of September 2008 finished the way it began, with a dire combination of volatility and panic. From Bear Stearns to Lehman to AIG, once the dominos began falling, there was no easy way to halt the progression. As traders sensed this, markets began accelerating to the downside; they got worse every week.

Into this cavalcade of collapse tripped the next major domino: Citigroup, the nation's biggest bank. Of the many players in our morality tale, the sprawling mess known as Citi was the oldest. It took two centuries of cautious risk management and careful growth to become the biggest and wealthiest of banks; it took less than five years for Citigroup to virtually collapse.

City Bank of New York was founded in 1812. A century later in 1919 it became the first U.S. bank with $1 billion in assets. Just as the stock market was topping before the 1929 crash, the National City Bank of New York (as it was known then) had become the largest commercial bank in the world.[2] This was a position the bank that would become Citigroup would frequently occupy for the rest of the twentieth century.

As a banking institution, National City introduced many firsts: traveler's checks, compound interest on savings accounts, unsecured personal loans to its depositors, negotiable certificates of deposit, consumer checking accounts with no minimum balance requirement, even the idea of a "Personal Loan Department" all originated with Citi. These innovations, combined with intelligent risk management, led to slow but steady growth.

When John Reed became CEO in 1984, he accelerated Citibank's growth-by-acquisition strategy. Under Reed, Citibank became the largest bank in the United States, the largest credit card issuer, and the largest charge card servicer in the world.[3] The bank eventually grew to 275,000 employees, with 200 million customer accounts in more than 100 countries.[4]

From antitrust laws to Glass-Steagall, Citi began running up against legal limits as to how much further it could bulk up. The law of big numbers caught up with Citi, and its growth strategy lost steam.

That was the case until 1998, the year of the $140 billion megamerger between Citicorp and Travelers Group. The deal was seen as a crowning moment for Citi Chairman and CEO Sandy Weil, widely regarded as the architect of the firm's "financial supermarket" strategy. When we trace where things really began to go awry for Citi, this is the tipping point. It marks the moment when Citi went from being a very large bank to becoming an unmanageable Goliath.

Ever since Continental Illinois had to be rescued by the Federal Deposit Insurance Corporation (FDIC) in the 1980s, the operative phrase concerning bailouts has been whether something is "too big to fail."[5] Following the Citi-Travelers merger, the question became whether Citigroup was *too big to succeed*. As we shall soon see, the answer was a resounding yes.

■ ■ ■

Among its peers, Citigroup was a unique banking creature. Not just because of its history and size; Citi was exceptional in that it had more to do with the repeal of the Glass-Steagall Act—the 1933 Depression-era legislation separating commercial and investment banks—than any other financial institution. Let's flash back for a moment to 1989 when Citi took what the *New York Times* called "another step in the battle to unshackle the banking industry from the restraints of the Glass-Steagall Act":

> In a securities deal announced last week, Citicorp, the bank holding company, said it was issuing $47 million of mortgage-backed securities through its Citibank Delaware Inc. subsidiary. The move was aimed at avoiding—some say circumventing—a Federal court order that would have blocked the New York–based Citibank from issuing securities backed by residential mortgages originated by the bank.[6]

In 1995, then Treasury secretary—and future Citigroup board member—Robert E. Rubin testified before the House Committee on Banking and Financial Services. He recommended that Congress should reform or repeal Glass-Steagall. This was an ongoing project for Rubin, and shortly after he retired as Treasury secretary, he would finally achieve victory. In late 1999, the Gramm-Leach-Bliley Act—or, as it was known in some circles, the "Citigroup Authorization Act"—repealed Glass-Steagall.[7]

The rules prohibiting bank holding companies from owning other financial firms were finally gone. "Today Congress voted to update the rules that have governed financial services since the Great Depression and replace them with a system for the 21st century," said then secretary of the Treasury and Rubin protégé Lawrence H. Summers. "This historic legislation will better enable American companies to compete in the new economy."[8]

Um, not exactly. While the repeal of Glass-Steagall was arguably not the primary cause of the 2008 credit crisis, it certainly made the outcome far worse. Had Glass-Steagall still been the law of the land, much of the damage banks like Citigroup are now suffering would have been minimized. They simply would not have been able to buy as many toxic assets as they did. Taxpayers are now spending trillions of dollars trying to get this toxic junk off the banks' balance sheets.

Despite his involvement in the debacle, Summers is now director of the National Economic Council for President Barack Obama. Talk about failing upward.

As to Rubin, the repeal of the 1933 Glass-Steagall Act was his "crowning achievement."[9] He stepped down as Treasury secretary in July 1999, and before the year was over, announced his new gig: chairman of Citi's executive committee. Annual compensation was $40 million.

Nice work if you can get it.

■ ■ ■

With the repeal of Glass-Steagall, the government pretty much repeated the same error it had made less than 20 years before. The cleanup for the savings and loan crisis—less a bailout than an insurance payout via the Federal Savings and Loan Insurance Corporation (FSLIC) guarantee to depositors—was about $200 billion.[10] The costs the next time would be far greater.

Citigroup was now a monster, bigger than any other Wall Street firm. A giant commercial bank, it also had bought investment bank Smith Barney and had added Salomon Brothers, the bond house Warren Buffett had rescued years earlier.

In the early 2000s, the men at the helm of Citi began urging a new and riskier strategy. Citigroup CEO Sandy Weil and influential director and senior adviser Robert Rubin sent the firm charging headlong into the booming housing market. The firm took up an even riskier expansion into derivatives, especially the issuance of collateralized debt obligations (CDOs). Citigroup was the seventh-ranked issuer by value of CDOs in 2000, cranking out $4 billion worth out of a world total of $68 billion. By 2007, Citi was the largest issuer of CDOs, responsible for more than 10 percent of all CDOs that year. It produced over $49 billion worth when the world's total production was $442 billion.[11]

The problem was not just what was done, but how. Citi charged recklessly into derivatives issuance. It did so in a slapdash and irresponsible way, with little oversight and even less risk management.

Citigroup CEO Chuck Prince—a lawyer who had been given the reins in 2003 by Sandy Weil in the wake of Eliot Spitzer's investigations into misconduct by the firm's sell-side research analysts—summed up the firm's attitude: "When the music stops, in terms of liquidity, things will be complicated. But as long as the music is playing, you've got to get up and dance. We're still dancing."

With that attitude from senior management, the day of reckoning was all but inevitable for the nation's biggest bank.

Writing in the *New York Times*, Eric Dash and Julie Creswell detailed how Citi was tripped up—by itself:

> For a time, Citigroup's megabank model paid off handsomely, as it rang up billions in earnings each quarter from credit cards, mortgages, merger advice and trading. But when Citigroup's trading machine began churning out billions of dollars in mortgage-related securities, it courted disaster. As it built up that business, it used accounting maneuvers to move billions of dollars of the troubled assets off its books, freeing capital so the bank could grow even larger. Because of pending accounting changes, Citigroup and other banks have been bringing those assets back in-house, raising concerns about a new round of potential losses.[12]

For most companies and corporate executives, Enron was a cautionary tale of what *not* to do. Citi learned the exact opposite lesson: It took its higher-risk assets and hid them away off its balance sheet in Enron-like side pockets. These are the now-infamous structured investment vehicles (SIVs) that Citi pioneered. The SIV market allowed firms to keep assets off their balance sheets as long as short-term credit was available to roll over the funds.

At their heart, the SIVs were a simple spread play. Citi made profits by selling short-term debt and using the proceeds to purchase much higher-yielding assets like bank debt, CDOs, and mortgage-backed securities.

And while this might be obvious, it bears repeating: *There is no free lunch*. Assets with higher yields are much riskier. Think of the yield as an inducement; all other things being equal, you can get people to purchase riskier assets only by bribing them with more money—or, in the case of these instruments, higher yield.

As any casino croupier will tell you, the longer shots usually lose. That is precisely what occurred with the Citi SIVs. As all that higher risk began to come up snake eyes, the entire model fell apart once credit markets froze and the value of the long-term debt began careening lower.

That was a major miscalculation by the SIV designers. As long as credit was readily available, the SIVs did the job of keeping the junky assets off balance sheets. What was apparently not contemplated was a simple cascade effect: The very same factors making these assets increasingly toxic would also impact credit availability. By 2007, house prices had fallen enough that foreclosures were increasing. In some regions of the country, mortgage delinquencies were spiking higher. Once short-term financing dried up, the company had no choice but to take the SIVs back in-house. As these billions in losing assets made their way back to Citi's balance sheet, its downward spiral began in earnest. By December 2007, Citi assumed $58 billion of debt to "rescue" $49 billion in assets.[13]

From July 2007 on, Citigroup's SIVs were festooned with $87 billion in toxic assets, mortgage-related CDOs, and other long-term paper. By the end of 2008, this had been pared down to $17.4 billion. It would take a monstrous government bailout to help Citi write down most of its SIVs.

In just about every imaginable way, Citigroup's wounds were self-inflicted. From the gargantuan company that was assembled, to the push for repeal of key regulations, to the way it ran daily operations—Citi was a classic case of "Be careful what you wish for."

■ ■ ■

As Citi was teetering at the height of the crisis, a joke was pinging across Wall Street trading desks: "I went to a Citibank ATM this morning, and it said 'insufficient funds.' I left wondering if it was them or me."

That was no joke for Ben Bernanke and Hank Paulson. The thought of the nation's biggest and best-known bank taking a face-plant gave nightmares to the country's top finance officials. There was simply no telling what sort of ripple effect that would have—on the economy, on investor confidence, on the markets. Let Citigroup suffer the fate of its own misjudgment? Who wanted to be the guy who let America's biggest bank go down on his watch? That's hardly a legacy to be proud of. It was time for some preemptive action. Shore up Citi, send a message, get ahead of the curve—for a change.

One might assume the government would cut a hard bargain with the biggest, stupidest, most irresponsible bank in the country, especially considering how self-inflicted Citibank's wounds were. Instead, the Treasury essentially handed over the keys to the kingdom for a mere song. For reasons still unknown, the banking behemoth got a helluva good deal.

Credit new CEO Vikram Pandit for scoring such a sweet deal. First, he sold his hedge fund, Old Lane, at an absurd price to the suckers running Citigroup. Then as Citi CEO, he pulled a coup, getting the government to absorb a huge slug of the bank's liabilities. The net liabilities for a full decade of terrible decision making were transferred from Citi's bond/shareholders to the taxpayers—a terrible deal for Uncle Sam, but a fantastic score for Citi.

Pandit's Coup

The deal is complex in its structure, but when all is said and done the government is on the hook for about $249 billion in toxic mortgage-backed assets in exchange for $27 billion in Citi preferred stock paying 8 percent. Terms of the $306 billion in loans:[14]

- The first $29 billion of losses from the portfolio will be absorbed by Citi entirely.
- The Treasury department will take 90 percent of the next $5 billion of losses, with Citi taking the rest.
- The FDIC will step in and take 90 percent of the next $10 billion of losses while Citi absorbs the balance.
- Losses beyond that will be taken by the Federal Reserve in the 90 percent government role.

In mathematical terms, the $306 billion in guarantees is $306 - 29 = 277 \times 0.90 = 249.3$ or $249.3 billion.

Citi took a $350 billion portfolio of assets—some junky, some not—and managed to get you and me to mark it at $306 billion. Never mind that other portfolios had taken 40 percent, 50 percent, even 65 percent haircuts. John Thain dumped some of Merrill Lynch's

assets—financing 75 percent of the sale to Lone Star—for what amounted to 5.47 percent on the dollar.[15]

How did Citi manage to suffer only an 11 percent haircut? Were its holdings that much superior to everyone else's? Or was the mere idea of a colossus like Citi collapsing that much more threatening to Bernanke and Paulson? Imagine what would have happened to the rest of the banking idiots holding the same crappy paper as Citi if they had to dump all those assets at once. Perhaps it is the Federal Reserve's desire to maintain confidence that was behind this obscene taxpayer-funded boondoggle.

Even worse, the Citigroup rescue deal is open-ended. The government has given Citi what is effectively an unlimited line of credit to carry these assets: no fire sales and no panics about marking to market.

■ ■ ■

While Citibank was slowly assembled over centuries, Bank of America, at least as we know it today, was a rather hastier creation. We'll skip its early but interesting history[16]—its roots go back to surviving the San Francisco earthquake in 1906, and it eventually created Visa—and fast-forward to the 1990s. That's when the firm began a 20-year acquisition spree that worked out somewhat less than ideally.[17]

Recall the original "too big to fail" doctrine that came about when Continental Illinois was rescued by the FDIC. Continental Illinois went into FDIC receivership in 1984, came out of receivership in 1991, and was ironically purchased by Bank of America in 1994.[18] Yes, Bank of America's track record of lousy acquisitions actually goes back decades.

It was in the 2000s when the management's acumen for killer acquisitions really shone:

- June 2005: Bank of America takes a 9 percent stake in China Construction Bank for $3 billion; China's market tops out in 2007 and then plummets 72 percent.
- January 2006: Bank of America acquires MBNA for $35 billion. The world's largest issuer of credit cards is taken over right before

the world's largest credit crunch occurs, and (whoops) just before the worst postwar recession begins.

- August 2007: Bank of America invests $2 billion in Countrywide Financial, the nation's biggest mortgage lender and loan servicer. It is a jumbo loser, dropping 57 percent in a few months' time.
- January 2008: Bank of America doubles down and announces a $4.1 billion acquisition of Countrywide. The timing is flawless, and the purchase is announced as the worst housing collapse in modern history is accelerating.
- September 2008: Bank of America pays $50 billion for Merrill Lynch, including Merrill's portfolio of toxic assets (along with some previously unannounced trading desk errors).

On February 20, 2009, Bank of America's stock hit a low of $2.53. Before the Countrywide acquisition went bust, Bank of America's stock was at $52 (October 2007).

As bad as those acquisitions may be, some were even worse than they appear. When Jamie Dimon, CEO of JPMorgan Chase, agreed to take Bear Stearns off the hands of the Federal Reserve, he managed to convince Ben Bernanke to backstop the transaction to the tune of $29 billion. It was a shrewd move, as Bear's subprime and derivative losses have accumulated not to JPMorgan, but to the Fed. Similarly, Dimon waited for the FDIC to put Washington Mutual through the receivership process before acquiring the thrift in late September 2008.

Bank of America CEO Ken Lewis was not quite as savvy. He failed to obtain a government guarantee at the time the Countrywide deal was done, and he vastly overpaid for Merrill Lynch's thundering herd. Without the Fed's explicit guarantee, he got precisely what a thundering herd of cattle leaves in its trail. He could have waited 24 hours for the firm to fail and then picked up assets for pennies on the dollar, as Barclays did with Lehman's asset management unit.

Instead, Lewis bought the firm lock, stock, and barrel—and the barrel was stuffed with nonperforming assets. You didn't need the benefit of hindsight to see this was a disaster waiting to happen.

■ ■ ■

And so September 2008 ended with the stock market in hasty retreat. The already weak stock market plummeted on September 29, 2008, when the House of Representatives rejected the $700 billion bank bailout. The Dow Jones Industrial Average suffered its largest-ever point decline in reaction, falling 777 points, or 7 percent. The S&P 500 took an 8.75 percent hit, its worst decline since the 1987 crash. The NASDAQ lost more than 9 percent, as Google fell below $400 for the first time in two years and Apple tumbled 18 percent. The following week (ending October 10) was the worst in the market's history. The Dow plummeted 20 percent to break under 8,000. One year earlier, the blue-chip index had been north of 14,000.

With markets in turmoil, it mattered little how the megabanks had been created—whether carefully assembled over two centuries or haphazardly over two decades. Their *past* was irrelevant, their *present* riddled with collapsing subprime derivatives, their *future* bleak. With too little capital and too much bad debt, management had no idea what to do.

Out of this maelstrom arose the Troubled Assets Relief Program (TARP): It was Treasury Secretary Hank Paulson's plan to save the big banks. Inject capital, buy the junk off their balance sheets, spend trillions in taxpayer monies to protect the banks from their own actions. Initial cost was $700 billion. By March 2009, the costs of this plan would rise to $2 trillion.

Why spend such an enormous amount of money rescuing such reckless, poorly run financial institutions? Perhaps the backgrounds of the men behind the bailouts are instructive.

The two Treasury secretaries of the bailout era each provide a cautionary tale for future presidents. Hank Paulson came to Treasury from Goldman Sachs. Over the course of three decades, he had risen through the ranks to become Goldie's CEO. His successor at Treasury is Timothy Geithner, the former president of the New York Federal Reserve Bank (or, as the credit trading desks call him, Turbo Tax Timmy). The New York Fed is a private Delaware corporation, owned in large part by its primary dealers—the 20 or so banks that purchase government Treasuries.[19] (Geithner is also a protégé of another Treasury secretary, Robert Rubin.) Paulson and Geithner are both creatures of the banking world (and both are Dartmouth alums). They didn't seem to make a smooth transition from being employed by private banks to being employed by the president, working for the public.

Verily, the danger of the sacred cow is revealed. Rather than pulling out all the stops to save the *banking system*, the Treasury secretary was flailing desperately to save the *banks*. All of Paulson's energies were misplaced. That should come as no surprise, given his (and later, Geithner's) background. They are bankers, first and foremost. As such, they do what most professionals do when their industry is under assault: protect the institutions. And if it happens to take ungodly amounts of taxpayer money to accomplish, so be it.

The obvious solution—put the insolvent banks into FDIC receivership, fire management, liquidate holdings, sell the assets off, wipe out shareholders, and pay the bondholders whatever was left over—was simply unthinkable.

This is reflected in Paulson's original TARP proposal. It was shockingly short on details, calling for a tremendous expansion of the Treasury secretary's powers, with no oversight or liability:[20]

> The Secretary will have the discretion, in consultation with the Chairman of the Federal Reserve, to purchase other assets, as deemed necessary to effectively stabilize financial markets. Removing troubled assets will begin to restore the strength of our financial system so it can again finance economic growth. The timing and scale of any purchases will be at the discretion of Treasury and its agents, subject to this total cap.[21]

For $700 billion, the country *literally* got a one-pager: no details, few specifics, and an enormous price tag. Whether it was hubris or something else entirely, it was emblematic of Paulson's response to the banking disaster. There was no consistency to the decision making, no discernible thought pattern. Every choice seemed to be on the fly, off the cuff, and by the seat of his pants. Hank Paulson's Treasury department was little more than an "adhocracy."

Is this anyway to run a Bailout Nation?

■ ■ ■

A modified version of the TARP, sweetened with pork to assure passage, flew though the House and Senate in early October. It was quickly signed into law by President Bush.[22] Treasury Secretary

Paulson called the government bailout plan "extensive, powerful and transformative."[23]

Shortly after the TARP was passed, Paulson added to its original intent—to use the funds to buy toxic debt from the banks—with a mishmash of programs and schemes, including:

- Injection of $250 billion into the nation's banks.
- The U.S. government would guarantee new debt issued by banks for three years; this was designed to prompt banks to resume lending to one another and to customers.
- The FDIC offered unlimited guarantees on bank deposits in accounts that don't bear interest—usually those of small businesses.
- The Treasury took preferred equity stakes in the nation's largest banks (Goldman Sachs, Morgan Stanley, JPMorgan Chase, Bank of America, Citigroup, Wells Fargo, Bank of New York Mellon, and State Street).

Beyond those massive expenditures, Uncle Sam was to "temporarily guarantee $1.5 trillion in new senior debt issued by banks, as well as insure $500 billion in deposits in noninterest-bearing accounts, mainly used by businesses."[24]

All told, the costs of the "bailout package came to $2.25 trillion, triple the size of the original $700 billion rescue package."[25]

Now for the punch line: It was all an elaborate ruse, a coverup of the fact that Citigroup was busted.

As of October 2008, the other banks, while somewhat worse for wear, neither wanted nor needed the capital injection. None of them were in the same trouble as Citi. Even Bank of America's problems via Merrill Lynch wouldn't become acute until December 2008. Washington Mutual, the most troubled on the list, had *already been put into FDIC receivership* the month before.[26] JPMorgan bought WaMu from the FDIC for under $2 billion, and Wachovia was swept up by Wells Fargo for about $15 billion. Thanks to a change in the tax law, Wells Fargo got to shelter $74 billion in profits from taxation. Instead of the FDIC absorbing a few billion in losses from Wachovia's bad assets, the taxpayers lost 35 times that amount.[27]

At the time of Paulson's gambit, only Citigroup was in dire straits. Paulson apparently feared what might happen if the rest of the world realized Citi was insolvent at the same moment the markets were cratering. Rather than stigmatize one reckless, poorly managed, overleveraged bank, the Treasury secretary decided to paint the entire banking sector with the same slanderous brush.

The solvent bankers chafed at the latest TARP plan. Paulson called a meeting of heads of the biggest banks—it was reminiscent of the Long-Term Capital Management meeting at the New York Federal Reserve, with a touch of *The Godfather* thrown in. The Treasury secretary presented his plan as an offer the banks could not refuse. "It was a take it or take it offer," said one person who was briefed on the meeting, speaking on condition of anonymity because the discussions were private. "Everyone knew there was only one answer."[28]

What a bizarre twist on the film's famous horse head scene: "Take this $25 billion or else."

■ ■ ■

As 2008 progressed, the usual snafus and foul-ups of any huge government program followed: The Federal Reserve refused to identify who were the recipients of nearly $2 trillion of emergency loans funded by taxpayers;[29] (Bloomberg sued the Fed under the U.S. Freedom of Information Act for a full disclosure).[30] A GAO report criticized the TARP's internal controls.[31]

But the real outrage began once financial institutions began using TARP bailout money to pay executive bonuses. The firms, of course, say it's different money and bonuses are key to retaining top employees. But if you need to come to the government for a handout, shouldn't your executives forgo a bonus? Or, as was the case in Europe, shouldn't the government make canceling bonuses a condition of getting aid?

Adding to the growing anger were new tax giveaways to bailout recipients. The Treasury department provided a tax break to banks involved in acquisitions that could amount to $140 billion. The *Washington Post* revealed the IRS quietly made changes to the tax code issued on September 30, while Congress was debating the $700 billion TARP bill.[32]

All the while, Citi and Bank of America executives kept returning for more handouts. They may not have been very good at managing risk, but they sure were quick studies. After the first round of TARP

money, it became apparent that their capital-raising options were limited. Following the first $25 billion in TARP cash, Citi went back for another $20 billion, and then the big one—$250 billion in full faith and credit from the U.S. government guaranteeing its toxic assets. Bank of America—a.k.a. "Bank owned by America"— also came calling thrice: $25 billion, $20 billion, and then $300 billion in asset guarantees. The winner (and still champ) for multiple trips to handout junction remains AIG; it took four trips to wrangle a total of $173 billion of bailout green.

Don't you think they earned their bonuses for *that*?

■ ■ ■

2009 was a new year . . . with a new president, a new Treasury secretary, and a new bailout plan. And as this book was going to press, Treasury Secretary Tim Geithner's long-awaited successor to TARP was finally out. He chose to extend and replace the TARP with PPIP—a Public-Private Investment Program. Administered by the FDIC, the program's focus is to move toxic assets—typically CDOs, mortgage-backed securities, and commercial real estate loans—off of the books of troubled banks.

The PPIP has two unique twists. The first is the private-partnership aspect of it. The FDIC will lend qualified funds up to 7 times leverage to buy bank holdings. These funds need only put up $12 to purchase $84 worth of distressed assets via an auction. The United States is apparently going to use more leverage to work its way out of a situation created by using too much leverage. That seems a bit like trying to drink yourself sober.

The second twist is the end run on Congress that the PPIP manages. Since it is administered by the FDIC and these are technically secured loans, no congressional approval is required.[33]

Treasury has come up with prior clever ways to backdoor Congress. As Felix Salmon wrote on the *New York Times* Op-Ed page:

> It's not the first time that Treasury has magicked billions of dollars from some hidden back pocket, just to avoid having to ask Congress for the money. In 1995, with Robert Rubin recently installed as Treasury secretary, Lawrence Summers, the deputy secretary, along with Tim

> Geithner, a deputy assistant secretary, wanted to bail out Mexico in the face of Congressional opposition. They found something called the Exchange Stabilization Fund, originally intended to stabilize the value of the dollar on world currency markets, and managed to repurpose it for another use entirely.[34]

Just what the nation needs—another page from the playbook of Robert Rubin. Meet the new boss . . . same as the old boss.

■ ■ ■

Who's next? Ironically, this part of the chapter has been rewritten six times. Originally, it was about Fannie Mae, but then I had to switch it to Lehman Brothers, then AIG, then General Motors, now Citi.

That was the last straw, for I began to wonder if it wasn't me who was damning these companies by even thinking about writing them up.

When the Detroit bailout occurred, I decided to swear off writing anything titled "Who's Next?" Besides, it was no longer a valid viewpoint. Perhaps a more appropriate title might be "Who's Left?" Rather than guess who is next, and thereby destroy that poor firm, I'd suggest you turn the page. Let's see how we got into this jam in the first place.

INTERMEZZO

Idiots Fiddle While Rome Burns

Sometimes I wonder whether the world is being run by smart people who are putting us on, or by imbeciles who really mean it.

—Mark Twain

Over the past two years of bailouts, the collection of clueless dolts, political hacks, and—oh, let's just be blunt and call them what they are—total idiots continues to expand into an ever wider circle.

While the republic burns due to the unsavory combination of incompetence, radical ideology, and casino capitalism, the clowns seem ever more determined to avoid any and all personal responsibility for the damage they have wrought. Instead, they flail about blindly, blaming everything and everyone—except their own horrific negligence.

This is financial incompetence writ on a scale far grander than anything seen for centuries.

As a nation, our institutions have failed us: Under Alan Greenspan, the Federal Reserve slept through the most reckless and irresponsible expansion of bank lending in history for reasons of ideological purity. As recently as March 2009 Greenspan actually contributed a *Wall Street Journal* op-ed renouncing any blame for the housing bubble.[35] In addition to his unprecedented monetary policy, his nonfeasance in failing to perform the Fed's regulatory role reached the point of criminal negligence long ago. History will be unkind to the Maestro.

As a nation, we have a choice to make: Either we place some reasonable regulations upon the banks and investment houses or we allow the vagaries of the free markets to punish those who trade with, or place their assets in, the wrong institutions.

If the taxpayers are ultimately on the hook for the losses of the financial sector, do they not have the right to insist that the riskiest of behaviors be restricted? If a business model is so inherently flawed that it causes a worldwide economic collapse, shouldn't the behavior that contributes to that collapse be prevented?

There is no middle ground; it is an either-or choice. But for God's sake, we cannot suffer the worst of both worlds—we cannot allow banks the freedom to make horrific but preventable mistakes (i.e., lending money to those who can't possibly hope to pay it back), but then expect the taxpayers to foot a multitrillion-dollar bill when they fail. It is not the responsibility of the taxpayer to act as guarantor to every counterparty, warrant all hedge funds' trades, and insure every Wall Street transaction.

That's not capitalism, it's not socialism, it's not regulation, and it sure as hell isn't what free markets are. Our language is insufficient to describe this hodgepodge system, this random patchwork of casino capitalism, cronyism, and politics as usual. *Ideological idiocy* is the only phrase I can muster that has any resonance with the daily insanity.

We cannot have privatized profits and socialized risks.

We have entered into a fit of Orwellian madness: American capitalists, long the globe's leading advocates for free markets, have become socialists. Halfway around the world, Chinese Communists have picked up the baton and are moving rapidly toward a form of capitalism. Ironically, it is the once-Communist nations—China and Russia—that hold most of Fannie's and Freddie's damaged paper.

Hey, comrades, who's selling the rope to whom?

Perhaps the government's rescue of "Phony and Fraudy," AIG, Bank of America, Citigroup, et al. is not so much a bailout of corporate America as it is a desperate attempt to stay in the good graces of our friendly global bankers. As the world's largest debtor nation, we have come to depend on the kindness of strangers—be they the Japanese, Europeans, oil-rich Gulf states, or even former Communists.

Back in the United States, something beyond cognitive dissonance is occurring—a full-blown case of dementia is unfolding in the public sphere. When this era of excess and absurdity is looked back upon in the future, the question I expect to be asked most is not why many of these people weren't jailed for their financial felonies. Rather, I expect future historians to wonder why so many of these folk weren't heavily medicated and placed in protective custody, for the only rational

explanation for their statements and behaviors is that they have gone so far round the bend as to be completely and totally insane.

Massively overleveraged companies? Blame short sellers.

Wildly undercapitalized financial firms? Blame rumors.

Heinously poor corporate management? Blame the messenger.

IndyMac goes belly-up, having lost $900 million in 2008 alone. Its shares fell 87 percent in 2007 and then its value dropped (on top of the prior year's utter collapse) another 95 percent in 2008. The stock was trading on the pink sheets for under a nickel as of mid-December.

Some estimates of the total bad loans made by IndyMac are in the neighborhood of $30 billion—and the head of the Office of Thrift Supervision (OTS) blames a senator who is investigating how much of the FDIC's $53 billion fund the rescue is going to eat up! The towering incompetence of OTS is incomprehensible, but it is its colossal gall that is truly stupefying.

Perhaps someone is running around Washington, D.C., with a ball-peen hammer, whacking senior government officials on their skulls. Blunt head trauma is a better explanation for the absurdities proffered than anything else we have heard. Books will be written about this period of time, and our descendants will wonder in awe as to how this was allowed to happen. *Tulip mania's got nothing on us!*

It's not just the total dollar value of the losses that has exceeded all other global fits of financial madness combined; rather, it's how so many warning signs were so blithely ignored by so many and for so long. Future authors and historians will wonder: *What was wrong with these people?* Did the antibiotics in the food supply drive them mad? Did the high-fructose corn syrup compromise their ability to think? Was it some form of viral plague? 'Roid rage? What else could have created such mass delusion among not just the populace, but their leadership and institutions? Once-proud investment houses have been replaced with casinos. Concepts such as risk management and capital preservation have become passé. Myths pass for wisdom, heuristics for knowledge.

Adam Smith would not know whether to weep or retch were he alive to see this today.

Part V

POST-BAILOUT NATION

Source: By permission of John Sherffius and Creators Syndicate, Inc.

Chapter 19

Casting Blame

The human mind cannot grasp the causes of phenomena in the aggregate. But the need to find these causes is inherent in man's soul. And the human intellect, without investigating the multiplicity and complexity of the conditions of phenomena, any one of which taken separately may seem to be the cause, snatches at the first, the most intelligible approximation to a cause, and says: "This is the cause!"

—Leo Tolstoy
War and Peace
Book IV, Part 2, Chapter 1, first paragraph

Now we come to what should be the most satisfying part of our exercise: assessing blame and assigning responsibility to all of the ne'er-do-wells who got us into this mess.

Fans of schadenfreude, brace yourselves: There are so many players responsible for the housing boom and bust, the credit crisis, and the financial collapse that it is difficult to blame any one person—it is a broadly shared culpability.

There are many who were rooting for the blame to be assessed to a given political party, a particular player, or a specific act of malfeasance. In reality, the situation is far more complex. The responsibility

is widespread, and there is plenty of shared blame. Joseph Stiglitz, the Nobel Prize–winning professor of economics at Columbia University, called it a "system failure"—not merely one bad decision, but a cascade of many decisions that produced tragic results.[1]

The recklessness and incompetence seemed to be a team effort. With no single villain and so much blame to go around, I fear missing some person or event that significantly contributed to the mess now enveloping the global economy.

That does not mean we cannot attempt to highlight those whose contributions have disproportionately led to the final catastrophe. After exhaustively reviewing this debacle, I assess responsibility in order of culpability as follows:

- Federal Reserve Chairman Alan Greenspan
- The Federal Reserve (in its role of setting monetary policy)
- Senator Phil Gramm
- Moody's Investors Service, Standard & Poor's, and Fitch Ratings (rating agencies)
- The Securities and Exchange Commission (SEC)
- Mortgage originators and lending banks
- Congress
- The Federal Reserve again (in its role as bank regulator)
- Borrowers and home buyers
- The five biggest Wall Street firms (Bear Stearns, Lehman Brothers, Merrill Lynch, Morgan Stanley, and Goldman Sachs) and their CEOs
- President George W. Bush
- Presidents Bill Clinton and Ronald Reagan
- Treasury Secretary Henry Paulson
- Treasury Secretaries Robert Rubin and Lawrence Summers
- FOMC Chief Ben Bernanke
- Mortgage brokers
- Appraisers (the dishonest ones)
- Collateralized debt obligation (CDO) managers (who produced the junk)
- Institutional investors (pensions, insurance firms, banks, etc.) for buying the junk

- Office of the Comptroller of the Currency (OCC); Office of Thrift Supervision (OTS)
- State regulatory agencies
- Structured investment vehicles (SIVs)/hedge funds for buying the junk

Let's look at the most significant players.

■ ■ ■

Many of the monetary and regulatory errors that directly led to the present crisis are attributable to the man they once called the Maestro. Under the guidance of Alan Greenspan, the Federal Reserve abused monetary policy, ignored critical lending issues, and failed to regulate new and irresponsible banking products.

Several of Greenspan's policies proved to be wildly misguided: the regular interventions to protect asset prices and bail out investors, the irresponsibly low rates after the post-2000 crash, and his nonfeasance in supervising lending. Most of all, it was his deeply held philosophical conviction that all regulations are bad, and are to be avoided at all cost. *We now know what that cost is, and it's astronomical.*

Alan Greenspan had spent his years at the Fed operating under an enormous philosophical misconception, as the former Fed chairman admitted in testimony before Congress on October 22, 2008: "I made a mistake in presuming that the self-interest of organizations, specifically banks and others, was such as that they were capable of protecting their own shareholders."[2]

Based on Greenspan's worldview, the events of the present crisis and many others that occurred over the past decade were impossible, given that the so-called wisdom of the free markets would prevent them. Only they did occur. Greenspan's faith was wildly misplaced, and the taxpayers are that much poorer for it. If we have to put our finger on the single intellectual flaw that underlies the housing collapse, the credit crisis, the economic recession, and the problems with toxic paper, it would be a misplaced belief that markets could self-regulate. One is reminded of the

Benjamin Disraeli quote: "He was distinguished for ignorance; for he had only one idea, and that was wrong."[3]

Given how enamored Greenspan was of free markets, it is increasingly difficult to reconcile many of the actions he undertook. The very concept of the champion of free markets repeatedly intervening in their inner workings is a contradiction of enormous proportions. It is a catch-22 worthy of Joseph Heller.

It is beyond my capacity to decipher how Greenspan justified his internal conflicts, but at least he later admitted that his primary philosophy "had a flaw." Unfortunately, his flawed economic belief system colored nearly every policy he enacted as Federal Reserve chairman. Most of today's crises trace their roots in part to his policies.

■ ■ ■

In 1836, Mayer Rothschild wrote, "Give me control of a nation's money, and I care not who makes the laws." If only that prescient warning had been heeded by the Federal Reserve. It might also serve as an admonition for Ben Bernanke, the current Fed chief.

The Greenspan era lasted 20 years (1987 to 2006). The Federal Open Market Committee (FOMC) must take responsibility for following him so obsequiously, especially in the latter years of his reign. Exceptions include Edward Gramlich, whose timely warnings about subprime and early concern with predatory lending were on target and ignored. So, too, William Poole deserves credit for his many cautionary warnings about the government-sponsored enterprises (GSEs) Fannie Mae and Freddie Mac. To our chagrin, neither man was paid much heed by Greenspan or the FOMC.

The single biggest fault found within the Fed is its inability to fulfill its responsibilities as bank regulator. The Fed not only failed to supervise lending institutions, but it also ignored the most significant shift in lending standards in the history of human finance. The results were disastrous.

The Fed, as an institution, failed the nation. It directly encouraged mass speculation. It failed to supervise innovative new forms of lending. The inflationary spiral that sent oil soaring from $16 in 2001 to $147 per barrel seven years later, along with other commodity and food prices, is attributable to its radical rate-cutting regime.

The current chairman, Ben Bernanke, deserves partial blame for the Fed's slumber during this inflationary spike. A renowned student of the Great Depression, it was then Fed Governor Bernanke who raised warning flags about *deflation* after the tech bubble burst. He provided the framework and intellectual cover for Greenspan's ultra-easy money circa 2001 to 2003.

As Fed chair, Bernanke was terribly slow to realize the subprime mortgage crisis was anything but "contained." By the time he did awaken to the crisis in August 2007, he responded with a series of programs that pushed the envelope of legality, dramatically expanded the Fed's balance sheet, and put the central bank's credibility at risk.

Of all the institutions that played a part in the current crisis, none had a more prominent role than the Federal Reserve.

■ ■ ■

The first telegraph message ever sent, "What hath God wrought," reflected Samuel Morse's deep concern for the repercussions of his own actions. If only Phil Gramm were so similarly introspective.

While Congress deserves much blame for the crisis, no one elected official looms larger in our drama than Gramm. He was the senator behind the Commodity Futures Modernization Act of 2000 (CFMA), and spearheaded the repeal of Glass-Steagall. The legislation that overturned it bears his name (Gramm-Leach-Bliley Act). Both legislative acts were WMDs—weapons of monetary destruction. These time bombs eventually led to mass financial destruction.

Barbara Roper, director of investor protection for the Consumer Federation of America, said: "Since the financial meltdown, people have been asking, 'Where was Congress? Why didn't they see this coming? Why didn't they provide better oversight?'" We now know the answer is that members of Congress were too busy pursuing a radical deregulatory agenda. Instead of protecting investors and defending the overall economic system, their misplaced concern was how to make life easier for Wall Street.

During the late-1990s era of deregulatory dogma, the GOP controlled the House and Senate, and Gramm was the point man on issues of deregulation. The Texas Republican was aided in his deregulatory quest in part by Senator Chuck Schumer, a New York Democrat. Perhaps Schumer represented the interests of New York's Wall Street too well.

To this day, Gramm *still* claims deregulation had no impact on the housing collapse or the credit crisis. The exempting of derivatives from all regulation—including state insurance supervision, reserve requirements, or clearing information—was not at all related to the eventual problems, according to Gramm. He remains unrepentant as to his impact. Placing any blame on deregulation was simply "an emerging myth," the retired Texas senator has said. Deregulation "played virtually no role" in the economic turmoil engulfing the globe, Gramm claimed in November 2008.[4]

What shameless nonsense. You will not come across a greater example of cognitive dissonance in your lifetime. Gramm's inability to recognize the results of his legislative handiwork is a function of a flawed mind protecting itself from the harsh reality. The inconsistency of his deeply held philosophy and the results thereof are logically incomprehensible to Gramm's conflicted brain. If he were ever to admit the truth, he would likely go stark, raving mad.

I'll give Alan Greenspan this much credit: At least he has come clean about the "flaw" in his philosophy. Gramm, by contrast, remains committed to his tainted brand of unregulated, free-market absolutism. Of all the players in the tragic drama that has unfolded, he alone remains unrepentant. Gramm is Bailout Nation's most intellectually bankrupt citizen. Like Greenspan, Gramm had only one idea; unlike Greenspan, he had no comprehension it was wrong.

■ ■ ■

From Ronald Reagan to George W. Bush, each president of the past 25 years bears some responsibility for contributing to the belief that we can let markets govern themselves.

Of the four, President George W. Bush has the greatest culpability—not because this crisis happened on his watch, though that should be reason enough. The more significant basis of his culpability is that he shared Greenspan's and Gramm's radical belief system—that markets could police themselves, that all regulation (indeed, most government) was inherently bad. This philosophy colored all of Bush's appointments to key supervisory positions, as well as his legislative agenda.

Former Presidents Clinton, George H.W. Bush, and Reagan each have some responsibility, but far less. The first President Bush is the least culpable. Reagan chose not to reappoint Fed Chair Paul Volcker, replacing him with Alan Greenspan. Regardless of other actions, this forever taints the legacy of the Gipper. However, in many ways, Ronald Reagan is the intellectual father to what became the radical deregulatory movement. As the *Washington Post* noted, "Ronald Reagan's unwavering belief in free markets—and his distaste for regulation that put hurdles in the way of entrepreneurs—had steadily spread through the government. 'The United States believes the greatest contribution we can make to world prosperity is the continued advocacy of the magic of the marketplace, "Reagan told a U.N. audience'" in 1986.

While some partisans have tried to paint the crisis as a purely Republican debacle, history informs us otherwise. Yes, the GOP did control Congress from 1994 to 2006. However, President Clinton, a Democrat, bears a significant responsibility also. He and his Treasury secretaries, Robert Rubin and Lawrence Summers, all bought into the deregulatory mantra. Clinton, Rubin, and Summers are right there with W. in the hierarchy of proximate causes of the debacle.

Until recently, Rubin has escaped much blame for both supporting Glass-Steagall's repeal as Treasury secretary and his participation in Citigroup's failure as a long-standing board member.[5] Citibank was one of the main proponents of repealing Glass-Steagall, and Rubin joined the bank's board shortly after leaving Treasury in 1999—quite an unsavory turn of events.[6]

At Treasury, Rubin strongly supported the Commodity Futures Modernization Act. He actively opposed the concerns of Brooksley Born, then head of the Commodity Futures Trading Commission. In 1997, Born was raising alarms to Congress about unregulated trading in derivatives, such as credit default swaps (CDSs).[7] Unregulated derivatives could "threaten our regulated markets or, indeed, our economy without any Federal agency knowing about it," she testified. Born called for a variety of fixes—now being enacted after the horse is out of the

barn—including greater transparency, disclosure of trades through a central clearing firm, and required reserves against losses. Born was shouted down by the likes of Greenspan, Rubin, and Summers.

President Clinton oversaw the passage of utterly ruinous legislation. He signed both the damaging Gramm-Leach-Bliley Act repealing Glass-Steagall and the odious Commodity Futures Modernization Act exempting derivatives from regulation. They may each have been sponsored by Senator Gramm, but they were both signed into law by President Clinton. He does not deserve the free pass for his misguided actions.

But it was George W. Bush's appointments who chanted the "laissez-faire, free markets reign supreme" mantra the loudest. The SEC chairs he appointed were terrible, and many of his other appointments—Office of Thrift Supervision, Federal Reserve, Treasury secretary, and other key regulatory roles—were similarly ill-advised.

Question: What do you get when a president who doesn't believe in government appoints those who share this philosophy to key regulatory and supervisory roles?

Answer: Neither regulation nor supervision.

Missed opportunities seem to be a hallmark of the Bush presidency: As the various crises unfolded, there were key choke points where the damage could have been contained. None were acted upon until after the crisis had fully flowered.

When appraisers petitioned the White House in 2001, complaining of inflated home appraisals filed by corrupt home inspectors, they were rebuffed. When state banking regulators recognized signs of lending fraud early on, their attempts to curtail it were prevented by Bush. The White House asserted that it was the federal agencies—and not the states—that had jurisdiction over federally chartered banks. That's a fine argument to make, until those federal agencies recognized lending problems and began proposing rules to curtail them on their own. They, too, were rebuffed by the White House—not state agencies, but the federal agencies the White House claimed had exclusive jurisdiction.

The Associated Press (AP) summed up why the very government regulators assigned to prevent abuse failed so miserably to do so: "The administration's blind eye to the impending crisis is emblematic of its governing philosophy, which trusted market forces and discounted the value of government intervention in the economy. Its belief ironically has ushered in the most massive government intervention since the 1930s."[8]

Let's get specific as to the sort of warnings the White House ignored: Bank regulators had proposed new guidelines for writing risky loans in 2005. These were basic administrative rules; had they been enacted, the worst of the housing and credit crisis might have been avoided. The Bush administration backed away from proposed crackdowns on the subprime, no-money down, interest-only mortgages that were critical contributors to the credit and housing crisis.

According to the AP, pressure from banks (many of which have since failed) was the prime reason:

> Bowing to aggressive lobbying—along with assurances from banks that the troubled mortgages were OK—regulators delayed action for nearly one year. By the time new rules were released late in 2006, the toughest of the proposed provisions were gone and the meltdown was under way. "These mortgages have been considered more safe and sound for portfolio lenders than many fixed-rate mortgages," David Schneider, home loan president of Washington Mutual, told federal regulators in early 2006. Two years later, WaMu became the largest bank failure in U.S. history.[9]

The list of banks that lobbied most aggressively against the proposed rules reads like a who's who of bankruptcy and FDIC conservatorship, including IndyMac, Countrywide Financial, Washington Mutual, Lehman Brothers, and Downey Savings.

What was so damning was that these proposals were all stripped from the final administrative rules by the Bush White House. None required congressional approval; they did not even require the president's signature. The proposals that were removed from the administrative rules were:

- Banks would have to increase efforts to verify that home buyers actually held jobs.
- Lenders would have to assess whether the borrower could afford the house.
- Regulators would inform bankers that exotic mortgages were often inappropriate for buyers with bad credit.
- Banks that purchased mortgages from brokers also would need to verify that buyers could afford their homes.
- Regulators proposed a cap on risky mortgages so a string of defaults wouldn't be crippling.

- Banks that bundled and sold mortgages would be told to be sure investors knew exactly what they were buying.
- Regulators urged banks to help buyers make responsible decisions and clearly advise them that interest rates might rise.
- Big increases in payments would need to be clearly disclosed, including how much more a loan would cost once it reset.

The administration also ignored remarkably prescient warnings that foretold the financial meltdown, according to an AP review of regulatory documents.

Similarly, the Office of the Comptroller of the Currency (OCC) "played a key role in the mortgage meltdown, both by actively blocking state consumer protection laws through the expansion of federal preemption, and by simultaneously failing to adequately monitor the nationally-chartered lending institutions under its purview," as Eric Stein, senior vice president of the Center for Responsible Lending, testified in October 2008 at a Senate hearing entitled "Turmoil in the U.S. Credit Markets: The Genesis of the Current Economic Crisis."[10]

The OCC bowed to pressure from National City and its subprime lending subsidiary First Franklin Financial in preempting "comprehensive mortgage reform legislation" passed by the state of Georgia, Stein testified.[11] There are other examples of the OCC thwarting legislation that could have prevented some of the most irresponsible bank loans, including predatory lending.

Despite his professed belief in free markets over government intervention, George W. Bush ended up overseeing the greatest nationalization of private industry the United States has ever had. The irony of the Bush administration's bailout fever was captured by Allan Mendelowitz, who observed: "The Bush administration, which took office as social conservatives, is now leaving as conservative socialists."[12]

■ ■ ■

Over the course of two terms, Bush appointed three misfit SEC chairmen, each ill-suited for the position. They formed a veritable parade of poor regulators, none right for the agency's role of being the investors' advocate.

Bush's first SEC appointment, Harvey Pitt, was a securities industry defense attorney. To say he was wholly unsuited to the position is to understate the case. Instead of representing the interests of investors, Pitt was a well-known industry lapdog. Pitt pledged a "kinder and gentler" SEC in the midst of a huge run of corporate misfeasance. He was the precise opposite of what was needed.

Even worse, in an era of corporate accounting scandals, Pitt had close ties with the accounting industry. As a Wall Street lawyer, Pitt had "recommended that clients destroy sensitive documents before they could be used against them—advice that seemed to find echoes in the SEC's investigations into Enron and its shredder-happy auditor, Arthur Andersen."[13] Pitt had to recuse himself from many of the SEC's votes, as they were frequently about the clients he had represented as a defense attorney. For inexplicable reasons, during *active* SEC investigations, Pitt would meet with the heads of companies under review.[14]

It should come as no surprise that Pitt's chairmanship demoralized the agency. To investor advocacy groups, having Pitt as SEC chief was "like naming Osama bin Laden to run the Office of Homeland Security."[15]

By July 2002, Senator John McCain was calling for Pitt's resignation.[16] Pitt resigned following a series of scandals.

The next SEC chairman Bush appointed was William Donaldson, the former chairman of the New York Stock Exchange (NYSE). He was also the "D" in DLJ (Donaldson, Lufkin & Jenrette), which eventually was acquired by Credit Suisse.

Donaldson was called upon to lend some gravitas to the SEC after Pitt's resignation. Given the former NYSE chairman's close ties to big Wall Street firms, we shouldn't be surprised at what came next. During Donaldson's watch, the net capital rule for the five biggest investment banks was exempted in 2004. Instead of being limited to 12 to 1 leverage, banks were allowed to lever up 30, 35, and even 40 to 1 after the waiver. It isn't glib to say the financial meltdown was three times as bad as it might have been but for Donaldson's SEC granting this waiver.

Then there is Christopher Cox, the third Bush SEC chair. He shared Greenspan's and Gramm's hostility to regulations. "Cox's long-standing support of a deregulated market and friendliness to business made him the wrong SEC chairman at the wrong time."[17]

In July 2007, Cox eliminated the so-called uptick rule, removing a modest restraint on shorting just as the credit crunch was getting started. The market peaked a few months later. When it began heading south, there was no uptick rule in place to prevent indiscriminate short selling and piling on. Even if only for psychological reasons, removing the uptick rule, which was put in place in the aftermath of the 1929 crash, turned out to be not very smart.

Then in September 2008, with the crisis in full flower, Cox made shorting financial stocks illegal. Apparently, he was unaware that fierce market sell-offs often end with short sellers covering their positions, locking in profits on their bearish bets. With short sellers out of the market, the downturn became even fiercer. From the market highs of October 2007, the S&P 500 and the Dow Jones Industrial Average were cut in half in 12 months. Much of the damage came *after* the no-shorting rule went into effect.

As the GOP presidential candidate in 2008, Senator John McCain called for Cox's resignation.

And as this book went to press, the latest SEC black eye was reaching a milestone: Bernie Madoff had finally been sent to prison after pleading guilty to stealing as much as $50 billion in investor assets in a giant Ponzi scheme. Madoff had "made off" with his clients' monies for several years, despite many warnings to the SEC.

Numerous people, including hedge fund manager Doug Kass and options strategist Harry Markopolos, had warned years before that the ability to provide such unusually smooth returns with so little volatility was more likely the result of fraud than investing acumen.[18]

Markopolos, particularly, made unveiling Madoff's fraud his passion. He sent numerous anonymous letters to the SEC and met with officials of the SEC's Boston office in 2001 to lay out his concerns, the *Wall Street Journal* reported. Around the same time, "*Barron's* and hedge-fund trade publication *MarHedge* suggested Madoff was front running for favored clients."[19]

Despite frequent tips, which led to at least eight examinations of Madoff's firm in 16 years by the SEC and other regulators, the fraud was discovered only after Madoff, faced with redemptions, confessed that the firm was nearly bankrupt.

Testifying before Congress on February 4, 2009, Markopolos blistered the SEC and other financial regulators for their "abject failure" to stop Madoff, "even when a multi-billion-dollar case [was] handed to them on a silver platter."[20]

Soon after Madoff's confession, the SEC was rocked by yet another major scandal surrounding Stanford Financial Group, whose namesake founder, Sir Allen Stanford, stands accused of overseeing an $8 billion fraud. As of March 2009, Stanford has refused to cooperate in the government's investigation of what the SEC alleges is fraud "of a shocking magnitude."[21]

What isn't shocking to anyone is that the SEC missed it for years.

■ ■ ■

Next up in our cavalcade of criticism: the mortgage brokers and originators. What did federal bank regulators have to say about this paradigm shift? Very little, even though the FBI warned of an "epidemic" of mortgage fraud in 2004.[22]

The lightly regulated industry was filled with aggressive salespeople who ruthlessly found ways to generate the highest commissions. The mortgage originations that were likely to have the highest vig were the 2/28 adjustable-rate mortgages (ARMs)—loans with cheap teaser rates that lasted for two years and then reset to a much higher, market-based rate for the rest of the 30-year term. These now-notorious loans allowed brokers to sell the highest dollar loan possible for the lowest monthly payment to the least qualified borrowers.

Much of the mortgage industry embraced these irresponsible, high-default products. All the parties involved knew the high likelihood of foreclosures, as detailed in Chapter 10. They abdicated traditional lending standards because the defaults would take place after the mortgages were off their hands. Indeed, these companies happily played dumb, so long as the loan didn't default within 90 days. By month four, it was someone else's headache, as far as the originator was concerned. Now it has become everyone's worry.

That hundreds of these firms have gone bankrupt is cold comfort to the rest of us.

■ ■ ■

Regardless of how low rates got, the fact remains that many borrowers took out mortgages regardless of their own ability to repay the monthly principle and interest. This was simply reckless behavior, and should be recognized as such. Innumeracy is no excuse.

Ultimately, banks have a fiduciary responsibility to their shareholders and depositors to lend money only to qualified borrowers. Hence, they have a greater liability in the lending crisis. This is especially true of the "lend to securitize" originators who *knew they would be causing future foreclosures.*

However, the lenders' irresponsible behavior does not exonerate those people who failed to do basic math. It is incumbent upon borrowers to know what they can afford each month—and to not get themselves into financial trouble. Perhaps it's time to teach basic financial literacy in public schools.

Then there are the flippers, the speculators, the Donald Trump wannabes who got caught when the market turned. Those of you who are defaulting on your mortgages: congratulations—you have achieved your dreams! You are now just like the Donald: In late 2008, Trump reneged on a $40 million debt to Deutsche Bank for a commercial property development.[23]

The many real estate speculators who got caught without a chair when the music stopped must accept their fair share of the blame. (Surprisingly, Mr. Trump remains blameless for the current mess.)

■ ■ ■

Other than CFMA and repeal of Glass-Steagall, I will not point to any single vote of the legislative body; those are political choices, which it is not my purview to second-guess. Instead, I want to specify two relatively new ways Congress carries out the people's business that are utterly reprehensible.

The first is the abhorrent practice of passing legislation sight unseen. This is simply beyond the comprehension of any rational person. It makes a mockery of the idea of a representative government elected by the people. Is there any meaningful difference between a dictatorship and an elected body that votes on legislation it has not so much as read?

It wasn't just the Commodity Futures Modernization Act that passed unread. The Patriot Act, the Digital Millennium Copyright Act, the

TARP, and other legislation have been voted on essentially unread. If proposed laws are going to be passed without so much as a single reading, then we might as well elect a Congress of illiterates; perhaps we already have. How could we tell the difference?

The second form of Congressional idiocy that has come into vogue is the "nonvote" vote. Rather than actually vote for a specific act, Congress grants authority to a third person to exercise judgment on behalf of Congress. The president and Treasury secretary have each received authority they claimed they wouldn't need or use. "If you've got a bazooka, and people know you've got it, you may not have to take it out," Paulson famously said in July 2008, explaining the rationale for giving him the power to nationalize Fannie and Freddie.[24]

One cannot tell whether it is sheer foolishness or cowardice that leads to this absurdity, but consider these nonvote votes that have occurred so far this decade:

- The Iraq war authorization
- The Fannie Mae recapitalization
- The Troubled Assets Relief Program

Such cowardice. Rather than actually confront the issue head-on, we get this foolish subterfuge. Anytime an administration obtains congressional authority to do something (go to war, spend money on bailouts), it is identical to actually authorizing the act—meaning yes, this is now guaranteed to eventually occur. Claiming you are merely granting authority only reveals your cowardice in not voting yea or nay on the act in the first place. The enabling vote may make the act more politically palatable, but it is obviously an attempt to hide it from the public. Don't ever kid yourself—it is no different than the actual act itself.

One understands how Mark Twain came to remark, "Suppose you were an idiot. And suppose you were a member of Congress. But I repeat myself."

■ ■ ■

Structured financial products, from residential mortgage-backed securities (RMBSs) to collateralized debt obligations (CDOs), lay at the heart of the global credit and financial meltdown. The process of creating, rating, and selling this paper is complex. As we have

learned after the fact, the rating agencies were not (as they claim) passive participants who just happened to underestimate the likelihood of future defaults. Rather, when they placed precious triple-A ratings on all sorts of mortgage-backed and related securities, they were active participants—collaborators, according to the *Wall Street Journal*.[25]

The subprime paper that eventually collapsed found its way onto the balance sheets of many banks, funds, and other firms. Had "the securities initially received the risky ratings" they deserved (and many now carry), the various pension funds, trusts, and mutual funds that now own them "would have been barred by their own rules from buying them."[26]

Nobel laureate Joseph Stiglitz, economics professor at Columbia University, observed:

> I view the ratings agencies as one of the key culprits. They were the party that performed that alchemy that converted the securities from F-rated to A-rated. The banks could not have done what they did without the complicity of the ratings agencies.[27]

In 2008, the House Oversight Committee opened a probe into the role of the bond-rating agencies in the credit crisis, and Congress held a hearing on the subject, featuring a now-infamous instant message exchange: "We rate every deal," one Standard & Poor's analyst told another who dared to question the validity of the ratings process. "It could be structured by cows and we would rate it."[28]

When they are not rating bovine structured products, the rating agencies can be found belatedly downgrading junk paper into bankruptcy. In March 2009, Moody's Investors Service came out with a new ratings list: The Bottom Rung.

"Moody's estimates about 45% of the Bottom Rung companies will default in the next year," the *Wall Street Journal* reported.[29] Perhaps the cliché about analysts is better applied to rating agencies: You don't need them in a bull market, and you don't want them in a bear market.

While it was the investment banks that sold the junk paper, it was the rating agencies that tarted up the bonds. It was the equivalent of putting lipstick on a pig: This paper could never have danced its way onto the laps of so many drooling buyers without the rating agencies' imprimatur of triple-A respectability.

Yet considering the massive damage they are directly responsible for, the rating agencies have all escaped relatively unscathed. Given their key role in the crisis—*were they corrupt or incompetent or both?*—one might have thought an Arthur Andersen-like demise was a distinct possibility. Warren Buffett should consider himself lucky—he is the biggest shareholder of Moody's, and is fortunate the scandal hasn't tarnished his reputation.

■ ■ ■

Of course, none of this would really have mattered if a few hedge funds and a much larger number of institutional investors—including foreign central banks—didn't suck up so much of this suspect paper (China evidently bought $10 billion in subprime mortgages). Through the indiscriminate use of leverage and by failing to know what they owned, the purchasers of the triple-A-rated junk paper must also shoulder some of the blame.

How did so much of the investment world manage to overlook these issues? Didn't anyone do *any* due diligence? Or was it simply a case of the casinos keeping the securitization process rolling? I've had conversations with CDO originators and insiders, as well as money managers, who unabashedly claimed: "We knew we were buying time bombs."

So we can rule out sheer ignorance. Rather, it appears that as long as deal fees could be generated, Wall Street kept the CDO factories running 24/7.

Talk about your misplaced compensation incentives. This is precisely the kind of self-destruction that Alan Greenspan believed was impossible in a free market system. The flaw he misunderstood was simply this: It wasn't that the free market would prevent it from occurring; it was that relentless competitive forces would drive such firms out of business. That is what began to happen in 2008. The free market actually worked as it should—firms that managed risk poorly were demolished by market forces. The trouble was, none of the erstwhile free market advocates had the stomach to live through the creative destruction Mr. Market was serving.

That is the risk that excessive deregulation brings: We can eliminate regulations that might prevent systemic risk. However, the free market advocates whine when the market doesn't do their bidding. Bad choices by management led to failure. That failure brought on a global recession, bankrupted over 300 U.S. mortgage companies, and turned many of the biggest banks and investment firms into tapioca.

The firms that allowed excessive risk taking and leverage found themselves on the wrong side of the corporate version of Darwin's laws—which was precisely where they belonged.

■ ■ ■

Several of the states with the biggest foreclosure problem today had an opportunity to confront the problem when it was much smaller. These are the states that now lead the nation in foreclosures. Their regulatory agencies had long lists of complaints brought to their attention. None acted upon them.

A 2008 exposé by the *Miami Herald* revealed that Florida allowed thousands of ex-cons, many with criminal records for fraud, to work unlicensed as loan originators. More than half the people who wrote mortgages in Florida during that period were not subject to any criminal background check. Despite repeated pleas from industry leaders to screen them, Florida regulators refused.[30]

And in California, attempts to regulate the many subprime mortgage lenders working in the state were beaten back, primarily by Democratic lawmakers who were protecting the then fast-growing industry.

Today, California and Florida are the nation's leading foreclosure factories.

Then there is Arizona. When Internet real estate service Zillow began publishing online housing price estimates in the state, it received a cease and desist order from the Arizona Board of Appraisal. Zillow's site makes it clear that its data are merely estimates and not actual appraisals. Regardless, misguided Arizona pols did not want some online firm horning in on their local business. It is no wonder Arizona is ranked fourth in the nation in terms of defaults and foreclosures listed by RealtyTrac.[31]

■ ■ ■

The misguided deification of markets is the primary factor that led us to being a Bailout Nation. Markets can and do get it wrong—not by just a little, either; occasionally they can be wildly wrong.

Recall those two Bear Stearns hedge funds that blew up in June 2007. The S&P 500 stumbled in August 2007 at that early sign of a brewing credit crisis. But in the market's infinite wisdom, it determined that credit wasn't such a significant problem after all. The S&P 500 and Dow Jones Industrial Average proceeded to set all-time highs a few months later, peaking in October 2007. That they got cut in half over the next year makes one wonder why anyone would call the stock market prescient.

This was not the only time Mr. Market has managed to get things precisely wrong. There are far too many examples to enumerate here.

■ ■ ■

In the final analysis, allowing markets to set policy is inherently *anti-democratic.* Free people are entitled to elect a representative government, which then enacts legislation on their behalf. Those elected representatives go to Washington, D.C., to do the people's will. If it is the people's will to prevent testosterone-addled traders from saddling the taxpayers with trillions in losses, that is their choice.

Americans have long recognized the advantages of economic freedom. We want the markets to be relatively free to operate. However, we do not want to allow the worst of human behaviors to have free rein. Complaints about regulating markets are actually objections to proscribing the worst behaviors of the people who operate in those markets. We want markets to operate intelligently, but not run roughshod over us. Blame the radical free-market extremists who insist on replacing representative government with the so-called wisdom of markets. This has proven to be misguided.

What the actual result of market-based decision making does is to eliminate those pesky human voters from exercising their will through a representative government. Ultimately, the free-market zealots are not only antiregulation, they are antidemocracy and antirepresentative government. Taken to illogical extremes, they would create a market-based dictatorship.

One part bad philosophy, one part mob rule. That pretty much sums up the financial markets, circa 2008–2009.

Chapter 20

Misplaced Fault

Ignorance more frequently begets confidence than does knowledge.
—Charles Darwin

One of the oddest things to come out of the 2008 U.S. presidential campaign was a series of accusations seeking to throw off blame for the current economic crisis. It wasn't radical deregulation, the Federal Reserve, or so-called ninja loans that were at fault, politicos claimed. Instead, they shifted blame to decades-old government policy.

Some of the arguments had merit—at least as policy criticisms. However, none of them made the leap to correctly identifying the proximate causes of the present crisis. Here we'll look at the targets of five such arguments: the mortgage interest deduction, naked shorting, the Community Reinvestment Act (CRA), securitization, and last, Fannie Mae and Freddie Mac.

Mortgage Interest Deduction

The Sixteenth Amendment to the U.S. Constitution was made in 1913, effectively reinstating an overturned 1894 tax law and making

income tax legal. Ever since, all forms of interest—including mortgage interest—have been deductible.

Indeed, the tax code provides a fairly generous benefit for being a mortgage-paying homeowner: The full interest deduction reduces your taxable income. Hence, if a renter and a homeowner are making similar monthly payments, the renter's after-tax costs are as much as 35 percent higher.[1]

Several commentators have criticized this, and some, such as Harvard economics professor Edward L. Glaeser, claim it to be a major factor in the housing collapse.[2] Glaeser recently wrote:

> Subsidizing interest payments encourages people to leverage themselves to the hilt to bet on housing markets. The size of the tax benefit is proportional to your debt. The deduction essentially encourages us to make leveraged bets on the swings of the housing market. That leverage means that housing price swings can easily wipe people out. We are currently experiencing the consequences of subsidizing gambles on housing.[3]

While the professor's basic premise is intriguing, his conclusions are suspect. Yes, we do encourage people to become homeowners by subsidizing interest payments. But is it worth it? Do we get the maximum benefit out of this subsidy? That is a worthy discussion for another time.

But the leverage side of the argument remains dubious. It was only recently that so many home buyers engaged in reckless, highly leveraged purchases. Since the interest deduction came into effect a century ago, most homeowners have used it responsibly.

It is a huge leap to get from that history to placing blame on the interest deduction as the root cause of the current maelstrom. When something has existed for almost 100 years without incident, we are better served looking for more recent, intervening factors that are probable causes. For housing, ultralow rates and the abdication of lending standards were those factors.

Naked Shorting

A recurrent theme in 2008 was the role of naked shorting in the fall of Bear Stearns, Lehman Brothers, and others. This is yet another case of misplaced blame.

To legitimately short a stock, one must first borrow the shares, then sell them. Upon covering the short ("buying in the shares"), the borrowed stock can be returned. Naked shorting is where this borrowing never takes place.

"Going naked" has been a dirty secret among Wall Street firms for years, and for good reason: It is very profitable. Not only does a commission get transacted that might otherwise not, but there is an even juicier vig on the trade. Whenever a short sale is made, the transaction takes place in a margin account. The broker-dealer gets to charge an annual margin fee of 9 percent or more.

There is a delicious irony to bank CEOs complaining about naked shorting destroying their firms when they had spent decades profiting from it.

While it may be an illegal and abusive practice, it had little to do with the fall of Bear or Lehman. These firms had by their own volition leapt off the roof of the Empire State Building; naked shorts were the people who threw stones at the bodies as they fell. More likely causes of death were the excess leverage, the undercapitalization, the lack of risk controls, the bad mortgage-related investments, oh, and a general insolvency—not naked short selling.

Back when my firm initiated a short in Lehman Brothers in June 2008, the stock was over $30. It was an easy borrow. There was no need to short naked; we simply called the stock loan desk and got an authorization number. My biggest regret about Lehman Brothers—aside from all the unfortunate souls who lost their jobs when the company imploded—was that I didn't think of buying put options, an even bigger, more leveraged bet against the company.

And no, option trading didn't kill the company, either.

Community Reinvestment Act (CRA)

Let me ask you, where in the CRA does it say to make loans to people who can't afford to repay? Nowhere.

—FDIC Chairman Sheila Bair[4]

As housing and credit collapsed into the heart of the 2008 presidential campaign, a mad dash began. Politicos sought to duck responsibility for

what occurred, with each side trying to lay the blame at the feet of the opposing party. Of all the flailing criticism and finger-pointing after the collapse, blaming the Community Reinvestment Act (CRA) was probably the oddest:

> On the Republican side of Congress, in the right-wing financial media (which is to say the financial media), and in certain parts of the op-ed-o-sphere, there's a consensus emerging that the whole mess should be laid at the feet of Fannie Mae and Freddie Mac, the failed mortgage giants, and the Community Reinvestment Act, a law passed during the Carter administration. The CRA, which was amended in the 1990s and this decade, requires banks—which had a long, distinguished history of not making loans to minorities—to make more efforts to do so.[5]

The purpose of the CRA was to encourage banks to lend money back to their own business customers and depositors. The CRA followed other legislation such as the Fair Housing Act of 1968, the Equal Credit Opportunity Act of 1974, and the Home Mortgage Disclosure Act of 1975. CRA compliance is part of the standard bank review by regulators—Federal Reserve, Federal Deposit Insurance Corporation (FDIC), and Office of the Comptroller of the Currency (OCC)—and includes a very soft rating system, not a hard quota. This modest legislation was designed to help overcome redlining. That was an illegal bank practice of literally encircling a neighborhood on a map with a red marker and not making any loans to residents within that red line, regardless of income or creditworthiness.

The CRA told banks that if they opened branches in Harlem, they could not suck up all the local businesses' and residents' cash deposits, then turn around and lend the funds only to Tribeca condo buyers. Banks were under no obligation to open Harlem branches, but if they did, they were required to at least try to lend the locals back some of their own money. There were no quotas, minimums, or mandates—just a good-faith attempt to make loans.

Those who insist the CRA was to blame for the current crisis have a hard time explaining some obvious logical flaws.

Why was there no credit or housing meltdown from 1977 to 2005? Why did dozens of other countries, from the United Kingdom to much of Europe to New Zealand and Australia—none of which are covered by American laws such as the CRA—have a remarkably similar housing boom and bust to the U.S. one? The pundits fail to address these questions. It's as if this legislation somehow manages to transcend both time and space.

It's even more dramatic when you see where the foreclosure crisis is concentrated in the United States. California leads the nation in defaults, delinquencies, and foreclosures, followed by southern Florida, Arizona, and the Las Vegas area. As of December 2008, year over year, California's foreclosure activity was up 51 percent. The foreclosures are concentrated primarily in bedroom communities in the suburbs of cities like San Diego and Los Angeles. These are not, as you would imagine, CRA regions.

Florida is in some ways worse: At the end of 2008, its foreclosure activity was up 68 percent from the year before. Blame the enormous overbuilding of condos for the real estate debacle. As Dan Gross pointed out in *Newsweek*, these weren't inner-city loans to minorities; they were the products of, for example, "WCI Communities, builder of highly amenitized condos in Florida (no subprime purchasers welcome there). . . . Very few of the tens of thousands of now-surplus condominiums in Miami were conceived to be marketed to subprime borrowers, or minorities—unless you count rich Venezuelans and Colombians as minorities."[6]

Oh, and WCI Communities filed for bankruptcy in August 2008.

There are additional errors with the "blame CRA" argument. The CRA applies to depository banks. But the financial institutions that made a headlong dive into the subprime market weren't regulated banks; they were the innovative new mortgage originators. Companies like Argent and American Home Mortgage and their ilk were not required to comply with the CRA. And these firms worked closely with Bear Stearns and Lehman Brothers to securitize their subprime mortgages. Neither Bear nor Lehman was covered by the auspices of the CRA.[7]

Of course the CRA did not force mortgage companies to offer loans to people with bad credit or whose incomes would not support the payments. And the no-money-down, no-income-check features were also innovations independent of the CRA. Throwing underwriting standards out the window was the creation of the mortgage originators alone. And

as far as I can tell, nothing in the CRA forced the credit rating agencies to slap AAA high-grade ratings on subprime debt that went into default in record numbers.[8]

Numerous studies have found the CRA blameless in the current mess. Fed Governor Randall S. Kroszner[9] and Federal Deposit Insurance Corporation Chair Sheila Bair[10] each, in unrelated speeches, drew the same conclusion.

Since the Bear Stearns collapse in March 2008, there has been a veritable parade of bankers, mortgage originators, lenders, fund managers, and investment bank CEOs all testifying before Congress. Curiously, not one blamed the CRA:

> It's telling that, amid all the recent recriminations, even lenders have not fingered CRA. That's because CRA didn't bring about the reckless lending at the heart of the crisis. Just as sub-prime lending was exploding, CRA was losing force and relevance. And the worst offenders, the independent mortgage companies, were never subject to CRA—or any federal regulator. Law didn't make them lend. The profit motive did.[11]

Consider this Federal Reserve Board data, as compiled by the McClatchy Company:

- More than 84 percent of the subprime mortgages in 2006 were issued by private lending institutions.
- Private firms made nearly 83 percent of the subprime loans to low- and moderate-income borrowers that year.
- Only one of the top 25 subprime lenders in 2006 was directly subject to the CRA.
- Only commercial banks and thrifts must follow CRA rules. The investment banks don't, nor did the now-bankrupt nonbank lenders such as New Century Financial Corporation and Ameriquest that underwrote most of the subprime loans.
- Mortgage brokers, which also weren't subject to federal regulation or the CRA, originated most of the subprime loans.

It was as a political talking point that the "blame CRA" meme seemed to find new life. (The same occurred with Fannie and Freddie.) It spread among the partisan crowd during the 2008 presidential campaign.

One thing it did was provide a valuable time saving service: Those who mindlessly repeated these talking points—in print, on television, or on radio—identified themselves as partisans, not serious housing or credit analysts. This allowed the informed reader or listener to quickly dismiss the talking heads they might have otherwise wasted time on.

Fannie Mae and Freddie Mac, aka "Phonie & Fraudie"

Contrary to another one of these talking points, the government-sponsored enterprises (GSEs) were not a significant factor in causing the mortgage or housing crisis.

They were, however, a mess of an entirely different making.

Understanding the GSE story requires grasping their role within the housing sector.

Fannie Mae was not a government entity, but an independent, publicly traded firm. Fannie and Freddie were allowed to borrow at better rates than banks because they were GSEs. They bought what they did in an attempt to grab share and profits—and they did a lot of dumb things as the housing boom expanded and lending got really silly from 2002 to 2007.

For decades, Fannie and Freddie took advantage of their quasi-government status for access to cheap cash to crank out reliable profits. But for the most part, they followed their charters and only bought conforming mortgages. Fannie and Freddie eventually changed their mortgage-buying rules, allowing each firm to buy lower-quality loans. But by then, the housing boom was already nearing its peak, and the crash was all but inevitable.

Ironically, many of the political hacks focused their energy on the wrong place. Subprime wasn't the GSEs' biggest problem; it was their medium-quality loans that were going bad at an alarming rate. According to *Barron's*, Alt-A mortgages were what caused their demise:

> A substantial portion of Fannie's and Freddie's credit losses comes from \$337 billion and \$237 billion, respectively, of Alt-A mortgages that the agencies imprudently bought or guaranteed in recent years to boost their market share. These are mortgages for which little or no attempt

> was made to verify the borrowers' income or net worth. The principal balances were much higher than those of mortgages typically made to low-income borrowers. In short, Alt-A mortgages were a hallmark of real-estate speculation in the ex-urbs of Las Vegas or Los Angeles, not predatory lending to low-income folks in the inner cities.[12]

No doubt the GSEs were important cogs in the great mortgage securitization machinery. One might have thought Fannie Mae, a firm that had been in the business of securitizing mortgages since 1938, would have some insight into what was actually going on in the mortgage markets. No such luck.

This was their biggest contribution to the current crisis: Given their expertise, they were ideally situated to identify the massive credit bubble as it was inflating—and they completely missed it.

I was never enamored with Fannie Mae, and my firm started shorting FNM at $42+ later in 2007. (Given the company's penny stock price, I wish we were still short.) There had been all sorts of issues: Fraud, incompetence, and corruption were just starters. Imagine in the era of quantitative mortgage analysis, their computer systems did a poor job analyzing risky loans. And on top of that, from 2004 to 2006, Fannie operated without a permanent chief risk officer.

They were a disaster waiting to happen.

■ ■ ■

The folks who want to place the crisis at Fannie and Freddie's doorstep seem to be focusing on minor factors and irrelevancies. This was not a "grand social engineering" experiment, as the radical right has called it. This was a profit-motivated private company that was poorly managed and rife with extreme shortsightedness.

When Fannie hired Daniel Mudd as its new CEO in 2004, he arrived to find a company in utter disarray. At the time, Fannie Mae was still recovering from a massive accounting scandal in which the company had overstated billions in profits. Senior management had pocketed hundreds of millions in illicit stock option gains based on this phony income.[13]

This was the GSEs' real crime: simple fraud. Fannie overstated profits by $6.3 billion from 2001 to 2003, and in 2008 the Office of Federal Housing Enterprise Oversight (OFHEO) sued former CEO

Frank Raines. The OFHEO recovered $24.7 million of ill-gotten stock option bonuses that were predicated on phony profits.[14] The stock options that Raines had exercised so profitably between 1998 and 2004 were priced at $77.10; Fannie Mae stock (FNM), now under federal conservatorship, recently traded at 37 cents.

Moreover, CEO Mudd arrived in 2004 to find "the company was under siege," as the *New York Times* described in an October 2008 autopsy on Fannie's failure:

> Competitors were snatching lucrative parts of its business. Congress was demanding that Mr. Mudd help steer more loans to low-income borrowers. Lenders were threatening to sell directly to Wall Street unless Fannie bought a bigger chunk of their riskiest loans. So Mr. Mudd made a fateful choice. Disregarding warnings from his managers that lenders were making too many loans that would never be repaid, he steered Fannie into more treacherous corners of the mortgage market.[15]

Those lenders included Countrywide Financial. Their CEO, Angelo Mozilo, was demanding that Fannie start buying the lender's riskier loans. When Fannie resisted, Mozilo threatened to terminate their partnership.

This was no idle threat. Countrywide was the nation's largest mortgage lender, and losing its business might have been fatal to Fannie. That's because by 2004, Fannie had lost 56 percent of its loan-reselling business to Wall Street.

When Mozilo said, "Jump," Fannie Mae said, "How high?"

Between 2005 and 2008, Fannie purchased or guaranteed at least $270 billion in loans to risky borrowers—more than three times as much as in all of its earlier years combined, the *New York Times* reported, citing company filings and industry data. "We didn't really know what we were buying," Marc Gott, a former director in Fannie's loan servicing department, told the *New York Times*. "This system was designed for plain vanilla loans, and we were trying to push chocolate sundaes through the gears."[16]

Meanwhile, over at Fannie's little brother, Freddie Mac:

> The chief executive of the mortgage giant Freddie Mac rejected internal warnings that could have protected the company from some of the financial crises now engulfing it, according to more than two dozen current and former high-ranking executives and others. That chief

> executive, Richard F. Syron, in 2004 received a memo from Freddie Mac's chief risk officer warning him that the firm was financing questionable loans that threatened its financial health.[17]

Poor risk management and poorer timing make for a dangerous combination.

■ ■ ■

It is a tenet of faith among right-wing supporters that abuses by Fannie Mae and Freddie Mac were aided and abetted by Democratic members of Congress, notably Representative Barney Frank. They blame much of the housing and credit crisis on the misuse of GSEs to further the liberal goal of maxing out home ownership for everyone, most notably minorities.

Many adherents of this "blame the Dems" viewpoint point to the 2004 House Finance hearings where then OFHEO director Armando Falcon was harshly treated for daring to so much as criticize the accounting breakdowns at Fannie and Freddie. A YouTube highlight reel of the hearing has received nearly three million hits as of this writing.[18]

The great irony is Fannie and Freddie spread around hundreds of millions of dollars corrupting members of Congress of both parties. A December 2008 AP story detailed Freddie Mac's "multi-million dollar campaign to preserve its largely regulatory free environment, with particular pressure on Republicans who controlled Congress at the time." Famed conservative Newt Gingrich was a notable recipient of Fannie's largesse.[19]

Indeed, Fannie and Freddie were among the most prolific lobbyists on K Street. For a long time they were successful in preventing closer oversight and in thwarting tighter regulation. The Republicans may have been a less natural ally than the Democrats when it came to Fannie and Freddie, but exonerating the GOP for the GSEs' misdeeds misses the larger point: Like much else in our Bailout Nation, it points to a bipartisan failure.

■ ■ ■

Fannie has been around since 1938, Freddie since 1968, and the CRA since 1977. Suddenly, all of housing goes to hell in 2006, and then credit collapses two years after—and the best explanation some people can come up with is Fannie, Freddie, and CRA? Gee, isn't that rather odd—especially after 70 years?

While reducing the complexities of economic history into bumper-sticker phrases is politically expedient, it does not help us get to the root cause of our problems. And it gets in the way of helping us fashion a solution for the future. This is why I hold the weasels who are attempting to obscure reality and rewrite history in such disdain.

For the nonpartisan, nonhacks among you, for the policy makers and academics and economists who are truly interested in how this came to pass and what we can do to fix it, the bottom line remains: The CRA was irrelevant to the current crisis, and Fannie Mae and Freddie Mac were mere cogs in a very complex financial machine with many moving parts.

But the primary cause of the mess? Not even close.

Chapter 21

The Virtues of Foreclosure

Home sales are coming down from the mountain peak, but they will level out at a high plateau, a plateau that is higher than previous peaks in the housing cycle.

—David Lereah, National Association of Realtors' chief economist, December 2005[1]

I don't know, but I think the worst of this may well be over.

—Alan Greenspan, October 2006[2]

By now, you may have noticed that housing has played a starring role in our Bailout Nation. It is the unifying theme that runs through much of the bailout narrative.

Housing was the prime driver of the economic cycle of 2001 to 2008: It was a disproportionate source of newly created jobs. Mortgage equity withdrawal (MEW) was an outsized contributor to consumer spending. Home mortgages were a huge portion of much of the twenty-first century's consumer debt creation. On Wall Street, the securitization of mortgages was a major factor driving revenue and profits; residential

mortgage-backed securities (RMBSs) were bundled by the Street, and then repackaged into collateralized debt obligations (CDOs). Pseudo insurance policies written on all those CDOs were credit default swaps (CDSs), a key element in the demises of Bear Stearns, Lehman Brothers, and AIG.

But that was *then*. Where does housing fit into the economy in our modern, postbailout world?

Today, housing presents a tricky catch-22. Allow me for a moment to be a two-handed economist: On the one hand, housing remains overpriced relative to historic norms; indeed, by nearly every major real estate metric, it has yet to revert to regular pricing levels. One the other hand, as prices fall, that leads to even more foreclosures, causing all manner of problems for the already battered banking sector.

Resolving the current crisis—the credit markets, the economy, the banking sector, and its toxic derivatives—is dependent on a nearly impossible goal. The ideal solution requires finding a way for home prices to normalize while simultaneously keeping foreclosure rates from spiking. It is quite a sticky balancing act.

Consider how interrelated these various elements are:

- Housing is a key part of the economy. Home purchases and refinancings drive other durable goods sales, like appliances, furniture, and automobiles. When housing sales run significantly below trend, as they have over the past few years, the negative economic impact is significant. For the economy to begin improving, housing must stabilize.
- During the five-year period from 2002 to 2007, the combination of ultralow rates and nonexistent credit standards created between five and seven million more home buyers than usual. Home ownership rose from 62 percent in 1960 to 66 percent in 2000. It peaked at just over 69 percent in the 2004–2007 period.[3] By Q4 2008, it had slipped to 67.5 percent.[4]
- The influx of new buyers helped drive prices several standard deviations higher (meaning more expensive than they should be). Even though home prices have since fallen more than 25 percent nationally (according to the Case-Shiller indexes[5]), housing still remains relatively overpriced in many areas.

- There have been over two million foreclosures in the United States as of the end of 2008. The many people who bought homes they could not afford are in the process of reverting back to being renters. There may be anywhere from another one to four million more foreclosures in the next few years. As disruptive as foreclosures are to families and neighborhoods, the silver lining is they help drive prices back toward normalized levels.
- A recent report by First American CoreLogic determined that 20 percent of homes with mortgages (8.3 million) are underwater—the mortgage debt is greater than the value of homes. Call them "home-*owers*." These properties tend to be at greater risk for walk-aways, jingle mail (mailing keys to lender), and foreclosures.[6]
- There have been over 5.1 million jobs lost so far in the recession that began in December 2007.[7] Employment generally lags the economic cycle, meaning it stays low even after the economy begins to recover. I would not be surprised to see another two to three million more job losses before the recession ends.
- Perhaps most significantly, as the recession continues, job losses are still rising and foreclosures increasing. The trillions of dollars in toxic paper held by banks and insurers become worth less and less with each economic downtick. More foreclosures = more bank failures = bigger FDIC/federal obligations.

This helps to explain why the Federal Reserve and the Treasury have been so desperate to stop foreclosures; it is also why the White House was willing to throw $75 billion at a foreclosure abatement program. While the intentions are good, the main issue remains: *Homes are still too expensive.*

This is the heart of our catch-22. It is an issue that seems sacrilegious to many economists: *Home prices remain too high for stabilization and/or a housing bottom to form.*

As Figures 21.1 to 21.3 show, the wreckage in the real estate sector has brought house prices down from wildly overvalued levels of a few years ago. But they are still too high by most valuation metrics. Consider such metrics as the ratio of median income to median home price, the cost of renting versus owning, and housing capitalization of gross domestic product (GDP); in each of these, home prices are still significantly elevated above historic norms.

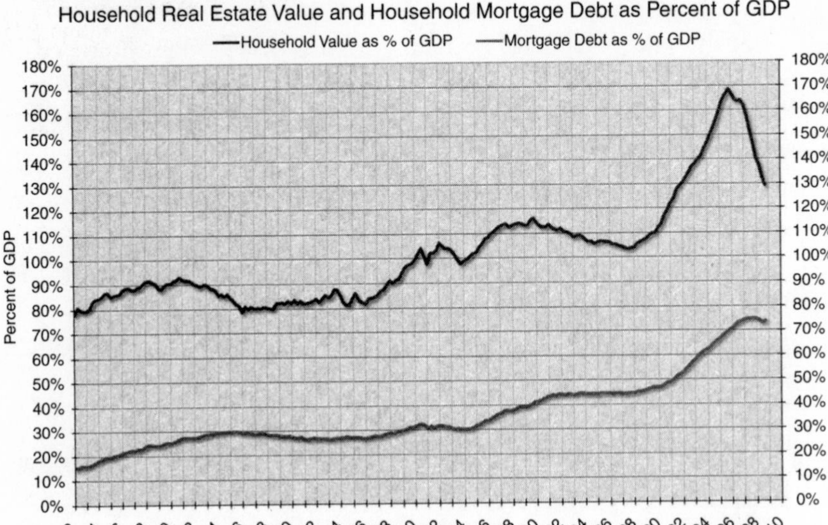

Figure 21.1 Home Prices as a Percentage of Gross Domestic Product
SOURCE: Chart courtesy of Calculated Risk, www.calculatedriskblog.com

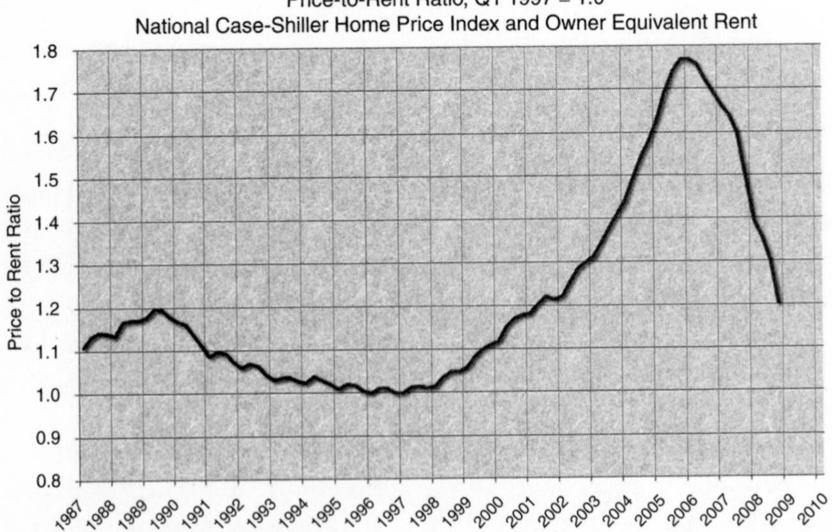

Figure 21.2 Price-to-Rent Ratio
SOURCE: Chart courtesy of Calculated Risk, www.calculatedriskblog.com

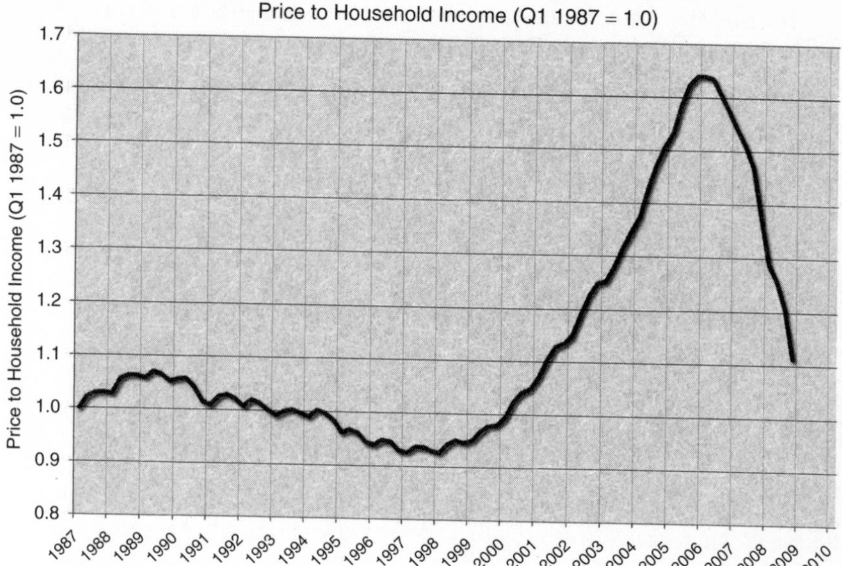

Figure 21.3 Home Prices versus Median Household Income
SOURCE: Chart courtesy of Calculated Risk, www.calculatedriskblog.com

In all of these charts, housing has come about half to two-thirds of the way back into line. But consider this grim reality about future home prices: Markets rarely revert just back to the mean. In most instances where assets have become dramatically overextended (stocks, commodities, bonds, and, yes, housing), the reversion tendency has been to overshoot to the downside.

Therein lies the crux of the problem: Propping up home prices or forestalling foreclosures might only serve to delay the inevitable. To effect true stabilization, including a real housing bottom and recovery, these overpriced assets will likely fall even further. (Either that, or a few million new buyers must come into the market.)

When prices drop enough, good things happen. The prime bubble areas—California, South Florida, Arizona, Las Vegas—each suffered enormous foreclosure surges of 80 to 120 percent, followed by huge price decreases of 40 to 50 percent. But now these states contain the few areas of the country where home sales are increasing—driven by sales of homes in foreclosure.

It's not that people are unwilling to buy real estate in the United States; it's that buyers are unwilling to overpay.

And therein lies the heart of the problem with most rescue plans. They are designed to prevent the continued downward spiral of the housing market, which unfortunately is precisely what is needed. The artificial demand of the ultralow rates and lax lending standards sent prices to unsustainable levels, and put millions of people into homes they could not afford. The markets are correcting these excesses as people trade out of those homes. It is a classic unwind of a bubble.

In much of the country, home prices remain too high, and the overpriced homes are not moving. That's reflected in the huge inventory overhang of unsold homes. (See Figure 21.4.) And the inventory data of homes for sale does not include the shadow inventory—all of the homes purchased as investments, by flippers, as second homes, or as rental units. These owners are waiting in the shadows for the opportunity to get rid of their properties. Any improvement in the real estate market is likely to bring forth this additional supply.

Figure 21.4 Existing Home Inventory
SOURCE: Chart courtesy of Calculated Risk, www.calculatedriskblog.com

Until prices revert back toward historical norms, the excess inventory will not be removed, the foreclosures will not stop, and the total sales will remain depressed. The sooner Washington, D.C., figures this out, the better off the economy and U.S. homeowners will be.

Real estate is unique. Unlike most goods and services, purchases are not independent from other parties to the sales transaction. Whether you buy 1,000 shares of stock, a used car, or a can of soup, only two parties are involved: the buyer and the seller. But buy a home (85 percent of all sales are existing homes) and you are involved in a transaction chain with four, five, even six or more other buyer/seller pairs.

Consider the newlywed couple who want to purchase a starter home. Their sellers are a family with a child on the way who want to move to a larger home. The sellers of *that* house have two teenage daughters driving them crazy, and they want to move to an even bigger house, whose seller is moving to a waterfront property, and so on. It is often a long chain of trade-ups, with increasing size and cost (and property taxes). The rub is that if any one of these sales falls apart, the entire chain collapses.

And therein lies the problem.

Go to any suburban neighborhood—even the one you live in. Look at the starter homes that our theoretical newlywed couple might consider: small Cape Cod cottages and two- or three-bedroom ranches. Assume that this couple are in their late 20s or early 30s, and are making decent (but not six-figure) salaries. I'm guessing that describes 80 percent of typical newlywed home buyers.

Can they afford that starter house? If not, then the real estate chain is partially frozen. What's left is mostly downsizing, laterals, and moves into different regions. As long as housing remains unaffordable for the majority of first-time buyers, it will significantly reduce total real estate sales.

House sales peaked in 2007 at well over 7 million units. We are now running about 4.25 million sales per year. A more normalized number would be between 5 and 5.5 million. That's not going to happen if the starter home market is dead. If the newlyweds cannot afford that first purchase, the entire chain gets bogged down.

How can we reduce foreclosures *and* lower home prices?

The real estate market would be much better off if policy makers recognized three things:

1. Falling prices help return the housing market to normalcy.
2. Those people who cannot afford to be in their houses (underwater, overpriced, too little income) should be helped to move into affordable housing (rental or purchased); keeping people in homes they cannot afford is counterproductive.
3. Those people who can afford to stay in their homes with a loan modification or workout are the best targets for legitimate foreclosure avoidance.

If they could, banks would prefer to avoid foreclosure. It's an expensive, time-consuming process; properties acquired through foreclosure are a messy, money-losing headache. Any intelligent proposal to reasonably avoid preventable foreclosures would give the banks a big incentive to voluntarily participate in loan modifications. I believe this is just such a plan.

In September 2008, I offered a housing proposal ("Fixing Housing & Finance: 30/20/10 Proposal"[8]) that provided a way to reduce foreclosures *and* lower home prices at the same time. Call it the "30/20/10" solution:

- **30:** Take up to 30 percent of any qualifying delinquent mortgage and separate it from the main mortgage; it becomes a second, interest-free balloon mortgage. It stays on the books of the present mortgage holder, be it the loan originator (bank) or MBS investor.
- **20:** The goal of the 30 percent part of the plan is to save 20 percent of the current delinquent and potential foreclosure properties; of the five million homes that are late in making payments (the first step along the road to delinquency, default, and foreclosure), the process should make 20 percent (one million) homes eligible.
- **10:** The balloon payment comes due in 10 years, and will be treated as a second mortgage, with interest charges accruing only as of September 1, 2019, when it can be refinanced or paid off in full.

There is no reason why those people who are underwater but current would not qualify for such a program. This plan would allow housing market prices to normalize, keep those loans that are savable from going into default, and avoid moral hazard. Note that this requires little if any taxpayer money. If you really want to motivate the banks to do this, however, Uncle Sam has to either guarantee some portion of the loans or provide low-interest-rate loans to the participating lenders.

A few other government actions are needed: The interest-free balloon loans should be made tax free; the lenders also need to be able to set aside these loans without taking a markdown immediately. The defaults (if any) wouldn't hit until 10 years hence. Banks should be permitted to carry these balloon loans not as a liability, but as a current nondelinquent loan (i.e., an asset).

■ ■ ■

The mad attempt to avoid any and all foreclosures is counterproductive. The foreclosure process is how an overpriced market returns back to normalcy. That is what is now happening, and excess interference will only slow down the eventual return to a healthy economy.

Chapter 22

Casino Capitalism

Speculators may do no harm as bubbles on a steady stream of enterprise. But the position is serious when enterprise becomes the bubble on a whirlpool of speculation. When the capital development of a country becomes a by-product of the activities of a casino, the job is likely to be ill-done.

—John Maynard Keynes

Bear Stearns opened the floodgates. Once the bailouts began, there was no end to them. Citigroup took $25 billion, and came back for another $20 billion, plus $250 billion in guarantees on its toxic assets. Bank of America—its name more appropriate now than ever—was also a three-time supplicant, getting the same $45 billion as Citi, plus $300 billion in guarantees. AIG has been back to the well four times—and counting—for a total of $173 billion of bailout green, so far.

Another hard lesson learned: Once executives get a taste of corporate welfare, they want more. Do you have any idea *how hard it is* to earn $30 billion in a year? Flying commercial—or even driving—to Washington, D.C., for an afternoon of hostile Q&A is a lot easier than having your company make $30 billion. The return on investment (ROI) on the day trip is *fantastic*.

The queen of corporate welfare is AIG. In addition to its multiple bailouts, it more or less threatened to blow up the rest of the world if more money wasn't forthcoming. In a special report to the Treasury Department titled *AIG: Is the Risk Systemic?*, AIG claimed that without a fourth bailout it would collapse, triggering a "chain reaction of enormous proportions" that would likely "bankrupt the entire system." Oh, and if you don't give us more money, we won't able repay the $135 billion we already owe the U.S. taxpayer.

It is casino capitalism at its finest. Heads, we win; tails, you lose.

■ ■ ■

The endless maw that the Treasury Department keeps feeding appears insatiable. First under Hank Paulson, now under Tim Geithner, the trillions in bailout monies paid out is beyond absurd—it is asinine.

With the conditions at the country's biggest banks deteriorating rapidly, the nation needs to move beyond the half trillion dollars paid out to the 10 largest banks so far. The money already dumped into the black holes of just the two largest financial institutions far exceeds their net worth. And in exchange for this foolish investment, taxpayers have received a small stake in each: at first, 6 percent of Bank of America and 7.8 percent of Citigroup (eventually converted into 36 percent). How an investment of 120 percent of a company's market capitalization yields only a *minor* ownership stake is simply beyond my comprehension.

There has to be a faster, fairer, cheaper, more efficient way out of the current credit and financial mess. There is, and it is called receivership—but you may know it under its more common name, nationalization.

The solution to the banks' problems, as well as this ridiculous investment posture, is relatively simple: Identify the banks that are insolvent, and temporarily nationalize them. Appoint new management, and give them six months to spin out 10 percent of each of the separate viable pieces, with the taxpayer retaining the rest as passive investors. Bank of America can spin out five major pieces: BoA, Merrill, Countrywide, a toxic holding company, and the rest of its holdings. The toxic assets put into the toxic holding section get wiped off the bank's balance sheet.

The derivatives exposure gets wound down (counterparties are unsecured creditors—except, for unfathomable reasons, in the case of AIG).

Stockholders get wiped out, as that is what occurs when you invest in a company that goes bankrupt. Bondholders take a haircut, and end up owning a piece of the new firm. Perhaps in exchange for fresh capital, they can have a preferred position in buying the new firms' bonds. As opposed to the small pro-rata share they would have gotten in liquidation, they get a convertible preferred in the new debt-free firm, as well as an opportunity to lend to the new banks at a generous convertible rate.

In January 2009, Adam S. Posen, deputy director of the Peterson Institute for International Economics, noted:

> The case for full nationalization is far stronger now than it was a few months ago. If you don't own the majority, you don't get to fire the management, to wipe out the shareholders, to declare that you are just going to take the losses and start over. It's the mistake the Japanese made in the '90s.[1]

It seems to be the least onerous, least offensive way to halt the downward spiral of America's largest financial institutions.

The current bailouts have shown themselves to be expensive, ineffective, and replete with moral hazard. Not only are we wasting vast sums of money, but we also are rewarding the incompetent management teams that created the mess in the first place. As this book was going to press, Treasury was forced to intervene to prevent AIG from giving out nearly $450 million in bonuses to "pay executives in the business unit that brought the company to the brink of collapse last year," according to the *Wall Street Journal*.[2]

How is it possible that the same collection of financial nincompoops who caused this problem not only are *still* in the employ of AIG, but somehow think they are entitled to *performance bonuses*?

■ ■ ■

Perhaps we should be looking to Sweden. Lars Jonung served as chief economic adviser to Swedish Prime Minister Carl Bildt from 1992 to 1994. That was when "the Swedish solution" was implemented.

The former professor at the Stockholm School of Economics sees the United States as having two options: go Swedish or turn Japanese:

> Banks all over the world are in deep trouble. This has created an interest in the successful bank resolution policy adopted in Sweden in the early 1990s. But can the Swedish model of yesterday be applied in other countries today?
>
> When Sweden was hit by a financial crisis in 1991–93, its response comprised a unique combination of seven distinctive features:
>
> 1) swift policy action, 2) political unity, 3) a blanket government guarantee of all bank liabilities (including deposits but excluding shareholder capital), 4) an appropriate legal framework based on open-ended government funding, 5) complete information disclosure by banks asking for government support, 6) a differentiated resolution policy by which banks were classified according to their financial strength and treated accordingly, and 7) an overall monetary and fiscal policy that facilitated the bank resolution policy.
>
> Two major banks were taken over by the government. Their assets were split into a good bank and a bad bank, the "toxic" assets of the latter being dealt with by asset-management companies (AMCs) which focused solely on the task of disposing of them. When transferring assets from the banks to the AMCs, cautious market values were applied, thus putting a floor under the valuation of such assets, mostly real estate. This restored demand and liquidity, and thus put a break on falling asset prices.[3]

The alternative is the Japanese model. When that country's economy crashed and its real estate bubble burst in 1989, Japan allowed banks to carry the bad assets on their books for years. They failed to take the painful write-downs or raise appropriate capital. The subsequent period is known as Japan's lost decade.

■ ■ ■

Perhaps the word *nationalization* scares some people, as if that is what would turn the United States into a banana republic. Why don't we call it by a more user-friendly name? How about "FDIC-mandated, prepackaged, government-funded Chapter 11 reorganization"?

That is an accurate description of what occurred with Washington Mutual (WaMu), now part of JPMorgan Chase, and with Wachovia, now part of Wells Fargo. The FDIC steps in and seamlessly transfers control of the assets to a new owner, while simultaneously wiping out the debt and the shareholders, and giving a big haircut to the bondholders.

Let's look at what these terms mean:

- **FDIC-mandated:** By law, the FDIC is required to handle the liquidation or reorganization of insolvent banking institutions. We have prevented that process from taking place by lending trillions of dollars in bailout monies.
- **Prepackaged:** The entire process is mapped out in advance so as to make it fast and seamless. Washington Mutual depositors did not notice a single change over the weekend their FDIC-mandated, prepackaged Chapter 11 workout, government-funded reorganization occurred. The only observable difference to WaMu customers was they were no longer charged a fee when they went to Chase ATMs.
- **Government-funded Chapter 11:** The full bankruptcy protection applies—meaning employees still get paid, secured creditors suffer the least, and debtor in possession (DIP) financing is available to the bank; Uncle Sam is the source of the DIP funding.
- **Reorganization:** This is just what it sounds like—a new board of directors is brought in, management transitions out to a new team, the company is recapitalized, bad debt is taken off of the books, and toxic assets are spun out.

What emerges is a clean, debt-free bank, well capitalized, without deadly toxic assets on its books. *Why would anyone find this state of affairs objectionable?*

If our choice is between going Swedish or turning Japanese, you can call me Inga.

■ ■ ■

In reality, the nationalization issue is moot. Miller Tabak's market strategist, Peter Boockvar, notes that the debate over nationalization is now mere wordplay:

> The raging debate over whether to nationalize Citigroup and/or Bank of America is semantics at this point. With politicians in Washington DC dictating executive pay, marketing expenses, employee trips, dividend policy, etc. . . . and the guarantee of almost a half trillion dollars' worth of assets, both are already wards of the state.
>
> But whatever step the government may or may not take, healing the banks directly is still only dealing with the symptoms and not the disease. That disease is "an overleveraged consumer and falling home prices"—when it's cured, it will heal the symptom that is a troubled bank sector. Shifting bad assets from the banks to the government is just a shell game, as we'll ultimately pay for it one way or another. The $64k question is what will happen to bond holders. . . . [4]

And it could get worse. If the recession intensifies, we should expect increased layoffs, weaker retail sales—and more foreclosures. As of this writing, the United States has had five consecutive monthly Non-Farm Payrolls releases of about 600,000 job losses or worse. If that number doesn't improve soon, foreclosures are going to increase. With most of the toxic paper banks hold primarily consisting of mortgage-backed securities, the need for more bailout money may be inevitable.

■ ■ ■

To get a handle on just how absurd the results of our casino capitalism have become, let's take a closer look at AIG. The bailouts of the insurance giant raise a disturbing question: Why are the taxpayers making good on hedge fund trades gone bad?

AIG was essentially two companies jammed under one roof. One was a highly regulated, state-supervised life insurance company—in fact, the biggest such firm in the world. It had a long history of steady growth, profitability, and excellent management, and made money (as the commercial goes) the old-fashioned way: They earned it.

This half of the company held the most important insurance in many families' financial lives: their life insurance. When an AIG policyholder passed away, the company paid off the policy, providing monies that were used to pay the mortgage, kids' college educations, and the surviving spouse's lifetime living expenses. Given the importance of this payment, one can see why the state has a vested interest in making sure there are sufficient reserves to pay off the life insurance policies. The actuarial tables used are conservative, the accounting transparent. The policy payoffs are rock solid, utterly reliable.

AIG, this insurance company, was well run. It made a steady income and provided a valuable service to its clients. It was also solvent, and had no need for a bailout.

The other half of the AIG firm was an unregulated structured finance firm, specializing in credit default swaps and other derivatives. Most people did not learn of the darker half of the firm until AIG faltered. This structured finance half was nothing that the life insurer was. Neither regulated nor transparent, it existed only in the shadow banking world, a nether region in the financial universe. This part of the company engaged in trading with hedge funds, banks, speculators, and gamblers from around the world. Huge derivative bets were placed, with billions of dollars riding on the outcome. Other than a legal pursuit of profit, it served no societal function.

This was the part of AIG that was nothing more than a giant structured finance hedge fund. Despite the fact this hedge fund had no credit rating, no supervision or regulatory oversight, and no reserves, it somehow managed to trade off of the good name—and triple-A rating—of the regulated half. Counterparties treated it as if it were triple-A, regulated and guaranteed by the government.

AIG "exploited a huge gap in regulatory oversight" to operate a hedge fund on top of its core insurance business," as Fed Chairman Ben Bernanke testified before Congress on March 3, 2009.

This was nothing more than a giant fraud, perpetrated by the people who were running AIG's structured products division. This side of the firm was exempt from any form of regulation or supervision, thanks to the Commodity Futures Modernization Act.

As you might have guessed by now, this portion of AIG is the insolvent half. As taxpayers, you should be asking yourself: Why have we paid $173 billion to bail out the speculation and derivative bets?

Of all the many horrific decisions that Hank Paulson made as Treasury secretary, the $143 billion to AIG may likely be his worst. And his successor at Treasury, Tim Geithner, is not too far behind, having already doled out $30 billion to AIG.

It's highly unlikely we're getting the money back. The main reason for the cash infusions so far seems to be bailing out AIG's counterparties, the firms for which AIG provided so-called insurance on collateralized debt obligations and other derivative instruments. Given that few of these CDOs are ever going to get back to par and that some of the policies have 30-year durations, we've only just begun the process of bailing out AIG and its policyholders, who have claims that some estimate run into the $450 billion range.

■ ■ ■

What should have been done? When AIG was nationalized, it should have immediately spun out the good, solvent life insurance company, which is a highly viable stand-alone entity. The hedge fund should have been wound down in an orderly fashion. Match up the offsetting trades; wind down the rest. End of story.

The credit default swap gamblers had no reasonable expectation that anyone other than the firm they placed their bet with was going to make it good. If they happened to place a bet with a firm run by incompetent management, well, then, that becomes their problem, not the government's. If they selected as a counterparty another hedge fund that did not reserve for the losses and was unable to make payments, well, that was a choice they made. It certainly is not the obligation of the taxpayer to assume the risk. As of March 2009, the bill for AIG is $173 billion—every last penny of which has been a needless waste.

At least as far as the taxpayers are concerned it's a waste. To the various counterparties, it was manna from heaven:

"AIG, under pressure from lawmakers to show how its bailout cash was spent, disclosed on March 15 that $105 billion flowed to states and banks, led by Goldman Sachs Group Inc., Société Générale SA and Deutsche Bank AG," Bloomberg reported.

"Banks that bought credit-default swaps or traded securities with AIG got $22.4 billion in collateral, $27.1 billion in payments from a U.S. entity to retire the derivatives and $43.7 billion tied to the securities-lending program, AIG said. States, including California and Virginia, got $12.1 billion tied to guaranteed investment contracts."[5]

Among those that have partaken of Uncle Sam's munificence were Goldman Sachs, Merrill Lynch, Morgan Stanley, Wachovia, and Bank of America. You might be surprised to learn that the rest of the charity recipients were overseas banks: Germany's Deutsche Bank and French bank Société Générale, as well as Calyon/Crédit Agricole (France), Danske (Denmark), HSBC (UK), Royal Bank of Scotland, Banco Santander (Spain), Lloyds Banking Group (UK), Barclay (UK), and Rabobank (Netherlands).

Not only are U.S. taxpayers subsidizing the bad decisions made by executives in the United States, but we are also bailing out the poor judgment of the rest of the world.

Adding injury to insult, "some of the billions of dollars that the U.S. government paid to bail out [AIG] stand to benefit hedge funds that bet on a falling housing market," the *Wall Street Journal* reported.[6]

In short, what looks like a government backdoor bailout of major financial institutions with AIG serving as the middleman is, in part, actually a bailout of private speculators. Hedge funds don't bear the responsibility for the collapse of our financial system, as some contend, but do they really deserve to double-dip on the real estate bust at taxpayers' expense?

▪ ▪ ▪

Hence, the call for nationalization is not a move toward socialism, but an attempt to prevent casino capitalism from bankrupting the country. (See Figures 22.1 to 22.5.)

Real capitalists nationalize; faux capitalists look for the free lunch.

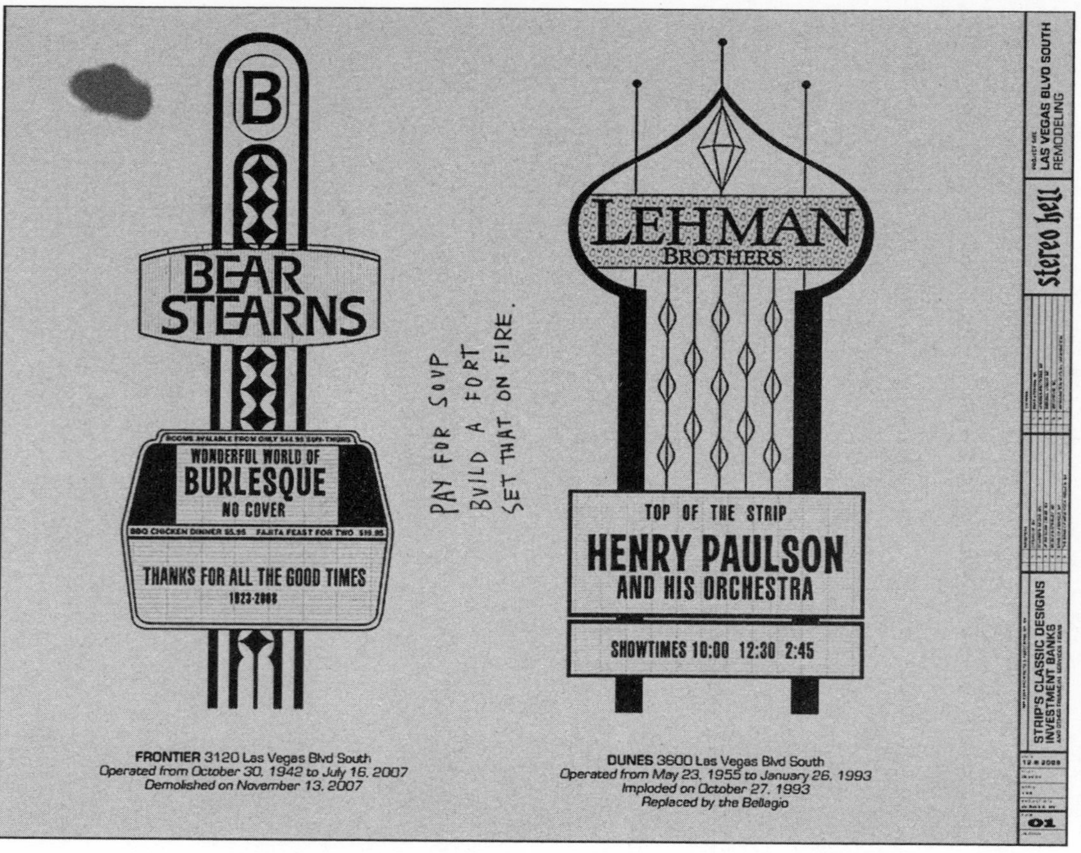

Figure 22.1

SOURCE: Strip's classic designs © 2008 Stereohell/JCC

Figure 22.2

SOURCE: Strip's classic designs © 2008 Stereohell/JCC

Figure 22.3

SOURCE: Strip's classic designs © 2008 Stereohell/JCC

Figure 22.4

SOURCE: Strip's classic designs © 2008 Stereohell/JCC

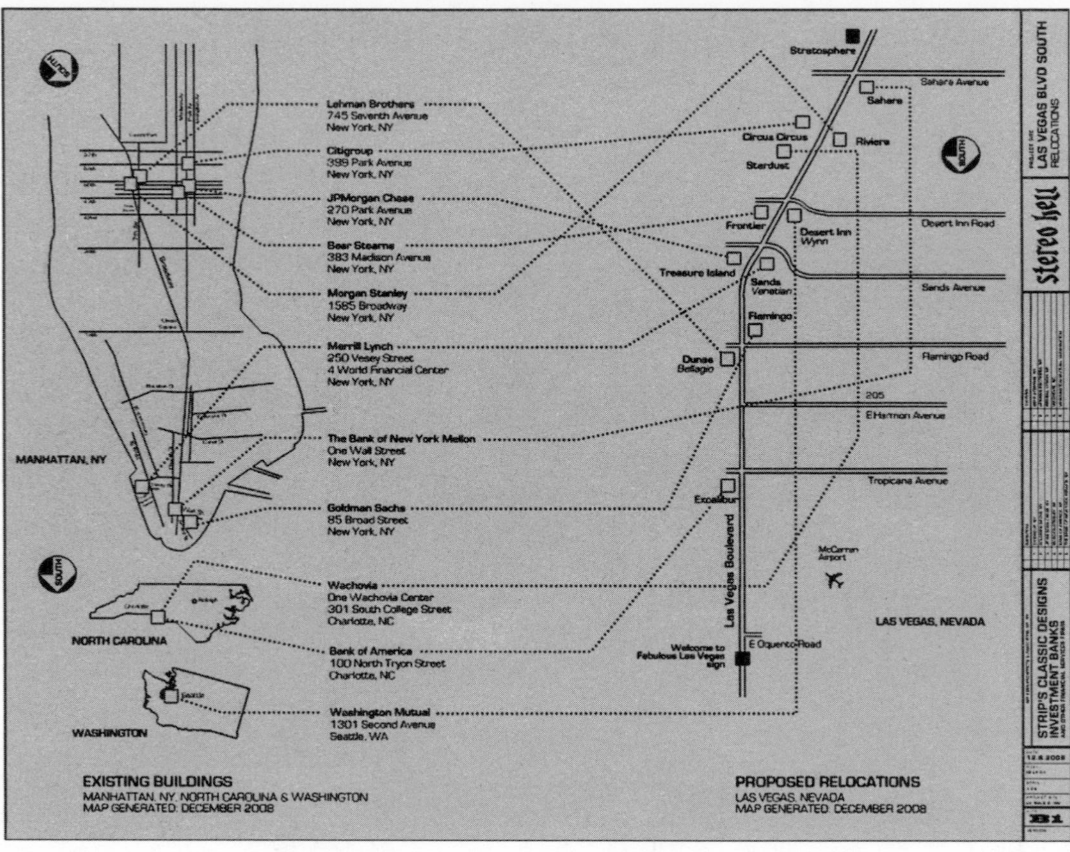

Figure 22.5
SOURCE: Strip's classic designs © 2008 Stereohell/JCC

Postscript

Advice to a New President

There can be few fields of human endeavor in which history counts for so little as in the world of finance. Past experience, to the extent that it is part of memory at all, is dismissed as the primitive refuge of those who do not have the insight to appreciate the incredible wonders of the present.

—John Kenneth Galbraith

I've detailed many of my own thoughts throughout the book, but I have two additional ideas. The first is simple: We need to start teaching basic financial literacy in public schools. That so many people willingly signed on the dotted lines for mortgages they could not possibly afford points to the terrible lack of basic financial knowledge.

Second, quantitative methods have become extremely important on Wall Street. Their ability to identify aberrational patterns and find trading opportunities is one of the biggest growth areas in finance today. It is a technique that could be easily adapted by the Securities and Exchange Commission for indentifying fraud. Perhaps the SEC could impanel practitioners, academics, mathematicians, and quants to develop a plan

to use the tools of quantitative analysis to ferret out Ponzi schemes such as Bernie Madoff's before they cause billions in losses and ruin lives.

These past 300 or so pages have criticized, castigated, and even castrated many of the worst citizens of Bailout Nation. For this last chapter, let's employ a different approach.

One of the terrific things about working on Wall Street is that you meet many astute, creative, intelligent people. Contrary to recent events, not everyone who works on the street of dreams is a reckless speculator, overcompensated executive, or Ponzi-schemist. Indeed, the vast majority of Wall Streeters are hardworking souls who are deeply upset about the way their industry has been hijacked and what that has done to our nation. They have many insights about the credit crisis, housing collapse, costly bailouts, and the ugliest recession of our lifetimes. And as you will see, they are not at all shy about expressing their views on how to fix the current mess, either.

Rather than ending our survey of malicious incompetence on a downbeat note, I would like to use this opportunity to present smart ideas from some of the best and brightest I know, offering constructive advice to a new president.

Their suggestions fall into a few broad categories: resolving the housing and credit mess, fixing the economy, improving monetary policy, energy innovations, and (for lack of a better phrase) presidential leadership.

■ ■ ■

Doug Kass manages a short hedge fund. (His optimism is such that he recently opened a long-only fund, too!) Doug warned early on that leverage, derivatives, and overvalued stocks were a dangerous combination. Now that his worst-case scenario has come true, he has an intriguing idea. Given that the problem in the housing market is one of excess supply relative to limited demand—too many houses, too few buyers—why not bring in more home buyers?

Doug writes: "For a long time the United States has had a policy of issuing green cards rapidly to foreigners willing to invest in a business here. If the U.S. had a new policy to issue rapid green cards (with all the usual security checks) to immigrants willing to buy a house or apartment for $200,000 or more and to eliminate overseas earnings from tax for 15 years, we could get a flood of good immigrants, with skills and assets, providing an immediate catalyst in soaking up the surplus of unsold housing inventory. These policies would cost the United States very little, and would bring in directed capital for housing and employment. U.S. residency/citizenship (sans the iniquitous foreign earnings tax policy) would be highly prized and desired among foreigners anxious to live in a stable society with opportunity, compared to the growing instability over much of the world."

Ed Easterling, president of Crestmont Research, explains why this might work: "The most significant intermediate economic issue is the excess supply of housing—currently more homes than qualified home buyers. Since we can't impact the supply of homes in the short run, we need to increase the availability of qualified homeowners. One solution would be to introduce a 10-year work visa program for foreigners who either have college degrees or agree to start a business (and can show that they have the capital to fund it). Both of those groups would be qualified to purchase a full range of excess housing stock and to contribute significantly to the economy."

And Michael Covel, producer of the documentary film *Broke: The New American Dream*, adds: "Increasing the population somehow or another is the only thing that can fix this mess. We need more people. Give tax breaks and dual passports immediately to those folks who pass an economic means test. Open the borders to money."

Newsletter writer John Mauldin concurs: "Bring in one million fairly affluent, legal immigrants, and you put a floor (and maybe some bounce) in the housing markets at all levels. They will figure out how to work and pay taxes (which we need). Many will start new businesses that will create jobs. With excess housing inventory gone, home building can start again, as well as a lot of related durable goods purchased to furnish those homes. And that is with just one million new immigrants. What if the number were two or three million?"

CNBC host Dylan Ratigan has a novel idea: He wants to update the GI Bill. Ratigan calls for a $50,000 housing tax credit provided to all veterans of the Iraq/Afghanistan wars and to every active member of the U.S. military. The idea is to help both the housing market and the veterans. And he advises, make it tradable. If they don't want to buy a

home, they can sell the credit to someone who does. It's more than an effort to prop up the housing market—it's a benefit for the servicemen and servicewomen in the armed forces.

Asset manager Jim Welsh advises preventing a repeat of mortgage securitization problems. In the future, any institution that originates a loan that will be securitized should be (1) required to keep 10 percent (or some significant percentage) of any loan that is securitized and (2) absorb the first X dollars of loss, rather than the loss going to the investors who purchased the securitized loan. Lenders will be far more attentive to maintaining good lending standards if they are at true risk of loss.

Jim further notes that we have a size problem. The credit crisis has resulted in a major consolidation among our largest financial institutions, with more than half of all nonfinancial debt (debt held by households, nonfinancial companies, and government) held by the top 15 institutions. The SEC, with the aid of Congress and the Federal Deposit Insurance Corporation (FDIC), should mandate that the 20 largest financial institutions be broken up into smaller firms within 10 years. Getting rid of these behemoth firms would go a long way toward preventing another financial meltdown.

Scott Frew runs Rockingham Capital Partners, a long/short hedge fund. He, too, foresaw a credit crisis before most economists and policy makers recognized it. His solution? "Bite the bullet. Recognize the insolvency of these banks, forcing them into receivership at the hands of the FDIC (a much more palatable framing than nationalizing them). Let's start dealing with the consequences sooner rather than later (as Japan did)."

The consequences from this action would be substantial: wiping out equity, preferred shareholders, and the subordinated debt. This action would have major ripple effects—including additional bankruptcies.

However, Scott argues that it is a necessary evil: "Pushing the big banks (and AIG needs to go there as well) into fully nationalized mode doesn't solve our problems by any means; it is merely the first step—but a step without which we can't make much progress—along a very difficult road. The extent of the deleveraging that we have to undergo, not simply among the banks, but by households and nonfinancial corporations as well, will take years to happen under the best of circumstances. My goal is putting banks in a position from which they are again able to lend."

On a related note, Robert Lenzner of *Forbes* suggests: "Get together a FASB-like institution for the SEC; populate it with wise men and lions with no axes to grind, such as Paul Volcker, Felix Rohatyn, and John Whitehead; and decide how to handle the treatment of the bank losses."

■ ■ ■

Stock Trader Almanac editor Jeffrey Hirsch suggests a Manhattan Project for energy technology. We have seen only incremental improvements in technologies, such as battery storage, solar energy conversion, and internal combustion efficiency. What we need is a breakthrough on a fundamental physics level—the sort of thing that only government can fund over long periods of time.

Silicon Valley executive Jeff Weitzman (Yahoo!, Coupons.com) adds, "With the billions that we dumped into AIG alone we could, for example, transform the solar industry: Subsidizing solar panel installations would at once pump money directly into the economy in the short term, significantly reduce our reliance on imported energy in the medium term, and push solar over the line of grid parity cost-effectiveness, creating a domestic industry that will *export* energy-producing equipment and create jobs in research, engineering, manufacturing, and more. We have to spend enough to send these industries into overdrive, setting ourselves on a course to transform our economy in a relatively short period of time."

Brian Gongol is a sales engineer, small-business owner, and radio talk show host. He thinks we can jump-start the nation's innovative energy entrepreneurs via inducement prizes. He wants the government (or a wealthy private benefactor) to offer $1 billion cash prizes for each of these energy innovations:

- Mass-produced solar roof shingles at a comparable cost to conventional shingles.
- Automobile engine modification that increases fuel efficiency by 10 miles per gallon for less than $1,000.
- Wallpaper-like insulation that increases the heating/cooling efficiency in homes.
- Reduction of transmission losses from power plants by 10 percent for less than the cost of the recovered power.

For a billion dollars each, it's virtually certain that someone or some organization would enthusiastically start seeking answers to each of these questions. The results would concentrate the diffuse social benefits of positive discoveries.

The simplest idea comes from James Altucher, managing partner, Formula Capital. James suggests: "No income taxes for one year. It's the most immediate way to make people feel wealthier and give them more confidence in the economy. The result will be new businesses started, a return of the multiplier effect in the economy, and over time much greater tax revenues."

■ ■ ■

Ned Davis (of Ned Davis Research) notes, "If President Obama wants to follow through on his pledge of fundamental change and trickle-up economic theory, I would have the government increase fixed investment in proven technologies with visible multipliers, and work with other countries to improve trade and financial stability, instead of providing bailouts. By putting out the prospect of new jobs, the government will help the future look more hopeful."

A few of Ned's ideas are:

- Installing modern equipment and software to make government more efficient, including the Pentagon.
- Improving transportation infrastructure, including bridges, roads, and mass transit to help Americans commute more safely, efficiently, and quickly.
- Developing nuclear, solar, wind, and other alternative energy facilities to cut our foreign energy dependence, which may reduce energy price volatility and help lower energy costs down the road. Upgrading the transmission grid.
- Improving water infrastructure, including drinking water, wastewater, dams, and ports.

Ned's bottom line is that a very strong correlation exists between gross domestic investment and nominal gross domestic product (GDP) (see Figure PS.1). If we need more stimulus, let it be directed toward needed investment, not bailouts.

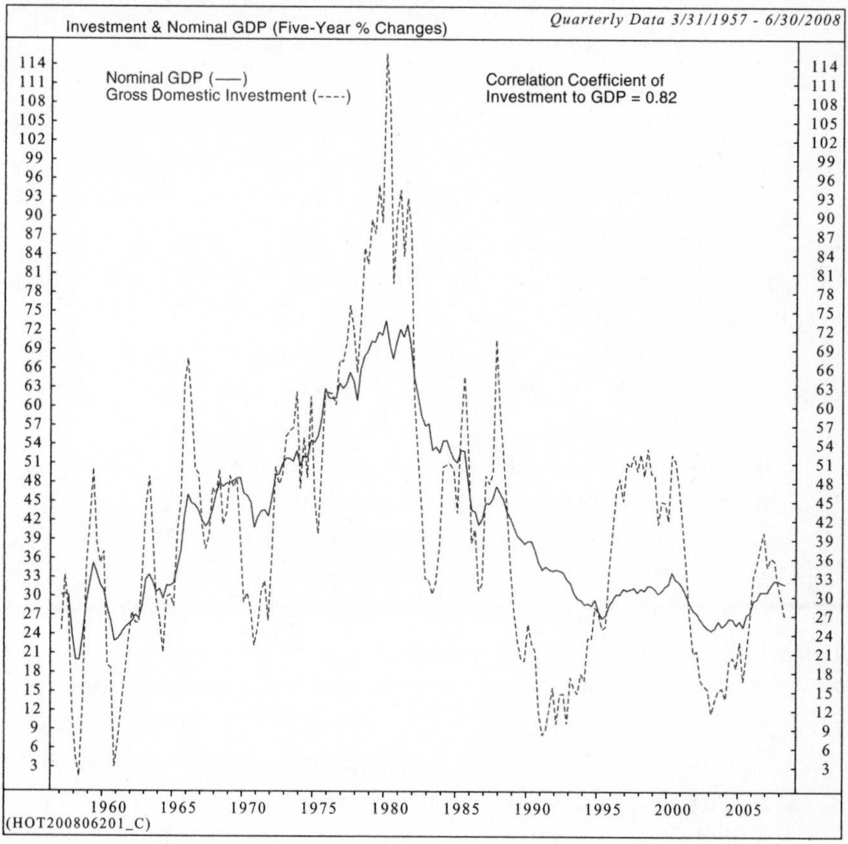

Investment & Nominal GDP (Five-Year % Changes)

Quarterly Data 3/31/1957 - 6/30/2008

Nominal GDP (——)
Gross Domestic Investment (----)

Correlation Coefficient of Investment to GDP = 0.82

(HOT200806201_C)

Figure PS.1 Investment and Nominal Changes (Five-Year Percent Changes)
SOURCE: Courtesy of Ned Davis Research

An overlooked economic fix would be to help the cash-starved state and local governments. That idea comes from David Rosenberg, the North American economist for Merrill Lynch. In a recent missive to Merrill's clients, David noted that "the economy is in dire need of a major positive exogenous shock." His idea: "The White House should instruct Congress to dole out a $1 trillion zero percent long-term loan to the beleaguered state and local governments that are being forced to cut back services and raise taxes at the worst possible time. What is not open for debate is the state of the economy, and we can no longer just label this a recession after the latest string of shockingly negative employment

reports. The government has to declare war right now . . . against this modern-day depression."

Jim Welsh concurs, noting that the primary focus of any federal government program should be to spend money on projects that will have the greatest multiplier effect. In the second quarter of 2008, the government spent more than $100 billion on rebate checks for individuals. Best estimates were that consumers spent only 20 cents of each $1 distributed, meaning the economy didn't get much of a boost. Spending on infrastructure projects, such as bridge and road repair, has historically generated more than $1 of economic activity for each $1 spent. I'm sure economists will be able to provide the Obama administration specific spending ideas that have the greatest multiplier effect.

Portfolio manager Carl Haefling suggests the Fed and Treasury "allow anyone in the nation who has a mortgage that is current to refinance the mortgage without fees at 4.5 percent for 30 years. This would be equal to a tax cut for large numbers of people. It could help stabilize the housing market and prevent more inventory being created. It would be offered one time only and available only for a designated period of time. (As long as we are considering government-guaranteed loans, we could also extend the low-interest-rate offer to well-qualified car buyers. That, or providing a $2,000 new car purchase tax credit would also add some activity to a weak section of the economy.)

Richard Lang, executive director of the Virtual Country Foundation, suggests that the United States "fund four years of public college education for every student in high school with at least a B average. This was calculated a few years ago at $35 billion. That sounded like too much money back then, but it seems like nothing now. It will provide a motivator for students to achieve reasonable academic goals, and the economic benefit will be felt immediately by every family with one or more children approaching college age."

On a strictly fiscal basis, Bob Agdern, retired counsel for BP Amoco, notes this key lesson from history: We should pay heed to the sheer number of empires that became overstretched militarily and then sunk under their own weight. We need a military and intelligence system structured for the next century, not the last one. And just as important, we need to be able to size these endeavors at a level we can afford. We can't continue to subsidize the entire free world by acting as the globe's policeman.

Several people, including *Greenspan's Bubbles* contributor Fred Sheehan, suggested disbanding the Federal Reserve entirely. Like unilateral nuclear disarmament, I somehow doubt that is likely to happen. And Seth Daniels, research analyst, wrote: "I find it interesting that not a single person advocated a laissez-faire recommendation."

Quite a few people had some interesting suggestions for the Fed.

David Merkel, chief economist of Finacorp Securities, who writes the Aleph Blog, notes that sometimes we have to take our medicine: "Alan Greenspan's unwillingness to allow for moderately stiff recessions led to an unsustainable buildup in the debt-to-GDP ratio." While we can smooth out the peaks and valleys of the business cycle, trying to eliminate it totally is a fool's errand.

Peter Boockvar, market strategist at Miller Tabak, goes even further, suggesting a more European Central Bank type model: "Change the responsibilities of the Fed to solely that of price stability. Eliminate the mandate of maximum employment, as the two conflict. The optimum environment for economic growth should be on the fiscal and regulatory front. The marketplace should set the proper level of interest rates. A stable currency and thus price stability are in the direct purview of monetary policy. It was unstable monetary policy—the shifting of the fed funds rate to manipulate economic activity—that created the basis for the boom/bust economy, without which bubbles would be dramatically less likely."

Gene Salomon is a music attorney and partner at Gang, Tyre, Ramer & Brown in Beverly Hills, whose clients include Neil Diamond, Pink, and Radiohead. Gene notes, "It has become common wisdom that we need a more robust regulatory scheme in the United States, and I agree. What is often overlooked in the discussion is the need to rebuild the regulatory agency manpower we used to have. Since the 1980s under Reagan, we have eliminated the professional civil servants necessary for regulation to work. Outsourcing has run amok and is ineffective and inefficient. Recruit and hire the best people (even if you have to pay more for them) as quickly as you can."

Last, Paul Brodsky and Lee Quaintance, who run asset management firm QB Partners, made the following bold suggestion: Make sound money the nation's highest economic priority. If U.S. dollars were to be thought of globally as a reasonable store of wealth—not just relative to other currencies but over generations—then global economies would

function far better and most if not all of the financial excesses we've been experiencing would go away. How to do that? Convert to the gold standard. (They admit that "our best ideas don't seem feasible at the moment.")

▪ ▪ ▪

Joe Moglia, chairman of TD Ameritrade, has an idea that is less about *what* the president should do than *how* he—along with Tim Geithner and Ben Bernanke—should approach their jobs. Joe's big complaint has to do with communication.

This is the first time we've had to handle this situation, and it's incredibly complex and difficult. While it takes great minds to devise a solution, when it's time to explain it to the typical family, it needs to be kept reasonably simple and clear. If a football coach has a brilliant game plan on the blackboard but cannot simplify it so it is crystal clear to the players, that plan will not get executed properly. The probability for failure increases.

Our president—as articulate as he is—is allowing his team to sound like philosophers and researchers when they explain what is going on in the marketplace and what the business plan is to fix it. He needs to speak to this country in a way people can understand. It will foster confidence that the fate of the nation is in good hands.

Vince Farrell of the Soleil Group offers this related suggestion: "Monthly (or quarterly) White House dinners. Take a page from New York City Mayor Michael Bloomberg and have regular dinners with people from different industries and walks of life. Include finance types at every dinner, along with academics and social workers, industrialists and health care workers. Everyone has to sing for their supper in two minutes or less with the most important issue on their minds."

▪ ▪ ▪

Good suggestions, all. I hope someone in the White House pays attention.

Notes

Chapter 1: A Brief History of Bailouts

1. Daniel Gross, *Pop! Why Bubbles Are Great for the Economy* (New York: HarperCollins, 2007).

Chapter 2: The Creation of the Federal Reserve, and Its Role in Creating Our Bailout Nation

1. Casimir Frank Gierut, *Taxpayers' Message to Congress: Repeal the Federal Reserve Banks; Pandora's Box of Criminal Acts* (Bunker Hill, IL: National Committee to Repeal the Federal Reserve Act, 1983), 31. (The Federal Reserve Act was passed in 1913 on a Sunday two days before Christmas when most of Congress was on vacation. Wilson's comments regarding the bill he signed into law were made years later.)
2. Steve Matthews, "The Improviser," *Bloomberg Markets*, June 2008, www.bloomberg.com/news/marketsmag/mm_0608_story2.html.
3. The Economic Club of New York, 395th Meeting, New York City, April 8, 2008, http://econclubny.org/files/Transcript_Volcker_April_2008.pdf.
4. "Jefferson's Opinion on the Constitutionality of a National Bank," 1791, The Avalon Project at Yale Law School, www.yale.edu/lawweb/avalon/amerdoc/bank-tj.htm.

5. Virtual Tour of Historic Philadelphia, "Second Bank of the United States/ Portrait Gallery: Biddle vs. Jackson," www.ushistory.org/tour/tour_2bank .htm.
6. Roger T. Johnson, "Historical Beginnings . . . the Federal Reserve," Federal Reserve Bank of Boston, December 1999, www.bos.frb.org/about/ pubs/begin.pdf.
7. Stephen Mihm, *A Nation of Counterfeiters: Capitalists, Con Men, and the Making of the United States* (Cambridge, MA: Harvard University Press, 2007).
8. Ibid., 6.
9. Johnson, "Historical Beginnings."
10. Robert F. Bruner and Sean D. Carr, *The Panic of 1907: Lessons Learned from the Market's Perfect Storm* (Hoboken, NJ: John Wiley & Sons, 2007), 7.
11. G. Edward Griffin, *The Creature from Jekyll Island*, 4th ed. (Westlake Village, CA: American Media, 2002).

Chapter 3: Pre-Bailout Nation (1860–1942)

1. Robert J. Shiller, "A Government Hand in the Economy Is as Old as the Republic," *Washington Post*, September 28, 2008, B01, www.washingtonpost .com/wp-dyn/content/article/2008/09/26/AR2008092602838. html.
2. Daniel Gross, *Pop! Why Bubbles Are Great for the Economy* (New York: HarperCollins, 2007), 29. (Morse was a reluctant entrepreneur who believed the telegraph was too important a public utility to be left to the private sector. He "repeatedly begged Congress to take control of the telegraph, and make the extension of lines a national project.")
3. Jonathan Alter, *The Defining Moment: FDR's Hundred Days and the Triumph of Hope* (New York: Simon & Schuster, 2006), 341.
4. Harriss, C. L., *History and Policies of the Home Owner's Loan Corporation* (Detroit: National Bureau of Economic Research, 1951), www.nber.org/books/ harr51-1.
5. "Profitable HOLC," *Time*, April 22, 1946, www.time.com/time/magazine/ article/0,9171,792832,00.html.
6. Alex J. Pollock, "A 1930s Loan Rescue Lesson," *Washington Post*, March 14, 2008, A17, www.washingtonpost.com/wp-dyn/content/article/ 2008/03/13/AR2008031303174.html.
7. Harriss, *History and Policies.*
8. Ibid.
9. Alan S. Blinder, "From the New Deal, a Way Out of a Mess," *New York Times*, February 24, 2008, www.nytimes.com/2008/02/24/business/24view.html.

10. Harriss, *History and Policies*.
11. James Butkiewicz, "Reconstruction Finance Corporation," in *EH.Net Encyclopedia*, ed. Robert Whaples, July 20, 2002, http://eh.net/encyclopedia/article/butkiewicz.finance.corp.reconstruction.
12. Wigmore, Barrie A., "The Crash and Its Aftermath: A History of Securities Markets in the United States, 1929–1933," Contributions in Economics and Economic History, no. 58 (Westport, CT: Greenwood Publishing Group, 1985), 540.

Chapter 4: Industrial-Era Bailouts (1971–1995)

1. The company placed the blame for these losses and its subsequent difficulties on military contracts arranged under the Total Package Procurement (TPP) procedure instituted by former Defense Secretary Robert McNamara, a system "designed to end overrun claims by setting a strict ceiling on the final cost of any project."
2. The TPP was a fixed contract purchasing program instituted by the Defense Department where defense contractors would bid for military programs based on their expected development and production costs and the government would pay only up to the contract ceiling. The losses involved in any contract would thus be shouldered by the contractor with the government liable only to the ceiling price.
3. Nick Barisheff, "August 15, 1971: Inflation Unleashed," Financial Sense University, May 11, 2006, www.financialsense.com/fsu/editorials/bms/2006/0511.html.
4. "The Biggest Bankruptcy Ever," *Time*, July 6, 1970, www.time.com/time/magazine/article/0,9171,878372,00.html.
5. "The Penn Central Reorganization Revisited—Again," News and Insights, DLA Piper, January 14, 2008, www.dlapiper.com/penn_central_reorganization/.
6. "Chrysler's Crisis Bailout," *Time*, August 20, 1979, www.time.com/time/magazine/article/0,9171,947356,00.html.
7. Jimmy Carter, "Chrysler Corporation Loan Guarantee Act of 1979: Remarks on Signing H.R. 5860 into Law," January 7, 1980, www.presidency.ucsb.edu/ws/index.php?pid=32978.

Chapter 5: Stock Market Bailouts (1987–1995)

1. Nell Henderson, "Backstopping the Economy Too Well?" *Washington Post*, June 30, 2005, D01, www.washingtonpost.com/wp-dyn/content/article/2005/06/29/AR2005062902841.html.

2. Robert T. Parry, "The October '87 Crash Ten Years Later," *Federal Reserve Bank San Francisco Economic Letter* 97-32, October 31, 1997, www.frbsf.org/econrsrch/wklyltr/e19-32.html.
3. Brett D. Fromson, "Plunge Protection Team," *Washington Post*, February 23, 1997, H01, www.washingtonpost.com/wp-srv/business/longterm/blackm/plunge.htm.
4. Zachary Roth, "Report Shows White House Engineered U.S. Attorney Firings," October 1, 2008, http://tpmmuckraker.talkingpointsmemo.com/2008/10/report_shows_white_house_engineered.php.
5. Lynn Thomasson and Eric Martin Bloomberg, "S&P 500 Index Drop Leaves 64 Industries with Losses," November 21, 2008, www.bloomberg.com/apps/news?pid=20601213&sid=am1FNznC.tNE&.
6. Carl E. Walsh, "What Caused the 1990–1991 Recession?" *Economic Review*, no. 2, Federal Reserve Bank of San Francisco, 1993, www.frbsf.org/publications/economics/review/1993/93-2_34-48.pdf.
7. Louis Uchitelle, "Greenspan's Authority Curtailed on Interest Rates, Officials Say," *New York Times*, April 8, 1991, http://query.nytimes.com/gst/fullpage.html?res=9D0CE0D8113DF93BA35757C0A967958260.
8. Paul R. Krugman, "Did the Federal Reserve Cause the Recession?" *U.S. News & World Report* 110, no. 12, April 1, 1991, 54, www.pkarchive.org/economy/FedRecession1991.html.
9. Federal Reserve Bank of New York, "Historical Changes of the Target Federal Funds and Discount Rates, 1971 to Present," www.newyorkfed.org/markets/statistics/dlyrates/fedrate.html.

Chapter 6: The Irrational Exuberance Era (1996–1999)

1. Alan Greenspan, Remarks at the Annual Dinner and Francis Boyer Lecture of the American Enterprise Institute for Public Policy Research, Washington, D.C., December 5, 1996, aka the "Irrational Exuberance Speech"; www.federalreserve.gov/boarddocs/speeches/1996/19961205.html.
2. Ibid.
3. Daniel Gross, "Wall Street Throws a Tantrum," *Newsweek*, February 11, 2008, www.newsweek.com/id/107571; Gillian Tett, "Markets Throw One Tantrum after Another," *Financial Times*, October 10, 2008, http://us.ft.com/ftgateway/superpage.ft?news_id=fto101020081422295531; "Carry On Screaming," *Economist*, October 9, 2008, www.economist.com/finance/displaystory.cfm?story_id=12381895.
4. Alan Greenspan, "Risk and Uncertainty in Monetary Policy," Remarks at the Meetings of the American Economic Association, San Diego,

California, January 3, 2004, www.federalreserve.gov/boarddocs/speeches/2004/20040103/default.htm.

5. Charles Mackay, *Extraordinary Popular Delusions and the Madness of Crowds*, published in 1841; Edwin Lefèvre, *Reminiscences of a Stock Operator*, published in 1922–1923; and John Kenneth Galbraith, *The Great Crash, 1929*, published in 1955, are examples.
6. Federal Reserve Press Release, November 17, 1998, www.federalreserve.gov/boarddocs/press/general/1998/19981117/.
7. "The Committee to Save the World: The Inside Story on How the Three Marketeers Have Prevented a Global Economic Meltdown—So Far," *Time*, February 15, 1999, www.time.com/time/covers/0,16641,19990215,00.html.

Chapter 7: The Tech Wreck (2000–2003)

1. Minutes of the Federal Open Market Committee meeting of August 20, 1996 (transcript).
2. Alan Greenspan, "Question: Is There a New Economy?" remarks at the Haas Annual Business Faculty Research Dialogue, University of California, Berkeley, California, September 4, 1998.
3. The full list of imploded mortgage lenders can be found at The Mortgage Lender Implode-O-Meter, http://ml-implode.com/index.html#lists.

Chapter 8: The Backwards, Rate-Driven Economy

1. Floyd Norris, "Dow Conquers 5,000 Mark, Riding Surge of Confidence," *New York Times*, November 22, 1995, http://query.nytimes.com/gst/fullpage.html?res=9F07E1DB1339F931A15752C1A963958260.
2. Ben S. Bernanke, "Deflation: Making Sure 'It' Doesn't Happen Here," remarks before the National Economists Club, Washington, D.C., November 21, 2002, www.federalreserve.gov/BOARDDOCS/SPEECHES/2002/20021121/default.htm.
3. Asha Bangalore, "Housing Market—Another Information Tidbit," Northern Trust Company, May 23, 2005, www.northerntrust.com/library/econ_research/daily/us/dd052305.pdf.
4. Christopher D. Carroll, Misuzu Otsuka, and Jiri Slacalek, "How Large Is the Housing Wealth Effect? A New Approach," NBER Working Paper W12746, December 2006, http://papers.ssrn.com/sol3/papers.cfm?abstract_id=949756.
5. Alan Abelson, "Hold the Bubbly," *Barron's*, January 2, 2006, http://online.barrons.com/article/SB113598787824035213.html.

Chapter 9: The Mad Scramble for Yield

1. Jesse Eisinger, *Portfolio*, September 2007, www.portfolio.com/news-markets/national-news/portfolio/2007/08/13/Moody-Ratings-Fiasco.
2. Aaron Lucchetti and Serena Ng, "How Rating Firms' Calls Fueled Subprime Mess," *Wall Street Journal*, August 15, 2007, http://online.wsj.com/article/SB118714461352698015.html.
3. Aaron Lucchetti, "As Housing Boomed, Moody's Opened Up," *Wall Street Journal*, April 11, 2008, http://online.wsj.com/article/SB120787287341306591.html.
4. Elliot Blair Smith, "Bringing Down Wall Street as Ratings Let Loose Subprime Scourge, Part I," *Bloomberg*, September 24, 2008, www.bloomberg.com/apps/news?pid=20601109&sid=ah839IWTLP9s&#.
5. Niall Ferguson, "Wall Street Lays Another Egg," *Vanity Fair*, December 2008, www.vanityfair.com/politics/features/2008/12/banks200812.
6. Ibid.
7. Ibid.
8. Ibid.
9. Ibid.

Chapter 10: The Machinery of Subprime

1. Anthony Ha, "Minorities Hit Hard by Foreclosure Crunch," *Hollister (CA) Free Lance*, May 3, 2007, http://hollisterfreelance.com/news/contentview.asp?c=213141.
2. Mara Der Hovanesian, "Nightmare Mortgages," *BusinessWeek*, September 11, 2006, www.businessweek.com/magazine/content/06_37/b4000001.htm.
3. Sarah Max, "Appraisal Fraud: Your Home at Risk; Appraisers Say They're Being Pressured by Lenders to Inflate Their Estimates of Home Values," *CNNMoney*, June 2, 2005, http://money.cnn.com/2005/05/23/real_estate/financing/appraisalfraud/index.htm.
4. Jeff Manning, "Chase Mortgage Memo Pushes 'Cheats & Tricks,'" *Oregonian*, March 27, 2008, www.oregonlive.com/business/oregonian/index.ssf?/base/business/120658650589950.xml&coll=7.

Chapter 11: Radical Deregulation, Nonfeasance

1. Peter S. Goodman, "Taking Hard New Look at a Greenspan Legacy," *New York Times*, October 9, 2008, www.nytimes.com/2008/10/09/business/economy/09greenspan.html.

2. Ibid.
3. Ibid.
4. Ibid.
5. Eric Lipton, "Gramm and the 'Enron Loophole,'" *New York Times*, November 17, 2008, www.nytimes.com/2008/11/17/business/17grammside.html.
6. "Blind Faith: How Deregulation and Enron's Influence over Government Looted Billions from Americans," Public Citizen, December 2001, www.tradewatch.org/cmep/energy_enviro_nuclear/electricity/Enron/articles.cfm?ID=7104.
7. Lipton, "Gramm and the 'Enron Loophole.'"
8. "Levin Lauds Congressional Approval of Close 'Enron Loophole' Law," press release, Office of Senator Carl Levin, May 15, 2008, http://levin.senate.gov/newsroom/release.cfm?id=297870.
9. Frank Partnoy, "Stock Gambling on the Cheap," *New York Times*, December 21, 2000, http://query.nytimes.com/gst/fullpage.html?res=9C06E6D81E39F932A15751C1A9669C8B63&sec=&spon=&pagewanted=2.
10. Lee A. Pickard, "SEC's Old Capital Approach Was Tried—and True," *American Banker* 173, no. 153 (August 8, 2008), 10, www.americanbanker.com/article.html?id=20080807ZAXGNH3Y&queryid=2110207978&.
11. Alan Greenspan, "Consumer Finance," remarks at the Federal Reserve System's Fourth Annual Community Affairs Research Conference, Washington, D.C., April 8, 2005.
12. Alan Greenspan, "Understanding Household Debt Obligations," remarks at the Credit Union National Association 2004 Governmental Affairs Conference, Washington, D.C., February 23, 2004.
13. Binyamin Appelbaum and Ellen Nakashima, "Banking Regulator Played Advocate over Enforcer," *Washington Post*, November 23, 2008, www.washingtonpost.com/wp-dyn/content/article/2008/11/22/AR2008112202213.html?nav=rss_print&sid=ST2008112300238&s_pos=.
14. "FBI Issues Mortgage Fraud Notice in Conjunction with Mortgage Bankers Association," press release, March 8, 2007, www.fbi.gov/pressrel/pressrel07/mortgagefraud030807.htm.
15. Terry Frieden, "FBI Warns of Mortgage Fraud 'Epidemic'; Seeks to Head Off 'Next S&L Crisis,'" CNN, September 17, 2004, www.cnn.com/2004/LAW/09/17/mortgage.fraud/.
16. Greg Ip, "Did Greenspan Add to Subprime Woes? Gramlich Says Ex-Colleague Blocked Crackdown on Predatory Lenders Despite Growing Concerns," *Wall Street Journal*, June 9, 2007, http://online.wsj.com/article/SB118134111823129555.html.

17. Ibid.
18. Edmund L. Andrews, "In Reversal, Fed Approves Plan to Curb Risky Lending," *New York Times*, December 19, 2007, www.nytimes.com/2007/12/19/business/19subprime.html.

Chapter 12: Strange Connections, Unintended Consequences

1. Frédéric Bastiat, "What Is Seen and What Is Not Seen," in *Selected Essays on Political Economy*, trans. Seymour Cain (Irvington-on-Hudson, NY: Foundation for Economic Education, 1995), www.econlib.org/library/Bastiat/basEss1.html.
2. Boskin Commission, "Toward a More Accurate Measure of the Cost of Living: Final Report to the Senate Finance Committee from the Advisory Commission to Study the Consumer Price Index," December 4, 1996, www.ssa.gov/history/reports/boskinrpt.html.
3. Kim Yeon-hee, "South Korea's KDB confirms talks with Lehman Ended," Reuters, September 10, 2008, www.reuters.com/article/businessNews/idUSSEO18673220080910?feedType=RSS&feedName=businessNews.
4. Lee A. Pickard, "SEC's Old Capital Approach Was Tried—and True," *American Banker* 173, no. 153 (August 8, 2008), www.americanbanker.com/article.html?id=20080807ZAXGNH3Y&queryid=2110207978&.
5. "Free Market Society," transcript of a discussion between David Gergen and Thomas Friedman, *NewsHour*, PBS, February 13, 1996, www.pbs.org/ newshour/gergen/friedman.html.
6. Paul S. Atkins, "Improving Financial Markets," remarks to the Vanderbilt University Financial Markets Research Center Conference on Securitization, Nashville, Tennessee, April 17, 2008, www.sec.gov/news/speech/2008/spch041708psa.htm.
7. Gretchen Morgenson, "Debt Watchdogs: Tamed or Caught Napping?" *New York Times*, December 6, 2008, www.nytimes.com/2008/12/07/business/07rating.html?pagewanted=1&hp.

Chapter 13: Moral Hazard: Why Bailouts Cause Future Problems

1. Alan Greenspan, letter to Senator Alphonse D'Amato, October 20, 1998, cited in *When Genius Failed: The Rise and Fall of Long-Term Capital Management*, by Roger Lowenstein (New York: Random House, 2000).
2. Allard E. Dembe and Leslie I. Boden, "Moral Hazard: A Question of Morality?" *New Solutions* 10, no. 3 (2000), 257–279.
3. E. S. Browning, "Fed Treads Moral Hazard," *Wall Street Journal*, August 13, 2007, http://online.wsj.com/article/SB118696170827295489.html.

4. Roger Lowenstein, *When Genius Failed: The Rise and Fall of Long-Term Capital Management* (New York: Random House, 2000).

5. "Questions about the $700 Billion Emergency Economic Stabilization Funds: The First Report of the Congressional Oversight Panel for Economic Stabilization," December 10, 2008, www.house.gov/apps/list/hearing/financialsvcs_dem/cop121008.pdf.

Chapter 14: 2008: Suicide by Democracy

1. Dawn Kopecki, "Fannie, Freddie 'Insolvent' after Losses, Poole Says," *Bloomberg*, July 10, 2008, www.bloomberg.com/apps/news?pid=20601087&sid=as4DEc5UFopA.

2. "Barney Frank on Bailouts, Welfare," *60 Minutes*, CBS, December 14, 2008, www.cbsnews.com/stories/2008/12/11/60minutes/main4663945.shtml.

Chapter 15: The Fall of Bear Stearns

1. Kate Kelly, "Lost Opportunities Haunt Final Days of Bear Stearns," *Wall Street Journal*, May 27, 2008, http://online.wsj.com/article/SB121184521826521301.html.

2. Kate Kelly, "Bear CEO's Handling of Crisis Raises Issues," *Wall Street Journal*, November 1, 2007, http://online.wsj.com/article/SB119387369474078336.html.

3. Gregory Zuckerman, "Hedge Funds, Once a Windfall, Contribute to Bear's Downfall," *Wall Street Journal*, March 17, 2008, http://online.wsj.com/article/SB120571237393540313.html.

4. David Einhorn, remarks at the Ira Sohn Investment Research Conference, May 21, 2008, www.tilsonfunds.com/EinhornIraSohn08.pdf.

5. Yalman Onaran and John Helyar, "Fuld Sought Buffett Offer He Refused as Lehman Sank," *Bloomberg*, November 10, 2008, www.bloomberg.com/apps/news?pid=newsarchive&sid=aMQJV3iJ5M8c.

6. Andrew Ackerman, "Court to Decide Fate of Lehman Contracts," *Bond Buyer*, December 15, 2008, www.bondbuyer.com/article.html?id=200812124023AG07.

7. Yalman Onaran, "Fed Aided Bear Stearns as Firm Faced Chapter 11, Bernanke Says," *Bloomberg*, April 2, 2008, www.bloomberg.com/apps/news?pid=20601087&refer=worldwide&sid=a7coicThgaEE.

Chapter 16: Dot-Com Penis Envy

1. Mike Sunnucks and Chris Casacchia, "CEO Pay: What Those Involved in the Financial Meltdown Made," *San Francisco Business Times*, September 23,

2008, (*The Puget Sound Business Journal* contributed to this story) http://www.bizjournals.com/eastbay/stories/2008/09/22/daily37.html.

2. "Bailout Should Cut the Cords of Golden Parachutes," *The Patriot Ledger*, Sep 23, 2008, http://www.patriotledger.com/business/x804155672/OUR-OPINION-Bailout-should-cut-the-chords-of-golden-parachutes.
3. Steve Lohr, "In Bailout Furor, Wall Street Pay Becomes a Target," *New York Times*, September 23, 2008, http://www.nytimes.com/2008/09/24/business/24pay.html.

Chapter 17: Year of the Bailout, Part I: The Notorious AIG

1. "AIG Ranks No. 1 in Financial Sector Capitalization," *Insurance Journal*, December 4, 2000, www.insurancejournal.com/news/national/2000/12/04/11570.htm.
2. Robert O'Harrow Jr. and Brady Dennis, "The Beautiful Machine," *Washington Post*, December 29, 2008, www.washingtonpost.com/wp-dyn/content/article/2008/12/28/AR2008122801916.html?sid=ST2009013000235.
3. Robert O'Harrow Jr. and Brady Dennis, "Downgrades and Downfall," *Washington Post*, December 31, 2008, www.washingtonpost.com/wp-dyn/content/article/2008/12/30/AR2008123003431.html.
4. Gretchen Morgenson, "Behind Insurer's Crisis, Blind Eye to a Web of Risk," *New York Times*, September 27, 2008, www.nytimes.com/2008/09/28/business/28melt.html?pagewanted=all.
5. Michael de la Merced and Gretchen Morgenson, "A.I.G. Allowed to Borrow Money from Subsidiaries," *New York Times*, September 14, 2008, www.nytimes. com/2008/09/15/business/15aig.html.
6. Brady Dennis and Robert O'Harrow Jr., "A Crack in the System," *Washington Post*, December 30, 2008, www.washingtonpost.com/wp-dyn/content/article/2008/12/29/AR2008122902670.html.
7. Ibid.
8. Mary Williams Walsh, "Tracking Firm Says Bets Placed on Lehman Have Been Quietly Settled," *New York Times*, October 22, 2008, www.nytimes.com/2008/10/23/business/23lehman.html.
9. "Fusion IQ's Ritholtz Expects More Writedowns at AIG: Video," *Bloomberg*, August 6, 2008, www.bloomberg.com/apps/news?pid=newsarchive&sid=avZEKuMTaGME.
10. Shannon D. Harrington, "AIG, Lehman, Merrill Lead Rise in Financial-Company Bond Risk," *Bloomberg*, September 12, 2008, www.bloomberg.com/apps/news?pid=20601087&sid=avRzVWkrgoyE&.
11. Ibid.

12. De la Merced and Morgenson, "A.I.G. Allowed."
13. Aaron Task, "Bernanke: Mad as Hell about AIG, But Bailouts Averting 'Disaster,' " Yahoo!, March 3, 2009, http://bit.ly/QEK9O.
14. Ibid.
15. Ibid.

Chapter 18: The Year of the Bailout, Part II: Too Big to Succeed?

1. William Safire, "Essay: Don't Bank on It," *New York Times*, April 16, 1998, www.nytimes.com/1998/04/16/opinion/essay-don-t-bank-on-it.html.
2. Time line of Citibank history, Citibank North America web site, www.citigroup.com/citi/corporate/history/citibank.htm.
3. Ibid.
4. Time line of major events since Citigroup and Travelers merged in 1998, Citibank North America web site, www.citigroup.com/citi/corporate/history/citigroup.htm.
5. "History of the Eighties—Lessons for the Future: Continental Illinois and 'Too Big to Fail,'" Division of Research and Statistics, Federal Deposit Insurance Corporation, December 1997, www.fdic.gov/bank/historical/history/235_258.pdf.
6. Jonathan Fuerbringer, "Talking Deals: Citicorp Strategy on Glass-Steagall," *New York Times*, March 23, 1989, http://query.nytimes.com/gst/fullpage.html?res=950DE2D81F39F930A15750C0A96F948260.
7. Robert Kuttner, "Friendly Takeover," *American Prospect*, March 18, 2007, www.prospect.org/cs/articles?articleId=12573.
8. Ibid.; see also "Rubin Calls for Modernization through Reform of Glass -Steagall Act," *Journal of Accountancy*, May 1, 1995, www.allbusiness.com/government/business-regulations/500983-1.html; Ken Brown and David Enrich, "Rubin, under Fire, Defends His Role at Citi," *Wall Street Journal*, November 29, 2008, http://online.wsj.com/article/SB122791795940965645.html.
9. Stephen Labaton, "Congress Passes Wide-Ranging Bill Easing Bank Laws," *New York Times*, November 5, 1999, www.nytimes.com/1999/11/05/business/congress-passes-wide-ranging-bill-easing-bank-laws.html.
10. "The S&L Crisis: A Chrono-Bibliography," FDIC web site, www.fdic.gov/bank/historical/s&l/.
11. Eric Dash and Julie Creswell, "Citigroup Saw No Red Flags Even as It Made Bolder Bets," *New York Times*, November 22, 2008, www.nytimes.com/2008/11/23/business/23citi.html; see also Eric Dash, "Citigroup Acknowledges Poor Risk Management," *New York Times*, October 16, 2007, www.nytimes.com/2007/10/16/business/16citi.html.

12. Dash and Creswell, "Citigroup Saw No Red Flags."
13. Shannon D. Harrington and Elizabeth Hester, "Citigroup Rescues SIVs with $58 Billion Debt Bailout," *Bloomberg*, December 14, 2007, www.bloomberg.com/apps/news?pid=20601087&refer=home&sid=aS0Dm.iV5BCI; see also "Citigroup Cuts SIV Size by $15 Billion," Reuters, December 11, 2007, www.reuters.com/article/ousiv/idUSL1111435920071211; George White, "Citigroup Finishes Winding Down SIVs," *The Deal*, November 19, 2008, www.thedeal.com/dealscape/2008/11/citigroup_finishes_winding_dow.php; "Citi Finalizes SIV Wind-Down by Agreeing to Purchase All Remaining Assets," Citigroup press release, November 19, 2008, www.citigroup.com/citi/press/2008/081119a.htm.
14. Hugo Dixon and Robert Cyran, "Vikram Pandit Scores a Great Deal for Citigroup," *New York Times*, December 2, 2008, www.nytimes.com/2008/12/03/business/economy/03views.html.
15. Barry Ritholtz, "Actual Merrill CDO Sale: 5.47 Percent on the Dollar," *The Big Picture*, July 29, 2008, http://bigpicture.typepad.com/comments/2008/07/merrill-writedo.html.
16. "Visa History," Visa web site, http://corporate.visa.com/av/about_visa/corp_history.jsp.
17. "The Making of the Bank of America," *Fortune*, September 5, 2005, http://money.cnn.com/magazines/fortune/fortune_archive/2005/09/05/8271409/index.htm.
18. Barry Ritholtz, "Citi & BofA Ain't No Continental Illinois Bank," *The Big Picture*, February 24, 2009, www.ritholtz.com/blog/2009/02/citi-bofa-aint-continental-illinois-bank/.
19. "Bylaws, Board of Directors," Federal Reserve Bank of New York, December 20, 2007, www.newyorkfed.org/aboutthefed/ny_bylaws.html.
20. "Fact Sheet: Proposed Treasury Authority to Purchase Troubled Assets," U.S. Treasury press release, September 20, 2008, www.treas.gov/press/releases/hp1150.htm; see also "Statement by Secretary Henry M. Paulson, Jr. on Treasury and Federal Housing Finance Agency Action to Protect Financial Markets and Taxpayers," September 7, 2008, http://treasury.gov/press/releases/hp1129.htm.
21. "Paulson TARP proposal," U.S. Treasury press release, September 20, 2008.
22. Alex Johnson, "Bush Signs $700 Billion Financial Bailout Bill," MSNBC.com, October 3, 2008, www.msnbc.msn.com/id/26987291/.
23. Ibid.
24. Mark Landler and Eric Dash, "Drama Behind a $250 Billion Banking Deal," *New York Times*, October 14, 2008, www.nytimes.com/2008/10/15/business/economy/15bailout.html.

25. Ibid.
26. Peter S. Goodman and Gretchen Morgenson, "Saying Yes, WaMu Built Empire on Shaky Loans," *New York Times*, December 27, 2008, www.nytimes.com/2008/12/28/business/28wamu.html; see also Greg Morcroft, "J.P. Morgan Pondering Buyout of Washington Mutual," January 11, 2008, www.marketwatch.com/news/story/jp-morgan-pondering-buyout-Washington/story.aspx?guid=percent7B89CA2071-2631-42C6-8936-22E745A3B6DA percent7D.
27. Binyamin Appelbaum, "After Change in Tax Law, Wells Fargo Swoops In," *Washington Post*, October 4, 2008, A01, http://www.washingtonpost.com/wp-dyn/content/article/2008/10/03/AR2008100301042.html?sub=AR.
28. Landler and Dash, "Drama."
29. Mark Pittman, Bob Ivry, and Alison Fitzgerald, "Fed Defies Transparency Aim in Refusal to Disclose," *Bloomberg*, November 10, 2009, www.bloomberg.com/apps/news?pid=20601087&sid=ahdVHk_Ccoeg&.
30. Mark Pittman, "Bloomberg Sues Fed to Force Disclosure of Collateral (Update 1)," *Bloomberg*, November 7, 2009, http://www.bloomberg.com/apps/news?pid=newsarchive&sid=aKr.oY2YKc2g.
31. John Carney, "TARP Trouble: GAO Report Rips Internal Controls, Bank Monitoring," Yahoo! Tech Ticker, December 3, 2008, http://finance.yahoo.com/tech-ticker/article/138232/TARP-Trouble:-GAO-Report-Rips-Internal-Controls,-Bank-Monitoring.
32. Amit R. Paley, "A Quiet Windfall for U.S. Banks: With Attention on Bailout Debate, Treasury Made Change to Tax Policy," *Washington Post*, November 10, 2008, A01, www.washingtonpost.com/wp-dyn/content/article/2008/11/09/AR2008110902155_pf.html.
33. Albert Bozzo, "Obama's Toxic-Asset Plan: End-Run around Congress?" CNBC.com, March 25, 2009, www.cnbc.com/id/29863145.
34. Felix Salmon, "How to Conjure Up $500 Billion," *New York Times*, March 26, 2009, www.nytimes.com/2009/03/27/opinion/27salmon.html.
35. Alan Greenspan, "The Fed Didn't Cause the Housing Bubble: Any New Regulations Should Help Direct Savings toward Productive Investments," *Wall Street Journal*, March 11, 2009, http://online.wsj.com/article/SB123672965066989281.html.

Chapter 19: Casting Blame

1. Joseph Stiglitz, "The Economic Crisis: Capitalist Fools," *Vanity Fair*, January 2009, www.vanityfair.com/magazine/2009/01/stiglitz200901.

2. Edmund L. Andrews, "Greenspan Concedes Error on Regulation," *New York Times*, October 23, 2008, www.nytimes.com/2008/10/24/business/economy/24panel.html.
3. Benjamin Disraeli, *Sybil*, Book IV, Chapter V.
4. Eric Lipton and Stephen Lebaton, "A Deregulator Looks Back, Unswayed," *New York Times*, November 16, 2008, www.nytimes.com/2008/11/17/business/economy/17gramm.html.
5. Ken Brown and David Enrich, "Rubin, Under Fire, Defends His Role at Citi," *Wall Street Journal*, November 29, 2008, http://online.wsj.com/article/SB122791795940965645.html.
6. Jonathan Fuerbringer, "Talking Deals: Citicorp Strategy on Glass-Steagall," *New York Times*, March 23, 1989, http://query.nytimes.com/gst/fullpage.html?res=950DE2D81F39F930A15750C0A96F948260.
7. Alan Katz and Ian Katz, "Greenspan Slept as Off-Books Debt Escaped Scrutiny," *Bloomberg*, October 20, 2008, www.bloomberg.com/apps/news?pid=20601170&refer=home&sid=aYJZOB_gZi0I.
8. Matt Apuzzo, "US Diluted Loan Rules before Crash," Associated Press, December 1, 2008, www.google.com/hostednews/ap/article/ALeqM5hTDPY8hFtJLxsv8i1Q7OvoRrlYrQD94PQ0JO0.
9. Ibid.
10. Eric Stein, "Turmoil in the U.S. Credit Markets: The Genesis of the Current Economic Crisis," testimony before the Senate Committee on Banking, Housing, and Urban Affairs, October 16, 2008, www.responsiblelending.org/policy/testimony/turmoil-in-the-u-s-credit-markets-the-genesis-of-the-current-economic-crisis.htm.
11. Ibid.
12. "Confronting Economic Meltdown," New America Foundation, www.newamerica.net/events/2008/confronting_economic_meltdown.
13. Jason Niss, "Harvey Pitt: Accounts Angel Who Supped with the Devil," *UK Independent*, August 11, 2002, www.independent.co.uk/news/business/analysis-and-features/harvey-pitt-accounts-angel-who-supped-with-the-devil-639450.html.
14. Simon English, "U.S. Watchdog Under Fire," *The Telegraph*, May 20, 2002, http://www.telegraph.co.uk/finance/2763231/US-watchdog-under-fire.html.
15. Arianna Huffington, "The SEC Goes AWOL," *Salon*, May 14, 2002, http://archive.salon.com/news/col/huff/2002/05/14/sec/print.html.
16. John McCain, "The Free Market Needs New Rules," *New York Times*, July 8, 2002, http://query.nytimes.com/gst/fullpage.html?res=9B00E3D61031F93BA35754C0A9649C8B63.

17. Dana Parson, "An Ironic Twist in the Tale of SEC's Christopher Cox," *Los Angeles Times*, January 30, 2009, www.latimes.com/news/local/la-me-parsons30-2009jan30,0,3244574.column.
18. Doug Kass, "Madoff Was Made Up," TheStreet.com, December 12, 2008, www.thestreet.com/story/10452909/1/kass-madoff-was-made-up.html.
19. Kara Scannell, "Madoff Chasers Dug for Years, to No Avail," *Wall Street Journal*, January 5, 2009, http://online.wsj.com/article/SB123111743915052731.html.
20. Congressional testimony of Harry Markopolos before the U.S. House of Representatives Committee on Financial Services, February 4, 2009, http://online.wsj.com/public/resources/documents/MarkopolosTestimony20090203.pdf.
21. Alex Spillius, "Sir Allen Stanford Refuses to Testify in Fraud Probe," *Telegraph*, March 12, 2009, www.telegraph.co.uk/finance/4976280/Sir-Allen-Stanford-refuses-to-testify-in-fraud-probe.html.
22. Mara Der Hovanesian, "Nightmare Mortgages," *BusinessWeek*, September 11, 2006, www.businessweek.com/magazine/content/06_37/b4000001.htm.
23. Floyd Norris, "Trump Sees Act of God in Recession," *New York Times*, December 4, 2008, www.nytimes.com/2008/12/05/business/05norris.html.
24. Tyler Cowen, "So We Thought. But Then Again . . . ," *New York Times*, January 13, 2008, www.nytimes.com/2008/01/13/business/13view.html.
25. Aaron Lucchetti and Serena Ng, "How Rating Firms' Calls Fueled Subprime Mess," *Wall Street Journal*, August 15, 2007, http://online.wsj.com/article/SB118714461352698015.html.
26. Ibid.
27. Stiglitz, "Economic Crisis."
28. Testimony of Deven Sharma, president, Standard & Poor's, remarks before the United States House of Representatives Committee on Oversight and Government Reform, October 22, 2008, http://oversight.house.gov/documents/20081022125052.pdf.
29. Jeffrey McCracken, "Moody's Aims to Be Ahead on Defaults," *Wall Street Journal*, March 10, 2009, http://online.wsj.com/article/SB123664643956778537.html; www.bloomberg.com/apps/news?pid=20601109&sid=ah839IWTLP9s&#.
30. Matthew Haggman, Rob Barry, and Jack Dolan, "Thousands with Criminal Records Work Unlicensed as Loan Originators," *Miami Herald*, July 20, 2008, www.miamiherald.com/static/multimedia/news/mortgage/originators.html; also, Jack Dolan, Rob Barry, and Matthew Haggman, "Ex-Convicts Active in Mortgage Fraud," *Miami Herald*, July 20, 2008, www.miamiherald.com/static/multimedia/news/mortgage/brokers.html.

31. Brad Linder, "Arizona Bans Zillow from Offering Real Estate Estimates," April 17, 2007, www.downloadsquad.com/2007/04/17/arizona-bans-zillow-from-offering-real-estate-estimates/.

Chapter 20: Misplaced Fault

1. Roger Lowenstein, "Who Needs the Mortgage-Interest Deduction?" *New York Times*, March 5, 2006, www.nytimes.com/2006/03/05/magazine/305 deduction.1.html.
2. Edward L. Glaeser and Jesse M. Shapiro, "The Benefits of the Home Mortgage Interest Deduction," Harvard University Discussion Paper 1979, October 2002, http://post.economics.harvard.edu/hier/2002papers/2002list.html.
3. Edward L. Glaeser, "Killing (or Maiming) a Sacred Cow: Home Mortgage Deductions," *Economix*, February 24, 2009, http://economix.blogs.nytimes.com/2009/02/24/killing-or-maiming-a-sacred-cow-home-mortgage-deductions/.
4. Kelly Curran, "FDIC's Bair Sets to Shatter CRA 'Myth,' " December 5, 2008, www.housingwire.com/2008/12/05/fdics-bair-sets-to-shatter-cra-myth/.
5. Daniel Gross, "Subprime Suspects," *Newsweek*, October 7, 2008, www.newsweek.com/id/162789.
6. Ibid.
7. Barry Ritholtz, "Misunderstanding Credit and Housing Crises: Blaming the CRA, GSEs," *The Big Picture*, October 2, 2008, www.ritholtz. com/blog/2008/10/misunderstanding-credit-and-housing-crises-blaming-the-cra-gses/.
8. Ibid.
9. Randall S. Kroszner, "The Enduring Challenge of Concentrated Poverty in America," remarks at the Confronting Concentrated Poverty Policy Forum, Board of Governors of the Federal Reserve System, December 3, 2008, www.federalreserve.gov/newsevents/speech/kroszner20081203a.htm and www.frbsf.org/cpreport/.
10. Curran, "FDIC's Bair"; also, Ronald D. Orol, "FDIC: Community Reinvestment Act Is Not Cause of Financial Crisis, FDIC's Bair Said," MarketWatch, December 4, 2008, http://tinyurl.com/fdic-cra.
11. Robert Gordon, "Did Liberals Cause the Sub-Prime Crisis?" *American Prospect*, April 7, 2008, www.prospect.org/cs/articles?article=did_liberals_cause_the_subprime_crisis; also see Aaron Pressman, "Community Reinvestment Act Had Nothing to Do with Subprime Crisis," *BusinessWeek*, September 29, 2008, www.businessweek.com/investing/insights/blog/archives/2008/09/community_reinv.html.
12. Jonathan R. Laing, "The Endgame Nears for Fannie and Freddie," *Barron's*, August 18, 2008, http://online.barrons.com/article/SB121884860106946277.html.

13. David S. Hilzenrath, "Fannie's Perilous Pursuit of Subprime Loans," *Washington Post*, August 19, 2008, www.washingtonpost.com/wp-dyn/content/article/2008/08/18/AR2008081802111.html.
14. James Tyson, "Former Fannie Mae Executives to Pay $31.4 Million," *Bloomberg*, April 18, 2008, www.bloomberg.com/apps/news?pid=20601103&sid=aMxLZLZWyFok&refer=us.
15. Charles Duhigg, "Pressured to Take More Risk, Fannie Reached Tipping Point," *New York Times*, October 4, 2008, www.nytimes.com/2008/10/05/business/05fannie.html?_r=1&pagewanted=all.
16. Charles Duhigg, "At Freddie Mac, Chief Discarded Warning Signs," *New York Times*, August 5, 2008, www.nytimes.com/2008/08/05/business/05freddie.html.
17. Ibid.
18. "Shocking Video Unearthed Democrats in Their Own Words Covering Up the Fannie Mae, Freddie Mac Scam That Caused Our Economic Crisis," video posted to NakedEmporerNews and YouTube.com, www.youtube.com/watch?v=_MGT_cSi7Rs.
19. Pete Yost, "AP IMPACT: How Freddie Mac Halted Regulatory Drive," December 7, 2008, http://seattletimes.nwsource.com/html/politics/2008479535_aptheinfluencegamefreddiemac.html.

Chapter 21: The Virtues of Foreclosure

1. "Historically Strong Home Sales Expected in 2006," NAR Publication, Business Wire, December 12, 2005, www.allbusiness.com/economy-economic-indicators/economic-indicators-existing/5174031-1.html; also, "Historically Strong Home Sales Expected in 2006," December 15, 2005, http://rodomino.realtor.org/research.nsf/htmlarchives/ResearchUpdate121505.
2. "Greenspan: Housing Market Worst May Be Over," Reuters, October 9, 2006, www.msnbc.msn.com/id/15198805/; also, "Greenspanity," *Economist.com*, August 14, 2008, www.economist.com/blogs/freeexchange/2008/08/greenspanity.cfm.
3. Historical Census of Housing Tables, www.census.gov/hhes/www/housing/census/historic/owner.html.
4. Ibid.
5. S&P/Case-Shiller Home Price Indexes, http://www2.standardandpoors.com/portal/site/sp/en/us/page.topic/indices_csmahp/0,0,0,0,0,0,0,0,0,1,1,0,0,0,0,0.html.
6. Amy Hoak, "Report: 20% of Home Mortgages Were Underwater," MarketWatch, March 4, 2009, http://online.wsj.com/article/SB123616863098628705.html.

7. Bureau of Labor Statistics, www.bls.gov/ces/.
8. Barry Ritholtz, "Fixing Housing & Finance: 30/20/10 Proposal," *The Big Picture*, September 22, 2008, www.ritholtz.com/blog/2008/09/fixing-housing-finance-302010-proposal/; also, http://makinghomeaffordable.gov/.

Chapter 22: Casino Capitalism

1. David Sanger, "Nationalization Gets a New, Serious Look," *New York Times*, January 25, 2009, www.nytimes.com/2009/01/26/business/economy/26banks.html.
2. Liam Pleven, "AIG to Pay $450 Million in Bonuses," *Wall Street Journal*, March 15, 2009, http://online.wsj.com/article/SB123707854113331281.html.
3. Lars Jonung, "Lessons from Swedish Bank Resolution Policy," Eurointelligence, March 6, 2009, www.eurointelligence.com/article.581+M50462bfd105.0.html.
4. Barry Ritholtz, "Debate over Nationalization Is 'Semantics,'" *The Big Picture*, February 23, 2009, www.ritholtz.com/blog/2009/02/debate-over-nationalization-is-semantics/.
5. Alison Vekshin, "AIG's Liddy Acknowledges 'Distasteful' Retention Pay," *Bloomberg*, March 18, 2009, www.bloomberg.com/apps/news?pid=newsarchive&sid=aECcRPKYAOx0.
6. Serena Ng, "Hedge Funds May Get AIG Cash," *Wall Street Journal*, March 18, 2009, http://online.wsj.com/article/SB123734123180365061.html.

Index